Effective Writing

ELEVENTH EDITION

Effective Writing

A Handbook for Accountants

Claire B. May, Ph.D.

Gordon S. May, Ph.D.

University of Georgia, Emeritus

 Pearson

New York, NY

Vice President, Business, Economics, and UK Courseware: Donna Battista
Director of Portfolio Management: Adrienne D'Ambrosio
Director, Courseware Portfolio Management: Ashley Dodge
Senior Sponsoring Editor: Neeraj Bhalla
Editorial Assistant: Elisa Marks
Vice President, Product Marketing: Roxanne McCarley
Senior Product Marketer: Tricia Murphy
Product Marketing Assistant: Marianela Silvestri
Manager of Field Marketing, Business Publishing: Adam Goldstein
Executive Field Marketing Manager: Nayke Popovich
Vice President, Production and Digital Studio, Arts and Business: Etain O'Dea
Director of Production, Business: Jeff Holcomb
Managing Producer, Business: Melissa Feimer
Content Producer: Sugandh Juneja
Operations Specialist: Carol Melville

Design Lead: Kathryn Foot
Manager, Learning Tools: Brian Surette
Content Developer, Learning Tools: Sarah Peterson
Managing Producer, Digital Studio and GLP, Media Production and Development: Ashley Santora
Managing Producer, Digital Studio: Diane Lombardo
Digital Studio Producer: Regina DaSilva
Digital Studio Producer: Alana Coles
Digital Content Team Lead: Noel Lotz
Digital Content Project Lead: Martha LaChance
Project Managers: Leah Grace Salazar and Sasibalan C, SPi Global
Interior Design: SPi Global
Cover Design: Laurie Entringer, SPi Global
Cover Art: Nick Brundle Photography/Getty Images
Printer/Binder: LSC Communications, Inc./ Crawfordsville
Cover Printer: LSC Communications, Inc./ Crawfordsville

The documents and related graphics contained herein could include technical inaccuracies or typographical errors. Changes are periodically added to the information herein. Microsoft and/or its respective suppliers may make improvements and/or changes in the product(s) and/or the program(s) described herein at any time. Partial screen shots may be viewed in full within the software version specified.

Microsoft® and Windows® are registered trademarks of the Microsoft Corporation in the U.S.A. and other countries. This book is not sponsored or endorsed by or affiliated with the Microsoft Corporation.

Library of Congress Cataloging-in-Publication Data

Names: May, Claire Arevalo, author. | May, Gordon S., author.
Title: Effective writing: a handbook for accountants / Claire B. May, Ph.D., Gordon S. May, Ph.D., University of Georgia, Emeritus.
Description: Eleventh Edition. | Hoboken : Pearson, [2017] | Includes index. Revised edition of the authors' Effective writing, [2015]
Identifiers: LCCN 2017046178| ISBN 9780134667386 | ISBN 0134667387
Subjects: LCSH: Business report writing. | Communication in accounting.
Classification: LCC HF5719 .M375 2017 | DDC 808.06/6657--dc23 LC record available at https://lccn.loc.gov/2017046178

1 18

ISBN 10:   0-13-466738-7
ISBN 13: 978-0-13-466738-6

Brief Contents

Contents

Preface

NEW TO THIS EDITION

- Emphasis on higher order thinking skills in solving accounting problems
- Expanded coverage of business documents: briefing documents, technical memos, discussion papers, in addition to general formats such as letters, memos, and reports
- Expanded coverage of writing for professional exams: CPA, CMA, CGMA
- Updated references for accounting research
- Current issues within the accounting profession, as reflected in assignments and examples
- Learning objectives for each chapter integrated into the text

SOLVING TEACHING AND LEARNING CHALLENGES

*Effective Writing: A Handbook for Accountants, 11*th *Edition* will help your students develop the communication skills they need to succeed in the profession. While the book's emphasis is writing skills, it also stresses other "soft skills" accountants need to be successful, including higher order thinking skills and problem solving, oral communication, listening skills, effective and responsible use of social media, and ethical considerations of the communication process.

Effective Writing guides the writer through all the stages of the writing process: planning, including analysis of audience and purpose; critical thinking about the problem to be solved or the job to be accomplished; generating and organizing ideas; writing the draft; revising for readable style and correct grammar; and designing the document for effective presentation. In addition to these basic writing principles, the book covers letters, memos, reports, and other formats used by accountants in practice, including email, social media, and other forms of electronic communication. Throughout the text, *Effective Writing* stresses coherence, conciseness, and clarity as the most important qualities of the writing done by accountants.

A special feature of this book is Chapter 8, which discusses accounting research. Here readers will find valuable material on topics such as:

- Where to find all types of accounting and financial information on the Internet, using online database services, and using other printed sources.

- How higher order thinking skills can be used to help solve problems and write persuasive documents.
- How to document sources of accounting information, including the *FASB Accounting Standards Codification*^{TM} and Internet sources.

Chapter 13 discusses writing for professional examinations including the CPA exam, the CMA exam, and the CGMA exam, all of which contain questions requiring candidates to demonstrate their writing ability.

Effective Writing is virtually unique in its application of communication skills to accounting topics and contexts. Throughout the text, students will see the relevance of communication strategies to actual situations encountered in accounting practice.

Effective Writing offers these features to help your students develop the communication skills they will need to succeed in their future careers:

- Examples and assignments use accounting topics and problems, so that students will practice learned skills in a context that will seem relevant to their future careers.
- Students are guided through all the steps of the writing process: planning for purpose and audience; generating and organizing ideas; drafting and revision, so that documents are clear, concise, and correct.
- Assignments are designed for students at different stages in their accounting education, from principles level courses to more advanced courses that incorporate accounting problem-solving and research.
- Updated reference materials will guide students when they research more challenging accounting problems.
- The *Instructor's Manual* contains valuable tips for integrating communication assignments into an accounting course: motivating and encouraging students to improve their skills; designing assignments that will improve communication skills while they reinforce course content; evaluating students' writing and oral presentations. The *Instructor's Manual* also contains teaching tips for each chapter.

DEVELOPING SKILLS FOR PROFESSIONAL SUCCESS

Accounting students need to be effective communicators if they are to succeed in their careers, yet many of them lack the communication skills they need. We notice their lack of communication skills in our classrooms, and also hear about problems from the professionals who hire them after graduation. Almost everyone in the field would agree that there is a need to help our students to become better communicators, especially better writers.

Writing skills are considered so important for the successful practice of accounting that they are tested in the major professional exams, such as the CPA exam, the CMA exam, and the new CGMA exam. *Effective Writing* discusses the specific criteria tested on these exams and shows students how to prepare for and take the writing portions of these exams as a step toward professional certification.

TABLE OF CONTENTS OVERVIEW

Effective Writing is divided into three parts: Communication Strategies, Business Documents, and Writing and Your Career.

Part 1: Communication Strategies – Here students will find discussions of why writing effectively is important to the practice of accounting, and a survey of the writing process. Several chapters cover particular elements of effective writing such as organization, style, use of Standard English, and document design. Discussions of higher level thinking skills and accounting research are also included.

Part 2: Business Documents – Chapters in this part of the book pay attention to the particular types of documents accountants may write in practice, such as, letters, memos, reports, and various types of e-communication and social media.

Part 3: Writing and Your Career – Here students will find chapters on how to write for academic and professional exams including the CPA, CMA, and CGMA exams, as well as how to write résumés and letters of application for employment. They will also find information on writing for publication and oral communication, including listening and speaking.

INSTRUCTOR TEACHING RESOURCES

At the Instructor Resource Center, *http://www.pearsonhighered.com/irc*, instructors can register to gain access to the Instructor's Manual available with this text.

Instructor's Manual and Slides

- Guidelines for incorporating writing assignments into an accounting course
- Using writing assignments to reinforce course content
- Designing writing assignments to supplement assignments in the end-of-chapter materials
- Evaluating writing assignments: two approaches
- For each chapter: teaching tips, trouble shooting, list of masters (for slides or handouts) to support the chapter, answers to exercises (where appropriate)
- Masters for hand-outs or slides

CHAPTER

Accountants as Communicators

1

Learning Objectives

After studying this chapter, you should be able to

1.1 Define "soft skills" and understand their importance to a successful accounting career.

1.2 Summarize the kinds of documents accountants write as part of their professional careers.

1.3 Summarize the six tips for effective writing.

1.4 Analyze an example of an accounting document and explain how it illustrates effective writing.

1.5 Gain confidence in your ability to write well.

1.6 Explain the interaction between writing and other forms of communication, such as reading, listening, and speaking.

1.7 Explain the connections between writing and problem solving, thinking, and ethics.

The accounting profession has changed dramatically in recent years, due in part to changing technology, the strength of the global business environment, increased regulation, and the evolving needs for accounting services. In spite of these changes, the ability to communicate effectively—whether through speaking or writing—is essential to success in the accounting profession and in the business world in general. It is the purpose of this book to help you master these essential skills.

THE IMPORTANCE OF "SOFT SKILLS"

LO1.1   Define "soft skills" and understand their importance to a successful accounting career.

Writing and speaking, interpersonal skills, leadership skills, the ability to think critically and to listen carefully are sometimes referred to as "soft skills," as opposed to the "hard skills" of technical knowledge and ability.

1

The major differences among competitors may often be found in the degree to which employees have mastered writing, speaking, higher order thinking, and other non-technical skills.

Soft skills, including communication and thinking skills, are essential for accountants in all areas of professional practice, including both public and managerial accounting. These skills are considered so important that they are evaluated on professional certification exams. The American Institute of Certified Public Accountants (AICPA) believes that cognitive and communication skills are as important as knowledge of professional content and evaluates these skills on the Certified Public Accountant (CPA) exam. Writing skills are also essential to success in managerial accounting and are evaluated on the Certified Management Accountant (CMA) exam offered by the IMA (formerly known as the Institute of Management Accountants).

The AICPA, in conjunction with the Chartered Institute of Management Accountants (CIMA), sponsors exams for the Chartered Global Management Accountant (CGMA) designation.[*] The CGMA exam requires candidates to demonstrate a wide range of management accounting skills, including communication. The International Accounting Education Standards Board (IAESB) also recognizes that successful accountants must be able to communicate clearly and concisely.

So, to be successful as well as competent, accountants must be good communicators, showing that they can think clearly and use words effectively. Many colleges and universities now stress effective writing and thinking in accounting coursework. And, as we have seen, these skills are evaluated on professional certification exams.

Effective communication, one of the soft skills necessary for professional success, is a broad area that includes formal and informal oral presentations, interpersonal communication, reading, listening, and skills in other related areas, including the ability to think carefully and critically. Ethical issues can also affect communication, both what accountants say and how they say it. Because this book is primarily about writing, we will now look at some of the documents accountants write on the job.

WHAT DO ACCOUNTANTS WRITE?

LO1.2   Summarize the kinds of documents accountants write as part of their professional careers.

In every type of accounting practice, writing is an essential part of the job. Whether in public accounting, management accounting, not-for-profit accounting, or government accounting, and whether specializing in tax, auditing, systems, or some other area, accountants write almost

---

[*]The AICPA and CIMA have established a joint venture called the Association of International Certified Professional Accountants, through which the CGMA designation is offered.

every day. Examples in four specialized areas—tax, auditing, systems, and management accounting—suggest a few of the many occasions that require accountants to write.

Tax accountants in accounting firms often write memos to other members of the firm that describe the results of their research. These memos may become part of the clients' files. A tax accountant might also write a letter advising a client about the best way to handle a tax problem. They must also write letters to the Internal Revenue Service (IRS) on behalf of clients and occasionally may even write a judicial brief.

Auditors write memos to be included in a client's files that describe work done on the client's audit. They may also write memos to their colleagues to request advice or to report research results. After an audit engagement, auditors may write advisory letters to management that suggest ways to improve accounting and internal control procedures.

Systems specialists write documents for readers with varying degrees of computer expertise. They may write a beginners' guide on how to use a software package, a highly technical report on a complex accounting system application, or a narrative description of an accounting information system, as we will see later in this chapter.

Management accountants may write reports or discussion papers intended for distribution inside or outside the company, memos to remind or inform employees about company issues or policies, briefing notes to be used by employees for various presentations, and emails for many different purposes.

No matter what their specialty, all accountants write memos to their supervisors, subordinates, and coworkers to request or provide information. They also write letters to clients, agencies, and a variety of other readers.

Technical reports and memos, both formal and informal, are also important ways in which accountants communicate. For instance, an accountant working for a corporation might write a report for management on alternative accounting treatments for a particular kind of business transaction. An accountant working for an accounting or business services firm might write a technical memo on how best to handle a client's unusual accounting problem.

Accountants may also write briefing documents, such as briefing memos or briefing notes. The purpose of these documents is to summarize important information on a particular issue for the decision makers in an organization, who then use this information as the basis of policy decisions or a presentation before some audience. When a problem or issue has several possible solutions, the briefing document will present the pros and cons for all the alternatives. Sometimes the briefing document will recommend one solution as the best among the choices, or it may just summarize the pros and cons of each solution, leaving the decision to the document's readers.

Yet another kind of writing prepared by accountants is the narrative portion of financial statements. Footnote disclosures communicate information that users may need to interpret the statements accurately. Unfortunately, the meaning of some footnote disclosures is not always clear to many financial statement readers. Several years ago, the Securities and Exchange Commission (SEC) issued a "plain English" disclosure rule requiring companies filing registration statements to write those statements in "plain English" so that readers would find them easier to understand. The rule enumerates several principles of "plain English" including the use of short sentences and clear, concise language.[1]

Not all professional writing appears on paper. Electronic communication, including email and social media, is nearly universal and will likely become increasingly important in the future.

To be effective, all written communication, whether electronic or print, must be carefully prepared, keeping the readers' needs in mind. How will clients react if, after reading a letter from their CPA, they are still confused about their income tax problem? How will management or one's supervisors react to a management accountant's report that is poorly organized and hard to follow?

We've seen that the ability to write well is essential for success in the business world. Some people believe the writing of business professionals is getting worse, in part because we have become so reliant on email, texts, posts, and other forms of electronic communication. Electronic communication in a purely social environment often emphasizes brevity over completeness, clarity, or attention to style. Therefore, we are being conditioned to use a type of writing that is not effective in many business situations. Yet email and all electronic communication can be written effectively, as Chapter 12 of this book shows.

SIX TIPS FOR EFFECTIVE WRITING

LO1.3   Summarize the six tips for effective writing.

What is good writing? The list of tips for writers in Figure 1–1 summarizes many qualities of effective business writing, including the writing done by accountants. These qualities are stressed throughout this book. Let's examine these tips in a little more detail.

The first tip concerns the *content* of the document. You must know what you are talking about, and the information you give should be accurate and relevant.

The second tip is *critical thinking*. You must analyze the issues with which you are dealing, including the questions and concerns of your readers. Can the issues be resolved in more than one way? If so, you will have to evaluate the alternatives carefully.

The third tip for effective writing is *to write appropriately for your readers*. You should write on a level your readers will understand and find meaningful, and you should anticipate and answer their questions.

FIGURE 1–1   Tips for the Effective Writer

1. *Content:* Be sure that the accounting content is correct and complete. Have you addressed all relevant accounting issues?
2. *Critical Thinking:* Using higher order thinking skills, think carefully and critically about the issues with which you're dealing. Anticipate questions and objections your readers might raise.
3. *Appropriateness for Intended Audience:* Write the document with a particular reader or audience in mind. Check that issues are discussed on a level they can understand. For most documents, it is better to focus on practical, explicit information and advice related to the case you are discussing rather than general accounting theory.
4. *Conciseness:* Write as concisely as possible, given the readers' needs and the issues to be addressed.
5. *Clarity:* Develop a style that is clear and readable. Choose words that convey your meaning with precision and clarity.
6. *Coherence:* Structure the document so that it is coherent. The organization should be logical and the train of thought easy to follow. Summarize main ideas near the beginning of the document and begin each paragraph with a topic sentence.
7. *Revision:* Revise the document so that it is polished and professional. It should be free of all spelling errors and typos; grammatical errors should not detract from the message.

The fourth tip is *conciseness*. Say what needs to be said in as few words as possible. To keep your writing concise, avoid digressions, unnecessary repetition, and wordiness.

Clarity is the next tip. Write as simply as possible, using words and phrases with which your readers are familiar. To improve the clarity of your writing, choose words that mean precisely what you intend so that your sentences are not confusing. Well-structured sentences also contribute to clear writing.

Coherence is the logical, orderly relationship of ideas. Coherent writing is well organized and easy to follow, with important ideas that stand out. Coherence is the sixth tip for effective writers.

The final tip is to *revise* your writing so that it is polished and professional. Documents should look attractive and be free of grammatical and mechanical errors.

EFFECTIVE WRITING: AN EXAMPLE

LO1.4   Analyze an example of an accounting document and explain how it illustrates effective writing.

You will find many examples of the kinds of documents accountants write throughout this text. One such document is the narrative description of an accounting information system (AIS). Figure 1–2 is

FIGURE 1–2   Narrative Description of Payroll Processing at S&S[2]

When employees are hired, they complete a new-employee form. When a change to an employee's payroll status occurs, such as a raise or a change in the number of exemptions, the human resources department completes an employee change form. A copy of these forms is sent to payroll. These forms are used to create or update the records in the employee/payroll file and are then stored in the file. Employee records are stored alphabetically.

Some S&S employees are paid a salary, but most are hourly workers who record their time on time cards. At the end of each pay period, department managers send the time cards to the payroll department. The payroll clerk uses the time card data, data from the employee file (such as pay rate and annual salary), and the appropriate tax tables to prepare a two-part check for each employee. The clerk also prepares a two-part payroll register showing gross pay, deductions, and net pay for each employee. The clerk updates the employee file to reflect each employee's current earnings. The original copy of the employee paycheck is forwarded to Susan. The payroll register is forwarded to the accounts payable clerk. The time cards and the duplicate copies of the payroll register and paychecks are stored by date in the payroll file.

Every pay period, the payroll clerk uses the data in the employee/payroll file to prepare a payroll summary report for Susan so she can control and monitor labor expenses. This report is forwarded to Susan with the original copies of the employee paychecks.

Every month, the payroll clerk uses the data in the employee/payroll file to prepare a two-part tax report. The original is forwarded to the accounts payable clerk, and the duplicate is added to the tax records in the payroll file. The accounts payable clerk uses the tax report to prepare a two-part check for taxes and a two-part cash disbursements voucher. The tax report and the original copy of each document are forwarded to Susan. The duplicates are stored by date in the accounts payable file.

The accounts payable clerk uses the payroll register to prepare a two-part check for the total amount of the employee payroll and a two-part disbursements voucher. The original copy of each document is forwarded to Susan, and the payroll register and the duplicates are stored by date in the accounts payable file.

Susan reviews each packet of information she receives, approves it, and signs the checks. She forwards the cash disbursements vouchers to Ashton, the tax reports and payments to the appropriate governmental agency, the payroll check to the bank, and the employee checks to the employees. She files the payroll report chronologically.

Ashton uses the payroll tax and the payroll check cash disbursement vouchers to update the general ledger. He then cancels the journal voucher by marking it "posted" and files it numerically.

an example of such a narrative description, in this case the payroll processing system of a hypothetical company, S&S, a small retail business owned by Scott and Susan. This description illustrates many of the characteristics of effective writing introduced here and explained more fully in later chapters of this text.

As you read the description, you will notice that it is organized logically, following the steps of the payroll process, so that the narrative is *coherent*. That is, readers will be able to understand how this system functions. Paragraphs are short and easy to follow. Sentences are *clear* and *concise*. The language is *correct*—written following the conventions of Standard English. The document is also written at a level *appropriate* to the intended audience, whom we assume to be the owners, managers, and other professionals who work with the payroll system at S&S.

YOU CAN BECOME A GOOD WRITER

LO1.5   Gain confidence in your ability to write well.

With all this talk about the importance of good writing to a successful career in accounting, you may feel overwhelmed or discouraged. Many people believe that they can never become good writers.

A word of encouragement is in order. Virtually anyone who succeeds in college work has the education and the skills to become at least an adequate writer, and probably even a good one. Problems with writing are often the result of two factors, both of which can be corrected: lack of adequate training in writing skills and lack of self-confidence.

Let's address the latter problem, the poor image some people have of themselves as writers. One reason to be optimistic about your writing ability is that you've already learned quite a bit about how to write from English courses and other writing classes, as well as from personal experience. Most people are better writers than they realize. They have the potential to become even more effective after they've mastered a few strategies such as the ones we'll cover in this book. As you read this book, note the techniques and principles you already use in your writing. Don't lose sight of your strengths while you work to improve the areas that could be better.

Another reason you should be able to write well as an accountant is that you will be writing about topics you understand and find interesting. If you have had unpleasant experiences with writing in courses other than accounting, the problem may have been that you were writing about topics you weren't interested in or didn't feel qualified to discuss. When you write about subjects you like and understand, it's much easier to write clearly and persuasively.

Finally, you may find it much easier to do the kind of writing recommended in this book because it is simple, direct writing. Some people believe that they must write in long, complicated sentences filled with difficult, "impressive" vocabulary. In fact, just the opposite is true: Effective business writing is written as simply as possible. It is therefore easier to do.

WRITING AND OTHER FORMS OF COMMUNICATION

LO1.6 Explain the interaction between writing and other forms of communication, such as reading, listening, and speaking.

Writing is only one of several forms of communication, along with such skills as reading, listening, speaking, and interpersonal communication. In fact, all these forms of communication work together to determine how well a person gives and receives information. Let's look at how reading, listening, and speaking skills can help you improve your writing.

Reading

Reading affects writing in several ways. Often you will write a memo or letter in response to a written communication from someone else. In public practice, for example, you might write a letter to clients to answer questions they have posed in a letter or an email to your firm. The ability to read the earlier correspondence carefully is essential to an effective response.

Careful reading is also important when you research accounting literature as background for the documents you write. The tax code, government regulations, financial accounting standards, articles in professional journals, and *The Wall Street Journal* are examples of the material you must read to stay informed on accounting issues and procedures as well as the broader business environment. You will need to understand this material and be able to apply it to particular situations.

You will also read information circulated and stored within your own firm or company, such as client files and memos or emails from colleagues. Reading this material carefully will provide many of the insights and facts you need to deal effectively with situations for which you are responsible.

Thus, careful reading, with an understanding of important ideas and key facts, can contribute to effective writing.

Listening

Along with reading, the ability to listen carefully determines how well you receive information from others. On the job, you interact with colleagues, supervisors, subordinates, or clients; at school, you interact with professors and other students. Listening carefully to these people provides important information you can use as the basis of your writing. Listening gives you facts about projects you are working on, along with insights into other people's expectations and concerns.

In many situations, listening skills contribute to effective writing. Instructions given by the professor in class, interviews with clients, requests from supervisors, and phone conversations with colleagues are a few examples. In all these situations, attentive listening is necessary to hear what people are saying. It's often a good idea to take notes and, when necessary, ask questions for clarification or additional information.

Careful listening to what others say is often a key ingredient in effective writing. By listening carefully, you learn much about what others know about a situation, what their concerns are, and what they expect from you.

Speaking

Oral communication is one of the soft skills we mentioned earlier as important to success in the accounting profession. Writing and speaking will often overlap in your professional activities. Informally, you may have meetings and conversations to discuss reports or memos you've written. Or you may use what you've written as the basis for formal oral presentations before a group. You might make a presentation to a board of directors, senior managers, or members of a professional organization, for example.

WRITING AND PROBLEM SOLVING

LO1.7 **Explain the connections between writing and problem solving, thinking, and ethics.**

Problem solving requires many skills, such as identifying key issues, researching relevant literature, and thinking critically and analytically. Often you must decide among several alternative solutions to a problem, a decision which may include ethical as well as practical considerations. At each step of the problem-solving process, writing can help you reach sound conclusions.

When faced with a problem on some topic, you might generate ideas on that topic by writing down what you already know about it, as well as what you have yet to find out. The act of writing about a subject can actually help you clarify your thinking. As one wit put it, "How do I know what I think until I see what I say?" There's more truth in this quip than might at first be apparent. Research into how people think and learn has shown that writers often generate ideas and improve their insights into a subject as they write down their thoughts.

Writing, thinking, problem solving, and decision making are often inseparable, interactive processes that are essential to the practice of accounting. The AICPA has stressed the importance of these skills for entry-level accountants and explicitly tests for cognitive skills on the

CPA and CGMA exams. Candidates must demonstrate critical thinking, problem solving, analytical ability, and professional skepticism. Cognitive skills are also evaluated on the CMA exam.

Writing and Ethics

Accounting communication, including writing, may involve ethical considerations as well as critical thinking and problem solving. In fact, these three processes—analyzing ethical and other accounting issues, thinking critically, and solving problems—are essential components of effective communication.

Ethics may be defined broadly as the standards we use to determine what is right and wrong, a set of moral principles or values that govern how we act. We learn these ethical principles in a variety of ways, from our families, religious communities, schools, or in general from the society of which we are a part. Professional people, including accountants, also acquire ethical standards as part of their professional training.

Accountants must adhere to very high ethical standards as they perform their professional responsibilities. CPAs must follow reporting rules established by the SEC and other governmental agencies, and they must adhere to ethical standards established by nongovernmental entities such as the Financial Accounting Standards Board (FASB) and the AICPA. In fact, the AICPA's Code of Professional Ethics is a major source of ethical standards for all accounting professionals, not just CPAs. The International Ethics Standards Board for Accountants® (IESBA®) also sets ethics standards, including auditor independence requirements, for professional accountants worldwide and publishes the *Code of Ethics for Professional Accountants™*. Management accountants also adhere to ethical requirements established by the IMA or CIMA, as well as by federal, state, and local laws. Individual firms and corporations may also have ethical codes for their employees.

Legal requirements and codes of professional conduct provide standards of ethical behavior for accountants as they perform their professional responsibilities. Yet these laws and codes alone may not always provide enough guidance for specific ethical dilemmas. Accountants sometimes face situations for which ready-made answers are not available. When you are faced with these dilemmas, you will need to think critically about the issues in light of your own personal ethical standards in order to make ethical decisions. Remember, too, that there may be a gap between what is legal and what is ethical. For many years, discrimination against ethnic minorities and women was legal in this country, but such discrimination was never ethical.

Ethical considerations often affect the way we communicate in a professional situation, whether orally or in writing. Remember that accounting is a process of measuring and *reporting* financial information. Ethical issues can relate to what we say and how we say it. The AICPA's Code of Professional Ethics requires that its members report all the information needed for a user of the information to make a reasonable decision; the Code also requires that financial data not be misrepresented. Thus, information must be reported in an honest, reasonably complete manner. Moreover, the information must be communicated clearly so that users can understand it. Accuracy, clarity, and completeness are all qualities of the ethical communication of accounting information.

Ethics also affects the attitude with which we regard other people, whether the public at large, our clients, or colleagues and coworkers. An important principle here is that we treat other people with courtesy and respect. Later chapters discuss such ethical considerations as writing with a courteous tone, the respectful use of titles and pronouns, and the need to write clear and concise documents so that readers can find the information they need as quickly as possible. We will also discuss analyzing readers' interests and needs as an essential step in the writing process. Finally, sections of this book that discuss higher order thinking skills and accounting research show how to analyze ethical dilemmas. You will learn how to decide what information to provide and how to provide it in a way that not only adheres to professional and legal standards, but also shows respect for the people who will use the information.

The AICPA believes that "a thorough understanding of professional and ethical responsibilities" is an essential requirement for all accountants, and tests for that understanding on the CPA exam.[3]

DEVELOPING SKILLS FOR YOUR CAREER

To be a successful accountant, you must master many skills. You must understand and be able to apply accounting principles, of course, but you must also be able to think critically and ethically, and to communicate effectively. A competent, ethical accountant who is also a critical thinker and an effective communicator usually is rewarded with professional success. In fact, these skills are essential even at the beginning of an accounting career. Experts who trace hiring trends in the profession of accounting note the increased importance of soft skills, including the ability to communicate effectively, in decisions to hire entry-level staff.

This text will help you develop these important skills. With study and practice, you'll be well on your way to professional success.

EXERCISES

Exercise 1–1 [General]

Consider the writing you find in one or two articles in *The Wall Street Journal* or the business section of another major business newspaper or magazine. How effective or ineffective do you find the writing? If you have trouble reading or understanding what you read, is the problem due to ineffective writing? If you find the material understandable and interesting to read, what qualities of the writing contribute to this effectiveness? You might consider the tips for effective writing in Figure 1–1 as the basis of your evaluation.

Exercise 1–2 [General]

Prepare a written report on why the SEC is so concerned that corporations use "plain English" in their filings and what it is doing about the issue. Among the materials you consult, be sure to look at the following SEC publications, but do not limit your sources to just these:

- *A Plain English Handbook: How to Create Clear SEC Disclosure Documents* at www.sec.gov/pdf/handbook.pdf.
- *Updated Staff Legal Bulletin No. 7* at www.sec.gov/interps/legal/cfslb7a.htm.
- *Plain English Disclosure Final Rules* at www.sec.gov/rules/final/33-7497.txt.

Exercise 1–3 [General]

Research the topic of "soft skills" and prepare an article for your company's staff newsletter or your school's newspaper on their definition and importance in the accounting and business world.

Exercise 1–4 [General]

The chair of the accounting department at a local college in your area has asked you to address beginning accounting students at an orientation session. The topic of your presentation is "A Competitive Edge: The Importance of Writing Skills for Accountants." Your purpose is to convince the students to take the need for good writing skills seriously.

Write an outline you can use as a basis for your presentation. As steps in preparing your outline, follow these guidelines:

- Analyze your audience for this presentation. How will you present your topic so that they find it meaningful and interesting?
- Think critically about the objections your audience might raise to your arguments. How will you respond to their objections?

- What material will you include in your presentation? Remember to anticipate your audience's objections and the way you will respond. Also, remember to arrange your ideas in a logical order.
- Using the guidelines found in Chapter 16—Oral Communication: Listening and Speaking, prepare, practice, and present your talk. Your instructor may ask you to make your presentation in class. As an alternative, you may ask a few friends to listen to your presentation.

Exercise 1–5 [General]

Assume that the talk you presented for Exercise 1–4 was very successful. In fact, you have been asked to write an article based on your talk for the accounting department's Web site, which is available to all accounting majors.

Using the guidelines given in Chapter 15—Writing for Publication, write the article.

Exercise 1–6 [General]

Research the following professional exams: CPA, CMA, and CGMA. How are these exams similar? How are they different? Write a memo to your classmates or departmental staff in which you compare and contrast the three exams. Chapter 10 provides information on writing memos.

Exercise 1–7 [Financial]

Look at several published corporate SEC Forms 10-K or annual reports for the most recent year and evaluate the financial statement disclosures they contain. Find examples of disclosures that are not written as clearly or concisely as they could be and rewrite them to be more clear and concise. Share your results with the class and discuss them. (Hint: You can access many 10-Ks and annual reports on the Internet by following the links to listed companies at the New York Stock Exchange (NYSE) Web site (www.nyse.com/index) or by going to www.annualreports.com/.

Exercise 1–8 [Ethics]

Ethics are an important part of any accountant's professional responsibilities. Prepare an article for your school's Web site or your firm's staff newsletter explaining why this is true and discuss sources of guidance for accountants in making ethical decisions.

Exercise 1–9 [Managerial/Systems/Auditing/Tax/Financial/International]

The publications below contain articles related to accounting. Choose one of the publications, search several recent editions, and find an article that interests you. Critique the writing using the tips for effective writing in Figure 1–1. How effective or ineffective do you find the writing? Does the writing style contribute to your understanding of the article? Why or why not?

- [Managerial/Systems] *Management Accounting Quarterly* (MAQ). (You can access MAQ on line at www.imanet.org/insights-and-trends/management-accounting-quarterly/maq-index. Access is on a subscription basis, so you may have to gain access through your school's library.)
- [Auditing/General] *AccountingWEB* (www.accountingweb.com/).
- [Tax, Auditing, or Financial] *Journal of Accountancy* and *The CPA Journal.* You may find these journals on line at www.journalofaccountancy.com/ or www.nysscpa.org/news/publications/the-cpa-journal/issue, respectively.
- [International] *The International Journal of Accounting.* You may find this journal on line at www.journals.elsevier.com/the-international-journal-of-accounting/.

Exercise 1–10 [Current Professional Issues]

In early 2016, The Association of Chartered Certified Accountants (ACCA), in cooperation with the Institute of Management Accountants (IMA), released a report entitled "From Share Value to Shared Value: Exploring the Role of Accountants in Developing Integrated Reporting in Practice" (available at www.imanet.org/insights-and-trends/external-reporting-and-disclosure-management/share-value-to-shared-value). The report encourages "integrated accounting" that includes financial information along with information about the social and economic impacts of a company's activities. Critique the writing in this report using each of the tips for effective writing in Figure 1–1. How effective or ineffective do you find the writing? Does the writing style contribute to your understanding of the report? Why or why not?

NOTES

1. "Plain English Disclosure." Securities and Exchange Commission. *Staff Legal Bulletin No. 7(CF).* www.sec.gov/interps/legal/slbcf7.htm (accessed 20 December 2016): 1–2.

2. Marshall B. Romney and Paul John Steinbart, *Accounting Information Systems,* 12th ed. Upper Saddle River, N.J.: Prentice Hall, 2012, p. 53. Used by permission.

3. American Institute of Certified Public Accountants, Exposure Draft, *Maintaining the Relevance of the Uniform CPA Examination*. (New York; AICPA, September 1, 2015), p. 3. Available at www.aicpa.org/BecomeACPA/CPAExam/nextexam/DownloadableDocuments/Next-CPA-Exam-Exposure-Draft-20150901.pdf (accessed 20 December 2016).

CHAPTER

The Writing Process: An Overview

2

Learning Objectives

After studying this chapter, you should be able to

2.1 Explain the writing process and apply it to your own writing.

2.2 Analyze the purpose for each writing task and plan a document that will achieve that purpose.

2.3 Identify the key issues to be addressed in each document you write and plan your document to address those issues.

2.4 Analyze the audience for each writing task and write appropriately for each audience.

2.5 Gather information for your writing and plan an effective organization for your documents.

2.6 Write a draft of your document.

2.7 Revise your document effectively.

2.8 Manage writer's block and time constraints.

2.9 Work with colleagues on writing critiques.

Effective writing is a process involving a sequence of steps. In this chapter, we discuss the writing process from beginning to end: planning for purpose and audience, including critical thinking about the issues; gathering information; generating and organizing ideas; drafting; revising; and proofreading.

STEPS OF THE WRITING PROCESS

LO2.1 **Explain the writing process and apply it to your own writing.**

Figure 2–1 summarizes the steps of the writing process. You will learn how to apply this process to overcome much of the anxiety you may feel about writing, including the problems of writer's block and time

FIGURE 2–1   The Writing Process

Plan

- Read the assignment or consider the task carefully.
- Analyze the purposes of the document.
- Identify the accounting issues, including different ways those issues might be addressed.
- Analyze the issues from the readers' point of view. What are their interests, needs, and expectations?
- Gather and organize material.

Draft

- Write down your ideas.
- Don't stop to edit.
- Write the parts of the paper in whatever order you want.
- Keep your readers in mind as you compose and organize your document.

Revise

- Reread the document from the readers' point of view. Is your treatment of the issues fair, thorough, and persuasive?
- Revise the document so that it is clear, coherent, and concise.
- Proofread for grammatical, mechanical, and typographical errors.

management. Throughout the chapter, we also discuss how computer technology can help you at every stage of the writing process.

In the previous chapter we identified seven tips for effective writing that focus on content, critical thinking, appropriateness for readers, conciseness, clarity, coherence, and revision (see Figure 1–1 in Chapter 1). In this and following chapters, we discuss specific guidelines and techniques that will help you achieve these goals.

GETTING STARTED: IDENTIFYING PURPOSE

LO2.2   Analyze the purpose for each writing task and plan a document that will achieve that purpose.

One of the first stages in the writing process—analyzing the purpose of the document—is easy to overlook. When you think about purpose, you decide what you want to accomplish with your letter, memo, or other document. Do you want to provide your readers with information about some topic, answer their questions, recommend a course of action, persuade them to do something, or convince them to agree with you on some point?

These are just a few of the purposes a document may have. You should think carefully about the purpose *before* beginning to write.

It might be helpful to think of your purpose in terms of three categories: to give information about something, to propose a course of action, or to solve a problem. The purpose of most writing tasks falls into one of these categories, or perhaps a combination of them. Be certain that you understand the document's purpose from your readers' point of view. For example, you may be asked to investigate several possible solutions to a problem faced by your organization. Your readers may expect you to recommend the preferred solution, or they may want you to summarize the pros and cons of each, which decision makers will evaluate before making the final decision.

As an example, assume you are the controller for Midwest Growth, Inc., a real estate development firm. Midwest's Board of Directors is considering the purchase of an office building for renovation and resale. A report on this possible purchase could have one or more of the following purposes:

- To inform Midwest's Board of the advantages (and/or disadvantages) of the purchase
- To recommend that Midwest purchase (or not purchase) the property
- To suggest a way to finance the purchase
- To explain the effects of the possible purchase on Midwest's tax liabilities.

One way to think about the purpose of a document is to identify the accounting issues it will address. Sometimes these issues are obvious, but at other times you must analyze the situation carefully before all the issues become apparent. For example, Midwest's Board might be eager to arrange the purchase of the office building so that the transaction will minimize Midwest's tax liabilities. As you analyze the possible purchase, you might become aware of accounting issues that would never occur to the Board, such as the need to record the transaction consistently with generally accepted accounting principles. You might also become aware of ethical or legal issues that the Board had not considered.

Identifying the issues can help you define the purposes of the document you are writing, because one purpose might be to explain the issues in a way your reader can understand.

After you have analyzed your purposes carefully, you should write them down. Be as specific as possible and try to define each purpose in a sentence. This sentence might later become part of the document's introduction.

When you analyze your purposes, *be specific*. Remember that you are writing to particular individuals in a particular situation. Relate the purposes of your writing to these people and their concerns. That is, state the purposes in the context of this specific situation rather than in broad, general terms. In the Midwest Growth example discussed above, suppose you were writing a report on how to finance the purchase of the office building. You would limit your discussion to the financing alternatives available to Midwest that are practical for the company to consider.

Sometimes, to determine the purpose or purposes of a document, you need to read previous correspondence on the subject, such as a letter or email from a client. Be sure to read this correspondence carefully, noting important information and questions you've been asked to address. You may also receive an oral request to write something, perhaps by your supervisor. If you receive such a request, listen carefully to the directions. If the purposes of the document are not clear, ask questions until you're sure what the document should include.

THINKING ABOUT THE ISSUES

LO2.3   Identify the key issues to be addressed in each document you write and plan your document to address those issues.

If a purpose for your writing involves analyzing complex accounting issues, think carefully about your topic as you plan your document, gather information, and write. A problem might have more than one reasonable solution, and some people might disagree with the course of action you recommend. As you plan your writing, keep alternative points of view in mind and evaluate the advantages and disadvantages of each alternative. Consider not only the reasons for your own opinion, but also the reasons other people might have a different view. How will you support your opinion, and how will you respond to the arguments of people who disagree with you? Critical thinking about the issues throughout the writing process helps ensure that the document you write is persuasive. Your readers will regard you as knowledgeable and fair, and they will take seriously what you write.

As we will see in later chapters, the AICPA regards the ability to analyze a problem and evaluate alternative solutions as essential to the practice of accounting. (Chapter 7 discusses these skills in more detail.)

ANALYZING THE READERS

LO2.4   Analyze the audience for each writing task and write appropriately for each audience.

When you are planning a writing task, it is important to consider who the readers will be. A memo on a highly technical accounting topic might be written one way for an accounting colleague, but another way for a client or manager with only limited knowledge of accounting procedures and terminology.

Effective writers analyze the needs and expectations of their readers before they begin to write. In writing a letter or memo, you will probably be writing to a limited number of people, perhaps to only one person. You also know, or can find out, important information about the reader or readers. Again, you ask certain questions: How much do the readers know about the subject being discussed? What else do they need to know? Have they already formed opinions on the issues? The answers to these questions, and perhaps others, will suggest the level at which you will write, including the terms and procedures you will explain, the background you will provide, and the arguments you will make.

Accountants who deal with the public should be particularly careful in analyzing the needs of their readers. A tax specialist, for example, might have clients with widely varying experience and knowledge of tax terminology. A corporate executive would probably understand such concepts as depreciation and accruals, but a small shopkeeper might not be familiar with this terminology. Business letters to these two clients, even on the same topic, should be written differently.

Consider the readers' attitudes and biases. Are your readers likely to be neutral to your conclusions and recommendations, or will they need to be convinced? The careful thinking you have already done about the issues will help you write to your readers in a convincing way. Remember your readers' interests and concerns as you write. How will they benefit, directly or indirectly, from what you propose? How can you present your arguments to overcome their objections and biases? To answer this last question, you must anticipate readers' questions, research the issues, and then organize your arguments into a convincing sequence.

Other important considerations when analyzing your readers' needs and expectations are tone and style. What are their attitudes and biases? Some readers react well to an informal, friendly style of writing, but other readers believe that professional writing should be more formal. Whoever your readers are, remember always to be courteous. Whether you write in a technical or conversational style, all readers deserve consideration, tact, and respect. Treating your readers with courtesy and respect will help ensure that your writing is ethical, as well as effective.

Word choices also contribute to an effective and responsible writing style. For example, many readers might find the following sentence troubling:

A successful *CEO* will treat *his* subordinates with respect.

Some readers might argue that the choice of pronouns (*CEO/his*) implies a gender bias. Whenever possible, use plural nouns and pronouns so that your language will be more inclusive:

Successful *CEOs* will treat *their* subordinates with respect.

Sometimes your readers will have additional expectations about your documents. In a classroom situation or in a business environment, you will usually be given directions, such as format and due date of the writing task you have been assigned. How well you follow the directions you are given will affect how your work is evaluated.

Readers' expectations are also important when you write on the job. In fact, meeting readers' expectations might actually be a matter of company policy. Policies often govern how certain documents are written and what procedures they must go through for approval. Many professional services firms do not let new staff members send letters to clients unless a manager or partner first approves them. If you were a new staff member in such a firm, you might draft the client letter, but a manager or partner would review it and possibly ask you to make revisions. Moreover, for certain documents, such as some engagement letters and auditing reports, the actual language used in the letter might be determined by company policy. You will be expected to follow these policies with great care.

In the example of the client letter discussed in the above paragraph, there are actually two or three readers: the manager and/or partner who reviews and approves the letter, and the client who receives it. This letter should be written on a technical level that is appropriate for the client, and it should address the client's concerns, but it should also meet the expectations of the manager or partner. Analyzing readers' needs, interests, and expectations is obviously more complex when there are several readers. Think carefully about the different readers and use your best judgment to meet the expectations of them all.

Analyzing readers' needs, expectations, and opinions is an important part of the preparation for writing. Planning, during which you think carefully about both your audience and your purpose, is an important part of the writing process.

GETTING YOUR IDEAS TOGETHER

LO2.5   Gather information for your writing and plan an effective organization for your documents.

After you have evaluated the purpose of the writing and the needs of the readers, you are ready for the second stage in the writing process: gathering information and organizing the ideas you want to present. This step might be quick and simple. A short letter may not require further research; organizing your ideas may involve only a short list of the main topics you want to include in the letter—perhaps one topic for each paragraph.

For much of the writing you do, gathering information and organizing might be a more complicated process that involves much thought and perhaps some research as well. Let's look at some techniques you can use.

Gathering Information

Before you begin to write the document, be sure you have complete and accurate information. For many projects, some information might already be available. If you're working on an audit, for example, information might be available from other members of the audit team as well as from the files of previous years' audits. Explore these sources of information fully. Review the files carefully and, when necessary, talk with the people who have already worked on the project.

Sometimes you might need to do additional research. This task can involve background reading on a technical topic or a careful review of professsional standards or law, such as FASB publications, the tax code, IRS publications, or SEC publications. As you read this material, take notes carefully and be alert for information that might be helpful when you write. Remember also that issues often have more than one possible solution. As you research, look for material that supports more than one point of view.

This research may require you to interview people who will be affected by the project that you are working on. Suppose you are writing a report to propose a new accounting information system for your company. You can gain important insights into topics your report should cover by talking with the people who would be affected by the proposed system. You can learn what they want the system to accomplish, what they might need to know about it, and whether they have already formed opinions that you should consider.

Generating Ideas

After you have gathered the information you need, you are ready to begin the next phase of the writing process: deciding exactly what to say.

If you have not already written your statement of purpose, now is the time to do so. Try to break up the purpose into several subtopics. Suppose the purpose of a client letter is to recommend that the client company update its accounting system. The statement of purpose for this letter could specify the different accounting jobs for which the expanded system would be useful, outline its major advantages, and respond to questions and objections the client might have.

Another useful technique for generating ideas is brainstorming. With this technique, you think about your topic and write down all your ideas, in whatever order they come to you. Don't worry about organizing the ideas or evaluating them; later, you can consider how these ideas fit into the outline you developed when you analyzed the purposes of the document.

As you assemble the keywords and phrases that occur to you, the phrases might start to become sentences and the sentences might flow together to become paragraphs. You may find that the faster you record your ideas, the more freely the ideas flow. Most people find that generating ideas on a word processing program will make this stage of the writing process easier.

Arranging Ideas: Organization

After you've decided what you want to say, you'll need to consider how best to arrange these ideas so the readers will find them easy to follow. In other words, it's time to think about how the document will be organized.

Much of the work you've already done will help you decide on the best pattern of organization. You may be able to use your statement of purpose as the basis of your organization, or your paper may be structured so that the readers' major concerns are your principle of organization—that is, each concern might be a major division of your paper. Some documents can be organized according to the issues they address.

When considering all these approaches to organization, remember this principle: The needs and interests *of your readers* should determine the document's organization. Arrange your ideas in the order they will find most helpful and easiest to follow. Anticipate when your readers are likely to raise objections or ask questions and respond to those needs when they are likely to occur.

There are a few other points of organization to consider. First, most writing has the same basic structure: an introduction, a concise summary of important ideas, development of the main ideas, and a conclusion. This structure is shown in Figure 2–2.

FIGURE 2–2   Basic Writing Structure

- *Introduction:* Identifies the subject of the document and tells why the document was written. Sometimes the introduction also provides background information about the topic or stresses its importance. You may also use the introduction to build rapport with your reader, perhaps by mentioning a common interest or concern or referring to previous communication on the topic. Finally, the introduction should identify the main topics the document will cover.
- *Concise statement of the main ideas:* Summarizes explicitly main ideas, conclusions, or recommendations. This part of a document may be part of the introduction or a separate section. It can be as short as one-sentence or as long as a three-page executive summary. Sometimes, the recommendation(s) will be part of the final section of the document, along with the conclusions.
- *Development of the main ideas:* Includes explanations, examples, analyses, steps, reasons, arguments, and factual details. This part of an outline or paper is often called the body.
- *Conclusion:* Brings the paper to an effective close. The conclusion may restate the main idea in a fresh way, suggest further work, or summarize recommendations, but an effective conclusion avoids unnecessary repetition.

In later chapters of this book, we will discuss more fully this basic structure as it is used for particular kinds of documents.

Another point is that ideas should be arranged in a logical order. To describe how to reconcile a bank statement, for instance, you would discuss each step of the procedure in the order in which it is performed.

Finally, you can often organize ideas according to their importance. In business writing, always arrange ideas from the most to the least important. Note that this principle means you start with the ideas that are most important *to the reader*.

Suppose you are writing a report to recommend that your firm purchase new accounting system software. Naturally, you will want to emphasize the advantages of this purchase, describing them in the order that is likely to be most convincing to the readers. However, this investment might also have drawbacks, such as the problems involved in converting from the old system to the new one. For your report to appear well researched and unbiased, you need to include these disadvantages in your discussion. You might use the following structure:

   I. Introduction, including your recommendation
  II. Body
     A. Advantages, beginning with those most appealing to the readers
     B. Disadvantages, including, when possible, ways to minimize or overcome any drawbacks
 III. Conclusion

One final word about organization: After you've decided how to arrange your ideas, it's a good idea to write an outline, if you haven't already done so. Having an outline in hand as you draft your paper will help you keep the paper on track. That way, you'll be sure to include all the information you had planned and avoid getting off the subject.

WRITING THE DRAFT

LO2.6 **Write a draft of your document.**

The next major step in the writing process is writing the draft. Most writers find that they can write a first draft more easily if they don't try to edit at this stage. Spelling, punctuation, and style are thus not important in the draft. What is important is to write the ideas so that you can later polish and correct what you have written.

If you did your brainstorming at the computer, you may already have parts of your draft if the list of ideas you began with evolved into sentences or paragraphs as you typed.

The outline you have prepared will guide you as you write. However, you may decide to change the outline as you go, omitting some parts that no longer seem to fit or adding other ideas that seem necessary. Feel free to change the outline as you write; when you revise the draft later, you can make sure your thoughts are still well organized.

Although you will use your outline as a guide to the ideas you want to include in your draft, you might find it easier to write the various parts of the document in a different order from the one used in the outline. Some people find introductions hard to write, so they leave them until last. You may also choose to write the easiest sections of your draft first, or you may start writing some parts of the draft while you are still getting the material together for other parts.

One final word of advice on the draft stage: Don't allow yourself to get stuck while you search for the perfect word, phrase, or sentence. Leave a blank space, or write something that is more or less what you mean. You'll probably find the right words later.

REVISING THE DRAFT

LO2.7   Revise your document effectively.

The next stage in the writing process is the revision of the draft. In this step, you check your spelling and grammar, polish your style, and make a final check to see that the ideas are effectively and completely presented. As you revise, read the document *from the readers' point of view*.

You'll need to revise most of your writing more than once—perhaps three or four times. The key to revising is to let the writing get cold between revisions; a time lapse between readings enables you to read the draft more objectively and see what you have actually said, instead of what you meant to say. Ideally, revisions should be at least a day apart.

Another technique is to have a colleague review the draft for both the content and the effectiveness of the writing. Choose a reviewer who is a good writer and evaluate the reviewer's suggestions with an open mind.

Most word processing software has the ability to check the text for grammar problems and certain errors in style, such as sentences that are too long and paragraphs that use the same word too often. The software may also identify some mistakes in punctuation, as well as most misspelled words.

A word of caution about these style analyzers, spell checkers, and grammar checkers—they're not infallible. They can't catch all the weaknesses in your text, and sometimes they flag problems that aren't really there. If you use a computer to analyze your writing, you still must use your own judgment about what changes to make.

Another revision technique is to print the document and edit the hard copy by hand. You can then make the revisions in your computer file later. Some writers find that they revise more effectively if they work with a hard copy rather than text on a screen.

The next four chapters of the handbook discuss what to look for when putting your writing in final form.

Document Design

After you have polished the style and organization of the paper, you will be ready to put it in final form. Consider questions of document design, such as the use of headings, white space, and other elements of the paper's appearance. We discuss document design more fully in Chapter 6.

Proofreading

Proofreading is an important step in the writing process. Here are some suggestions:

1. Proofreading is usually more effective if you leave time between typing and looking for errors. You will be able to critique the paper more clearly if you have been away from it for awhile.
2. Use your computer's spell check program to help eliminate spelling and typographical errors. Remember that the computer program may not distinguish between homonyms such as *their* and *there* or *affect* and *effect*.
3. In addition to your computer's spell checker, you may also need to use a dictionary to look up words that could possibly be misspelled, such as words the computer doesn't recognize or homonyms it may not have flagged. Check also that you've spelled people's names correctly. If you are a poor speller, have someone else read the paper for spelling errors.
4. If you know that you tend to make a certain type of error, read through your paper at least once to check for that error. For example, if you have problems with subject-verb agreement, check every sentence in your paper to be sure the verbs are correct.
5. Read your paper *backwards*, sentence by sentence, as a final proofreading step. This technique isolates each sentence and makes it easier to spot errors you may have overlooked in previous readings.

WRITER'S BLOCK AND TIME MANAGEMENT

LO2.8   Manage writer's block and time constraints.

Writer's block is a problem everyone faces at some time or another. We stare at blank paper or at a blank screen with no idea of how to get started. The ideas and the words just don't come.

Many of the techniques already discussed in this chapter will help you overcome writer's block. Thinking of writing as a process, rather than a completed product that appears suddenly in its final form, should help make the job less formidable. Any difficult task seems easier if you break it down into manageable steps.

The discussions of the steps in the writing process, especially the section on writing the draft, include suggestions that will help you overcome writer's block. Here is a summary of these techniques:

1. Plan before you write so that you know what you need to say.
2. Write with an outline in view, but write the paper in any order you want. You can rearrange it later.
3. Don't strive for perfection in the draft stage. Leave problems of grammar, spelling, style, and so forth to the revision stage.
4. Begin with the easiest sections to write.
5. Don't get stuck on difficult places. Skip over them and go on to something else. You may find that when you come back to the rough spots later, they are not as hard to write as you thought.

Another challenge you'll face in writing is to manage your time. Throughout this chapter, you've seen how writing is easier if you break the project down into steps. It's easy to manage these steps when you have plenty of time to plan, research, draft, revise, and polish.

What about situations in which you don't have the luxury of time? What about writing answers to discussion questions on an exam, or on-the-job writing tasks where you have only a little time to produce a letter or memo?

The truth is that any writing project, no matter how hurriedly it must be done, will go more smoothly if you stick with the three basic steps of the writing process: plan, draft, and revise. Even if you have only a few minutes to work on a document, allow yourself some of that time to think about who you're writing to, what you need to say, and the best way to organize that material. Then draft the paper. Remember to allow time to revise your writing.

Much of the writing you will do as a professional accountant will be for electronic transmission, such as email or other documents that are sent over the Internet. Documents sent electronically should be planned, written, and revised with the same care you would use for hard-copy versions. This may be obvious for formal documents, but even email and instant messaging, which we often send in haste and consider to be extremely informal, requires care in order to be effective. Chapter 12 gives guidance on the use of electronic communication, including advice on the use of email.

HELP FROM COLLEAGUES: CRITIQUING

LO2.9   Work with colleagues on writing critiques.

Once you have improved your document as much as you can, you may have another source of help: constructive feedback from one or more colleagues. If you are preparing an assignment for a course, this help may come from other students in the class. In a job situation, you might

ask a colleague to review your writing. You will, of course, be willing to return the favor if your colleagues ask you to critique their writing.
Here are some tips for giving helpful critiques:

- Reviews of the writing should be both tactful and honest.
- Always point out strengths of the writing, and then make a few suggestions if you see ways the writing could be improved.
- Make suggestions in positive ways, and be as specific as possible. For example, you wouldn't say, "I can't make any sense of this, and your grammar is deplorable!" Rather, you might say, "Can you explain this concept more clearly? Perhaps shorter sentences would help. Also, you might want to check your verbs."
- Ask the writer if you can write your feedback on the hardcopy paper or insert your feedback in the electronic file you've been given. Alternatively, ask if you can make a copy of the hardcopy or electronic file to do this. Then be prepared to discuss what you liked about the paper, as well as ways it could be improved.
- For specific guidelines on what to look for in the papers you critique, use Tips for the Effective Writer found in Figure 1–1 in Chapter 1.

If a colleague critiques your writing, here are some things to keep in mind:

- Whenever possible, ask people to critique your writing who are themselves good writers.
- Keep an open mind, and resist the natural temptation to be defensive. On the other hand, remember that final responsibility for the document is yours; you'll decide which suggestions to use. Not all advice, however well intended, is helpful.
- Thank the reviewers for their help.

EXERCISES

Exercise 2–1 [General]

Analyze the letter in Figure 2–3. How would you react if you received this letter?

1. Think about these questions and then discuss them with your classmates:
   - What are the strengths of this letter? (It does have some strengths!)
   - What are the weaknesses of the letter? (Hint: Can you find all the typos and spelling errors? In addition to these problems, the letter has a number of less obvious weaknesses. What are they?)

2. Revise the letter so that it is more effective. Invent any details you may need. We discuss letter writing in Chapter 9.

FIGURE 2–3   Letter for Exercise 2–1

> Wright and Wrongh, CPAs
> 123 Anystreet
> Anytown, US 12345
>
> Corner Bike Shop
> 123 Anyother Street
> Anytown, US 12345
>
> Gentleman
> We are in receipt of your correspondence and beg to thank you.
> After extensive research we have found what we hope will be a satisfactory responce to your questions, we hope you will find our work satisfactory. It is the goal of our firm to alway offer the best, most expert and reliable service possible to all our clients, all of whom are value and with whom we hope to have a lont-term working relationship to our mutual advantage.
> There were two possibilities for the resolution of this issue that we considered after a careful analyses of the applicable IRC sections to your situation. If the first possibility proved relevant, then you would be subject to a fine of $5500, plus penalties and interest. If athe other possibility was the best solution, then you would receive a $4400 credit because of a loss carryforard to your current year returns. As you no doubt know, IRC Sec.341(6)a [paras. 5-9] stipulate that the regulations we must follow. Thus, to be in compliance with the rules and regs. you must follow the provisions of the pertinent sections.
> As your CPAs, we are most concerned that we be in complianse with all standards of professional ethics, and we always keep this in mind when we advise you on your tax and accounting questions. We don't want to go to jail, and we're sure you don't either!
> After extensive research, we advise you to file an amended return immediately because the first possibility enumerated in the above paragraph proves to be the correct solution to your problem.
> Thanking you in advance, we remain
>
> Yours with highest regards,
>
> *M. Ostley Wrongh*
>
> M. Ostley Wrongh
> Wright and Wrongh, CPAs

Exercise 2–2 [General]

The chair of the accounting department at your school, John Lee, has decided to initiate a Web site that will provide useful information for the school's accounting majors. Dr. Lee has asked you to write an article for the site concerning the CGMA exam. In particular, he wants you to explain the exam's components. For what skills and knowledge will the exam test? How will these components be measured? What weight will be accorded to the various components?

Dr. Lee also suggests that your article discuss the advantages for professional success if an accountant obtains the CGMA certification.

Write the article for Dr. Lee, using the principles of writing discussed in this chapter. You may also include a table or other graphic illustration, if you think such an inclusion would be helpful to your readers. Chapter 6 discusses document design, including graphic illustration, and Chapter 15 discusses writing for publication.

Exercise 2–3 [General]

You are a member of Beta Alpha Psi (the accounting honorary society) at a major university. A large local high school has contacted your chapter of the honorary society and asked it to prepare a two-page flyer about opportunities provided by an accounting career and the skills (hard and soft) required to succeed both as an accounting student and as an accounting professional. You have been asked by the president of the honorary society, Sandy West, to write the flyer. She has asked that you send it to her as an email attachment. Write the flyer and the cover memo that you will send to Ms. West. Chapter 10 provides information on writing memos, and Chapter 12 discusses email.

Exercise 2–4 [Managerial]

Jim Kakes, CEO of Kakes Manufacturing Company, needs to hire a new controller as the current controller is retiring. Several other CEOs he knows have suggested he look for someone who is a Certified Management Accountant (CMA). Mr. Kakes is not familiar with this designation and has asked you what it is and whether you believe hiring a CMA would be a good idea, given the extra amount he will have to pay in salary.

Write a memo to Mr. Kakes responding to his request. You may wish to consult Chapter 10 for suggestions on memo organization and format and the Web for information on the CMA designation (www. imanet.org).

Exercise 2–5 [Systems]

You are employed by the consulting division of a large professional services firm. Your expertise is in information systems auditing. You have become interested in gaining professional certification in this area and are aware of an organization, ISACA (formerly known as the Information Systems Audit and Control Association and now known by its acronym only) which offers certification as a CISA (Certified Information Systems Auditor). Write a memo to the head of the consulting division, Mr. John

Shipley, requesting that your firm provide the funds for you to attain this certification. You should, of course, explain what this credential is and the benefits to your firm of having a CISA on staff. You have researched the possibility and believe you will need approximately $1,100 to cover the expenses of preparing for and taking the CISA exam.

Chapter 10 provides advice on how to write a memo. For more information on the CISA designation, go to www.isaca.org/.

Exercise 2–6 [Managerial/Current Professional Issues]

The AICPA and CIMA have jointly developed a credential called the Chartered Global Management Accountant (CGMA). Write an article for your school's Web site discussing this credential, what its advantages are, and how to obtain it. You can find more information about the CGMA at www.cgma.org.

Writing for publication is discussed in Chapter 15 of this handbook.

Exercise 2–7 [Auditing]

You are a partner in a medium-size CPA firm and want to convince your partners that your firm should update the way it conducts audits in order to become more competitive. Specifically, you believe the company should make use of up-to-date data analytics technology.

Write a memo to your partners to explain what data analytics technology is and the advantages to using it. Chapter 10 contains suggestions on memo organization and format.

Exercise 2–8 [Tax]

Your school's accounting honorary society maintains a Web site on which it includes short articles on various accounting topics. The readers of this Web site are primarily other accounting students. The Web master has asked you to write an article explaining the differences among progressive, proportional, and regressive tax systems, including their advantages and disadvantages. Write the article, including specific examples of ideas you develop. Chapter 15 discusses writing for publication.

Exercise 2–9 [Financial]

For decades, there has been a debate about whether different Generally Accepted Accounting Principles (GAAP) should be established for private companies as opposed to public companies. Often, this has been referred to as the "Big GAAP vs. Little GAAP" controversy. In mid-2012, the Financial Accounting Foundation's (FAF) board of trustees voted to establish a Private Company Council to determine whether the FAF should make exceptions or modifications to GAAP for privately held companies.

Prepare an outline you can use for a speech to your accounting club on the pros and cons of modifying GAAP for privately held companies. Chapter 16 provides more information on oral presentations.

Exercise 2–10 [International]

For many years, the International Financial Reporting Standards Foundation, through its standard-setting body, the International Accounting Standards Board (IASB), has worked to develop and promote the adoption of a single set of International Financial Reporting Standards (IFRSs) that are globally accepted.

Assume you are a staff accountant for a medium-size regional public accounting firm. Your managing partner, Alan Rhodes, as been asked to give a talk on the progress of the IFRS Foundation toward global adoption of its standards. He has in turn asked you to prepare a briefing memo for him on this topic that he can use in preparing his presentation. Include in your memo the pros and cons of global adoption of IFRSs, the progress made toward global adoption, and prospects for completion of the effort. Chapter 10 provides more information on memos and briefing memos. You can find information at www.ifrs.org/The-organisation/Documents/2015/WhoWeAre_ENGLISH_July%202015.pdf. But you may want to look at other sources as well.

CHAPTER

Coherent Writing: Organizing Business Documents

3

Learning Objectives

After studying this chapter, you should be able to

3.1 Write unified documents that focus on main ideas and readers' concerns.

3.2 Write with summary sentences.

3.3 Respond to readers' questions and concerns.

3.4 Write with transitions that contribute to unified, coherent documents.

3.5 Write paragraphs that focus on main ideas and develop those ideas so they are clear and coherent.

3.6 Organize longer documents, such as essays and discussion papers, so they are coherent, with main ideas that are focused and developed.

Coherence is one of the seven tips for effective business writing discussed in Chapter 1 (see Figure 1–1). Coherent writing is organized so that important ideas stand out. The flow of thought is logical and easy to follow.

Chapter 2 introduced several techniques that will help you make your writing more coherent: analyzing the purpose of the document and readers' needs, then outlining before you begin to write. This chapter discusses additional ways to ensure that your writing is coherent. You'll learn how to write with unity, use summary sentences and transitions, and structure effective paragraphs and longer documents, such as essays, discussion papers, and other business documents.

WRITING WITH UNITY

LO3.1 Write unified documents that focus on main ideas and readers' concerns.

The key to unified writing is to establish the main idea of each document. An office memo or email may contain only one paragraph, but that paragraph has a central idea. A report might be many pages long, but it still has a central idea or purpose, and probably secondary purposes as well. It's important to determine your purpose and main ideas before you begin writing, as discussed in Chapter 2.

You should be able to summarize a main idea in one sentence. In a paragraph, this sentence is called the topic sentence. In longer documents involving two or more paragraphs, this sentence may be called the thesis statement or statement of purpose.

The main idea is the key to the entire document. Any sentences or details that are unrelated to the main idea, either directly or indirectly, are irrelevant and should be omitted. In longer documents, entire paragraphs may be irrelevant to the main purpose. These irrelevant sentences or paragraphs are called digressions.

When you remove digressions and irrelevant sentences, your writing becomes unified; every sentence is related to the main idea.

The following paragraph is not unified. Which sentences are irrelevant to the topic sentence, and which is the first sentence?

> (1) Incorporation offers many advantages for a business and its owners. (2) For example, the owners are not responsible for the business's debts. (3) Investors hope to make money when they buy stock in a corporation. (4) Incorporation also enables a business to obtain professional management skills. (5) Corporations are subject to more government regulation than are other forms of organization.

Sentence 1, the topic sentence, identifies the main idea of the paragraph: the advantages of incorporation. Sentences 3 and 5 are off the subject.

Writing with unity is an important way to make your writing coherent.

USING SUMMARY SENTENCES

LO3.2 Write with summary sentences.

In coherent writing, the main ideas stand out. You can emphasize your main ideas by placing them in the document where they will get readers' attention.

First, as Chapter 2 suggested, it's usually a good idea to summarize your main ideas at the beginning of the document. A long document, especially a report, should have a separate summary section at or near the beginning of the paper. This formal summary may be called an abstract, an executive summary, or simply a summary. The document will also end with a conclusion that again summarizes your main ideas and recommendations.

When writing these summary sections, be specific and remember your readers' interests and needs. Let's say you are writing a memo to the management of Turnipseed Importers to explain the advantages of an accounting software package that it will use to manage its inventory. You'll need to summarize those advantages specifically and relate them to Turnipseed. One of these advantages might be stated this way:

> This software is particularly easy to use because it provides online help for the type of inventory control issues we often encounter with our seed stores. Competing software companies do not offer this type of online support.

The summary at the beginning of a document can be several sentences, or even several pages long, depending on the length of the document and the complexity of the main ideas or recommendations. Here is an example of a summary:

> The following procedures will ensure a smooth transition to the new software:
>
> • Management should designate a representative from each department to attend the training workshop provided by the vendor. This workshop will be offered on October 15. (Details will be provided later.)
> • Each department should plan a training session for its employees to emphasize the department's use of the system.
> • A two-week transition period should be allowed for converting from the old system.
> • Troubleshooters should be available to all departments to solve any problems that occur.

Summary sentences are important in other places in a document, especially at the beginning of each section and in the conclusion.

Any paper that is longer than three or four paragraphs probably has more than one main idea or recommendation; each of these ideas is suggested in the introduction or in a separate summary section. Often, the logical way to organize the remainder of the document is to use a separate section of the paper to discuss each idea further. Each section should begin with a summary statement to identify the main idea, or the topic, of that section. The reader will then have a clear idea of what that section is about. To make your document more readable, vary the wording from that used in the beginning of the paper.

The principle we've been discussing sounds simple: Begin with your conclusion and then give your support. However, many writers have trouble putting this advice into practice. The difficulty may occur because this order of ideas is the reverse of the process writers go through to reach their conclusions. That is, the typical research process would be to gather information first and then to arrive at the conclusions. A writer might try to take the reader through the same investigative steps as those he or she used to solve the problem or answer the question.

Think about your readers' needs. They're mainly interested in the findings of your research, not in the process you went through to get there. They might want to read about the facts you considered as well as your analytical reasoning; in fact, some readers will carefully evaluate the soundness of your data and methodology. However, their first concern is with the conclusions.

As we already mentioned, conclusions will be presented again in a final section, especially if the document is very long. Once again, you may need to remind the reader of your main ideas, but be careful not to sound repetitive. The length and complexity of the document determine how much detail to include in your conclusion.

RESPONDING TO READERS

LO3.3   Respond to readers' questions and concerns.

Earlier chapters discussed planning a document so that it responds to your readers' concerns. That is, you anticipate questions they may have as well as objections they may raise to your recommendations. As you plan the organization of your document, consider the best places to address these concerns. Questions are simple to handle: Anticipate where the readers are likely to have questions and answer them at that part of your paper.

Where you place your responses may also depend on how many objections there are and how complicated your responses are. Sometimes responses to readers' concerns are better addressed in a separate section of the paper. For example, suppose you are recommending a certain accounting treatment for a transaction, but you realize that your readers might disagree with you. The first part of the document might explain the reasons for your recommendation, and the final part of the document might explain the disadvantages of other treatments.

TRANSITIONS

LO3.4   Write with transitions that contribute to unified, coherent documents.

Transitions, which are another element of coherent writing, link ideas together. They can be used between sentences, paragraphs, and major divisions of the document. Transitions show the relationship between two ideas: how the second idea flows logically from the first, and how both are related to the main idea of the entire document.

As an example of how transitions work, consider this paragraph. The topic sentence (main idea) is the first sentence; the transitional expressions are in italics:

> (1) Financial statements are important to a variety of users. (2) *First,* investors and potential investors use the statements to determine whether a company is a good investment risk. (3) These users look at such factors as net income, the debt-to-equity ratio, retained earnings, and economic value added (EVA). (4) *Second,* creditors use financial statements to determine whether a firm is a good credit risk. (5) Creditors want to know whether a firm's cash flow is large enough and sufficiently timely to pay its debts. (6) *Third,* government agencies analyze financial statements for a variety of purposes. (7) *For example,* the Internal Revenue Service wants to know whether the company has paid the required amount of taxes on its income. (8) These examples of financial statement users show how diverse their interests can be.

The sentences beginning *first* (2), *second* (4), and *third* (6) give three examples of the paragraph's main idea: the variety of financial statement users. These three sentences relate to one another in a logical, sequential way, which the transitions make clear. These sentences also relate directly to the topic sentence; they illustrate it with specific examples. Sentence 7, which begins with *for example*, relates only indirectly to the main idea of the paragraph, but it relates directly to sentence 6. Sentence 7 identifies one reason why government agencies need access to financial statements.

Transitions can express a number of relationships between ideas. In the sample paragraph, the transitions indicate an enumerated list (2, 4, and 6) and a specific illustration of a general statement (7). Transitions can also imply other relationships between ideas—conclusions, additional information, or contrasts, for example.

To see the importance of transitions within a paragraph, look at the following example, which lacks transitions:

> Incorporation offers several advantages to businesses and their owners. Ownership is easy to transfer. The business is able to maintain a continuous existence even when the original owners are no longer involved. The stockholders of a corporation are not held responsible for the business's debts. If the Dallas Corporation defaults on a $1,000,000 loan, its investors will not be held responsible for paying that liability. Incorporation enables a business to obtain professional managers with centralized authority and responsibility. The business can be run more efficiently. Incorporation gives a business certain legal rights. It can enter into contracts, own property, and borrow money.

Now see how much easier it is to read the paragraph when it has appropriate transitions:

> Incorporation offers several advantages to businesses and their owners. *For one thing,* ownership is easy to transfer, *and* the business is able to

maintain a continuous existence even when the original owners are no longer involved. *In addition*, the stockholders of a corporation are not held responsible for the business's bad debts. If the Dallas Corporation defaults on a $1,000,000 loan, *for example*, its investors will not be held responsible for paying that liability. Incorporation *also* enables a business to obtain professional managers with centralized authority and responsibility; *therefore*, the business can be run more efficiently. *Finally*, incorporation gives a business certain legal rights. *For example*, it can enter into contracts, own property, and borrow money.

Transitional Words and Phrases

Following is a list of commonly used transitional expressions, their meanings, and example sentences showing how some of them work.

- **Adding a point or piece of information:** *and, also, in addition, moreover, furthermore, first/second/third, finally.*

  Example: We appreciate the opportunity to conduct your audit this year and will send you a detailed schedule of our work next week.

- **Making an exception or contrasting point:** *but, however, nevertheless, on the other hand, yet, still, on the contrary, in spite of . . ., nonetheless.*

  Example: Most of our divisions showed a profit his quarter. However, the Houston division was not so successful.

- **Giving specific examples or illustrations:** *for example, for instance, as an illustration, in particular, to illustrate.*

  Example: Financial statements serve a variety of users. For example, investors use them to evaluate potential investments. Other users include . . .

- **Clarifying a point:** *that is, in other words, in effect, put simply, stated briefly.*

  Example: The basic accounting equation is *assets equal liabilities plus owners' equity.* That is, A = L + OE.

- **Conceding a point to the opposite side:** *granted that, it may be true that, even though, although.*

  Example: Although upgrading our equipment will require a large capital outlay, increased efficiency will more than justify the use of funds.

- **Indicating place, time, or importance:**
  Place: *above, beside, beyond, to the right, below, around.*
  Time: *formerly, hitherto, earlier, in the past, before, at present, now, today, these days, tomorrow, in the future, next, later on, later.*
  Importance: *foremost, most importantly, especially, of less importance, of least importance.*

Example: In earlier centuries there was no need for elaborate accounting systems. However, the size and complexities of today's businesses
make modern accounting a complicated process indeed.

- **Indicating the stages in an argument or process, or the items in a series:** *initially, at the outset, to begin with, first, first of all, up to now, so far, second, thus far, next, after, finally, last.*

  Example: The accounting process works in stages. First, transactions
  must be analyzed.

- **Giving a result:** *as a result, consequently, accordingly, as a consequence, therefore, thus, hence, then, for that reason.*

  Example: Generally accepted accounting principles allow flexibility in
  their application. Therefore, it is easier for accountants to meet changing needs of the business world.

- **Adding emphasis:** *indeed, clearly*

  Example: Indeed, good writing skills are essential for professional
  success.

- **Summing up or restating the central point:** *in sum, to sum up, to summarize, in summary, to conclude, in brief, in short, as one can see, in conclusion.*

  Example: In conclusion, transitions often make writing much easier
  to read.

Repetition of Key Words and Phrases

Another way to add coherence to your writing is to repeat key words
and phrases. Such repetitions are particularly useful for connecting
paragraphs and major divisions of documents. These repetitions are
typically located at the beginning of a new paragraph or section.

The following outline of a student's essay shows the structure of
a discussion on alternatives to the historical cost basis of accounting.
Notice how the combination of transitional expressions and repeated
key phrases holds the report together. These techniques also tie the
parts of the report to the main idea of the paper, which is summarized in the thesis statement. Notice how summary sentences appear
throughout the outline.

THE MONETARY UNIT ASSUMPTION

  I. Introductory paragraph
    A. Introductory sentences
      One of the basic assumptions made by accountants is that
money is an effective common denominator by which the
operations of business enterprises can be measured and analyzed. Implicit in this assumption is the acceptance of the stable and unchanging nature of the monetary unit. However,

the validity of this assumption has been questioned not only by academicians and theorists, but by practitioners as well.

B. Thesis statement (main idea of entire paper)

Several solutions have been proposed by accountants to correct for the changing value of the monetary unit.

II. Body

A. Nature of the problem

The unadjusted monetary unit system has been criticized because it distorts financial statements during periods of inflation.

B. First solution to the problem

1. One solution to overstating profits solely because of inflation is to adjust figures for changes in the general purchasing power of the monetary unit. (This paragraph describes the solution and its advantages.)

2. However, the general purchasing power approach has been criticized for several reasons. (This paragraph describes the disadvantages of this approach.)

C. Second solution to the problem

1. Instead of the general purchasing power procedure, some favor adjusting for changes in replacement cost. (This paragraph describes this solution.)

2. One of the major advantages of the replacement cost approach ... (This paragraph discusses several advantages.)

3. One authority has summarized the criticisms of replacement cost accounting: "Most of the criticisms . . ." (This paragraph discusses the disadvantages of this approach.)

D. Third solution to the problem

1. Still others favor a mark-to-market (fair value) approach in which current exit values are used to value assets when possible.

2. For certain assets, the FASB now requires the use of this approach. In general, the advantages are ...

3. Critics of wide-spread use of this approach argue that ...

III. Concluding paragraph

Adjusting for changes in the general purchasing power, adjusting for changes in replacement cost, and the use of the mark-to-market (fair value) approach represent attempts to correct the problems of the stable monetary unit assumption in times of inflation.

Pronouns Used to Achieve Coherence

Another tool you can use to achieve coherent writing is the pronoun. A pronoun stands for a noun or a noun phrase that has previously been identified. The noun that the pronoun refers to is called its *antecedent.* Consider this sentence:

Investors expect that, over time, their portfolios will increase in value.

In this sentence, the pronoun *their* refers to the noun *investors.* Put another way, *investors* is the antecedent of *their.*

Because pronouns refer to nouns that the writer has already used, pronouns help connect the thoughts of a paragraph. Look at how the pronouns work in this paragraph:

The audit staff reviewed the financial statements of Western Manufacturing to determine whether the statements had been prepared in accordance with generally accepted accounting principles. *We* found two problems that may require *us* to issue a qualified opinion. First, Western has not been consistent in *its* treatment of accounts receivable. Second, *we* identified several transactions that may violate the matching principle. *We* suggest a meeting with Western's management to discuss these issues.

Pronouns require a word of warning, however. Unless a writer is careful, the reader may not be sure what noun the pronoun refers to. Look at the problem in this sentence:

The managers told the accountants that they did not understand company policy.

Who didn't understand company policy—the managers or the accountants? This sentence illustrates the problem of ambiguous pronoun reference.Chapter 5 discusses this problem further.

Problems with Transitions

A few problems can occur with transitions other than the failure to use them when they are needed. One problem occurs when a writer uses transitional expressions too often. These expressions are necessary to make the relationship of ideas clear when there might be some confusion. Often this logical relationship is clear without the use of transitional expressions. Consider this paragraph:

Accountants never finish their education. They work hard for their college degrees; after college they must continue studying to stay current on the latest developments in the profession. They must be thoroughly familiar with changing government regulations and new pronouncements by professional organizations such as the FASB. To improve their professional competence, they participate in a variety of continuing education programs sponsored by such organizations as the AICPA and state accounting societies. Well-qualified accountants are lifetime students, always seeking better ways to serve their clients and the public.

Notice how easy this paragraph is to follow, even though it doesn't use a single transitional expression.

Another problem with transitions occurs when the writer uses the wrong expression, suggesting an illogical connection of ideas. Consider these examples:

FAULTY TRANSITION: GAAP are not established by federal law. For instance, organizations such as the FASB issue these standards, and the FASB is not part of the federal government.

REVISED: GAAP are not established by federal law. Rather, organizations that are not part of the federal government, such as the FASB, issue these standards.

FAULTY TRANSITION: If accountants do not follow GAAP, they may lose their CPA licenses. Therefore, they must follow GAAP to conform to their code of professional ethics.

REVISED: If accountants do not follow GAAP, they may lose their CPA licenses. They must also follow GAAP to conform to their code of professional ethics.

Transitions, when used correctly, are valuable tools for clarifying the relationship between ideas. If you use transitions carefully, along with summary sentences and a logical organization, your writing will be easy to follow.

The next sections of this chapter show how to use these techniques to write coherent paragraphs, discussion questions, and longer forms of writing, such as essays and discussion papers.

PARAGRAPHS

LO3.5   Write paragraphs that focus on main ideas, and develop those ideas so that they are clear and coherent.

This section of the chapter is devoted to techniques of paragraphing: how to plan length, structure, and development so that your paragraphs are coherent.

Length

You might not be sure how long paragraphs should be. Are one-sentence paragraphs acceptable? What about paragraphs that run on for nearly an entire typed page?

One rule is that a paragraph should be limited to the development of one idea. Thus, the length of most paragraphs is somewhere between one sentence and an entire page. However, an occasional short paragraph, even of only one sentence, can be effective to emphasize an idea or to provide a transition between two major divisions of the writing.

Be wary of long paragraphs, which look intimidating and are often hard to follow. You may need to divide a long paragraph into two or more shorter ones. Appropriate transitions can tie the new paragraphs together and maintain a smooth flow of thought. Limit most of your paragraphs to four or five sentences.

Structure

Another feature of well-written paragraphs is an appropriate structure. We have already suggested that a strong topic sentence can contribute to a unified, coherent paragraph. A topic sentence states the main idea of the paragraph. It is usually the first sentence in the paragraph, and sometimes contains a transition tying the new paragraph to the previous one. All other sentences in the paragraph should develop the idea expressed in the topic sentence.

Two patterns of paragraph organization are useful for most writing tasks that accountants will tackle: the simple deductive paragraph and the complex deductive paragraph. The simple deductive arrangement states the main idea in the first sentence (topic sentence); all other sentences *directly* develop that idea by adding details. A concluding sentence is sometimes helpful. Look again at this paragraph, which illustrates a simple deductive organization:

> (1) Accountants never finish their education. (2) They work hard for their college degrees, but after college they must continue studying to stay current on the latest developments in the profession. (3) They must be thoroughly familiar with changing government regulations and new pronouncements by professional organizations such as the FASB. (4) To improve their professional competence, they participate in a variety of continuing education programs sponsored by such organizations as the AICPA and state accounting societies. (5) Well-qualified accountants are lifetime students, always seeking better ways to serve their clients and the public.

In this paragraph, sentence 1 is the topic sentence, sentences 2 through 4 develop the main idea, and sentence 5 is the conclusion. A simple deductive paragraph has a simple structure such as this one:

1. Topic sentence—main idea
   2. Supporting sentence
   3. Supporting sentence
   4. Supporting sentence
5. Concluding sentence (optional)

A complex deductive paragraph has a more elaborate structure. This paragraph is complex deductive:

> (1) Financial statements are important to a variety of users. (2) First, investors and potential investors use the statements to determine

whether a company is a good investment risk. (3) These users look at such factors as net income, the debt-to-equity ratio, retained earnings, and economic value added (EVA). (4) Second, creditors use financial statements to determine whether a firm is a good credit risk. (5) Creditors want to know whether a firm has a timely and large enough cash flow to pay its debts. (6) Third, government agencies analyze financial statements for a variety of purposes. (7) For example, the Internal Revenue Service wants to know whether the company has paid the required amount of taxes on its income. (8) These examples of financial statement users show how diverse their interests can be.

In this paragraph, sentence 1 (the topic sentence) states the main idea. Sentence 2 directly supports the main idea by giving an example, but sentence 3 explains sentence 2. Thus, sentence 3 directly supports sentence 2, but only indirectly supports sentence 1. Complex deductive paragraphs have a structure similar to this one:

1. Topic sentence—main idea
   2. Direct support
      3. Indirect support
   4. Direct support
      5. Indirect support
   6. Direct support
      7. Indirect support
8. Conclusion (optional)

Complex deductive paragraphs can have numerous variations. The number of direct supporting sentences can vary, as can the number of indirect supports. Sometimes direct supports do not require any indirect supports.

Consider another example of a complex deductive paragraph:

(1) Two of the most popular inventory flow assumptions used by businesses today are FIFO (first-in, first-out) and LIFO (last-in, first-out). (2) FIFO assumes that the first goods purchased for inventory are the first goods sold. (3) Therefore, ending inventory under FIFO consists of the most recent purchases. (4) Because older, usually lower costs are matched with sales revenues, FIFO results in a higher net income and thus higher income tax liabilities. (5) The LIFO flow assumption, on the other hand, assumes that the most recent purchases are the first goods sold. (6) Cost of goods sold, however, is based on more recent and higher prices. (7) Thus, LIFO usually results in lower net income and lower income tax liabilities. (8) This advantage makes LIFO very popular with many businesses.

This paragraph can be outlined to reveal the following structure:

I. Topic sentence (1): Two popular inventory flow assumptions
   A. FIFO (2-4)
      1. Description (2)
      2. Effect on inventory (3)
      3. Effect on net income and taxes (4)

B. LIFO (5–8)
  1. Description (5)
  2. Effect on inventory (6)
  3. Effect on net income and taxes (7)
  4. Popularity (8)

The descriptions of FIFO and LIFO in this paragraph are very condensed, probably too condensed for most purposes. Moreover, the paragraph is really too long. It would be better to divide it between sentences 4 and 5, resulting in two shorter but closely related paragraphs:

(1) Two of the most popular inventory flow assumptions used by businesses today are FIFO (first-in, first-out) and LIFO (last-in, first-out). (2) FIFO assumes that the first goods purchased for inventory are the first goods sold. (3) Therefore, ending inventory under FIFO consists of the most recent purchases. (4) Because older, usually lower costs are matched with sales revenues, FIFO results in a higher net income and thus higher income tax liabilities.

(5) The LIFO flow assumption, on the other hand, assumes that the most recent purchases are the first goods sold. (6) Cost of goods sold, however, is based on more recent and higher prices. (7) Thus, LIFO usually results in lower net income and lower income tax liabilities. (8) This advantage makes LIFO very popular with many businesses.

Both paragraphs now have simple deductive structures. However, the first paragraph is a modified version of a simple deductive structure because the main idea of this paragraph is in the second sentence.

The important idea about both simple and complex deductive paragraphs is their unity: All sentences, either directly or indirectly, develop the main idea of the paragraph as expressed in the topic sentence.

One advantage of deductive paragraphs is that they enable a reader to skim the document quickly and locate main ideas. A busy reader may scan a document, reading only the first sentence of each paragraph.

Some writers might wonder about a third type of paragraph organization: paragraphs with an inductive structure. Inductive paragraphs put the main idea last. Supporting sentences lead up to the topic sentence, which is the last sentence in the paragraph. For most business writing, inductive paragraphs are not as effective as simple or complex deductive paragraphs. Business readers like to identify main ideas from the start. They don't like to be kept in suspense, wondering, "What's all this leading up to? What's the point?" Thus, it's a good idea to stick with deductive organization for most business writing.

Paragraph Development

An effective paragraph is not only well organized, but it is also well developed. That is, the idea expressed in the topic sentence is adequately explained and illustrated so that the reader has a clear understanding of what the writer is saying.

Several techniques are useful for paragraph development: descriptive and factual details, illustrations or examples, definitions, and appeals to authority.

Descriptive and factual details give a more thorough, concrete explanation of the idea that is expressed in a general way in the topic sentence. Factual details give measurable, observable, or historical information that can be objectively verified. Descriptive details are similar to factual details. They give specific characteristics of the subject being discussed.

When you use details with which your readers are familiar, they can better understand your observations and conclusions. In the following paragraph, the main idea is stated in the first sentence. The paragraph is then developed with factual details:

> Our net income for next year should increase because we've signed a contract with an important new customer. Flip's Frog Ponds, Inc., which last year had more than $4 billion in revenue, has ordered a million lily pads from our horticultural division. This new business should increase our revenues by at least 15%.

Another useful paragraph development technique is using illustrations or examples—typical cases or specific instances of the idea being discussed. Illustrations can take a variety of forms. A paragraph might combine several brief examples, or use one long, extended illustration. The examples can be factually true, or they may be hypothetical, invented for the purpose of illustration.

Definitions are useful to explain concepts or terms that might be unfamiliar to the reader. A definition can be formal, such as the meaning given in a dictionary or an accounting standard, or it can be a more informal explanation of a term. Often a definition is more effective when combined with an illustration.

The following paragraph is developed by definition and illustration:

> *Assets* can be defined as things of value (economic resources) owned by a business. For example, cash is an asset; so are the land, buildings, and equipment owned by a business. Sometimes assets are resources owned by a business, though not tangible. An example of this kind of asset is an account receivable.

Finally, some paragraphs are developed by appeals to authority—facts, illustrations, or ideas obtained from a reputable source such as a book, article, interview, or official pronouncement. Appeals to authority can be paraphrases—someone else's idea expressed in your own words—or direct quotations from the source being used. Chapter 8 gives more information on the correct use of quotations and paraphrases.

By using a variety of techniques, you can fully develop the ideas expressed in the topic sentences of your paragraphs. Factual and descriptive detail, illustration, definition, and authority all give the reader a clear understanding of what you want to explain.

However you decide to develop your paragraphs, remember the importance of your readers' interests and needs. It's better to select supporting details and examples with which readers are already familiar.

ORGANIZING LONGER DOCUMENTS

LO3.6   Organize longer documents, such as essays and discussion papers, so they are coherent, with main ideas that are focused and developed.

We've seen that a well organized paragraph begins with a topic sentence that states the paragraph's main idea and then develops that idea more fully with details, explanations, and other forms of support. Many situations call for discussions of more than one paragraph, however. Some exam questions in accounting coursework, as well as professional certification exams, may require answers that will necessitate two or more paragraphs, or even several pages. Many business documents, such as memos, letters, and reports, require multiple paragraphs or pages. The principles discussed in this chapter are useful for all longer documents. You will find more information about specific business documents, as well as discussion papers, in later chapters.

The principles for organizing longer documents are similar to those for organizing paragraphs: begin with important ideas, and then develop those ideas with adequate support. In answering a discussion question on an academic or professional exam, the question may suggest the first sentence of the answer. Consider this example of a question that might appear on a course exam:

Discuss the sources of authoritative accounting principles.

The answer to this discussion question might begin with the following sentence, which gives the main idea of the answer:

Authoritative accounting principles derive from many sources.

The answer might then go on to discuss accounting principles promulgated by the FASB and its predecessor organizations. A second paragraph might then discuss accounting principles promulgated by the SEC and other governmental agencies. Finally, a third paragraph might discuss other less authoritative sources such as textbooks and articles in professional accounting publications. The third paragraph might begin with this topic sentence:

Although less authoritative, textbooks and articles in professional accounting publications can also be important.

Short paragraphs with strong topic sentences, as in the answer outlined in the preceding paragraphs, will help the exam grader identify your main ideas and give you credit for what you know.

Organizing Essays and Discussion Papers

The documents you will write as a professional accountant will usually be longer than single paragraphs, as long as several paragraphs or even many pages. In practice, you will typically write in business formats, such as letters, memos, or reports, but occasionally you may be asked to organize your writing into an essay format or discussion paper. This is true, for example, on some professional certification exams. The CMA exam may require you to write an essay, and the CGMA exam may call for a discussion paper.

Essays and discussion papers use similar strategies of effective organization, which we discuss below. In fact, the terms "essay" and "discussion paper" sometimes overlap. Generally, an essay is shorter than a discussion paper, perhaps five to six paragraphs. Discussion papers may be considerably longer, even many pages. We will begin by discussing how to organize an essay, since the principles for writing coherent essays apply equally well to discussion papers and other longer business documents.

Essays

Essays, which usually have four or more paragraphs, will have a complex deductive structure. That is, the paper will include both major and minor supports of the paper's main idea, or thesis. The paper's paragraphs offer direct support of the paper's thesis. The sentences within each paragraph develop the topic sentence of the paragraph, and thereby directly support the paragraph's main idea and indirectly support the thesis, or main idea of the paper.

Sometimes with a longer discussion the thesis may come at the end of the first paragraph, in which case it may be preceded by sentences that give background on the topic or otherwise interest the reader in what is being discussed.

An essay usually ends with a conclusion, which may be a sentence or a paragraph.

Below is the outline of a six-paragraph essay followed by an explanation of several of its components. Following the outline are explanations of several of the outline's components.

    I. Introduction—first paragraph
        A. Attention-getting sentences (optional)
        B. Thesis statement—main idea of the essay, usually expressed in one sentence
    II. Body of the essay—develops the thesis through analysis, explanation, examples, proofs, or steps.

A. Major support—second paragraph

   1.
   2. Minor supports—sentences that develop the paragraph
   3. in a simple or complex deductive organization

B. Major support—third paragraph

   1.
   2. Minor supports
   3.

C. Major support—fourth paragraph

   1.
   2. Minor supports
   3.

D. Major support—fifth paragraph

   1.
   2. Minor supports
   3.

III. Conclusion—sixth paragraph

   A. Repeats the essay's main idea (a variation of the thesis statement) or otherwise provides closure

   B. Forceful ending (optional)

Attention-Getting Sentences

Some longer discussions begin with attention-getting sentences, which are intended to get the reader interested in the subject. Several techniques can be used:

- Give background information about the topic. Why is the topic of current interest?
- Pose a problem or raise a question (to be answered in the essay).
- Define key terms, perhaps the topic itself.
- Show the relevance of the topic to the reader.
- Begin with an interesting direct quotation.
- Relate a brief anecdote relevant to the topic.
- Relate the specific topic to a wider area of interest.

The following essay introduction uses two of these techniques. It poses a question and then suggests the relevance of the topic to the reader, assuming that the essay was written for accountants. The final sentence of the paragraph states the paper's thesis, or main idea.

> Do accountants need to be good writers? Some people would answer "No" to this question. They believe an accountant's job is limited to arithmetical calculations and computer applications with very little need to use words or sentences. But this picture of an accountant's responsibilities is a misconception. In fact, good writing skills are essential to the successful practice of accounting.

Sometimes you might choose not to use attention-getting sentences, but decide instead to begin your discussion with the thesis statement. This is a particularly good strategy to use for exam questions.

Thesis Statement

The thesis statement summarizes the main idea of the essay, usually in one sentence. It can be a *simple* thesis statement, such as the following:

> Good writing skills are essential to the successful practice of accounting.

Alternatively, the thesis statement can be *expanded*. That is, it can summarize the main supports of the discussion. Here is an example of an expanded thesis statement:

> In fact, successful accountants must have good writing skills to communicate with clients, managers, agencies, and colleagues.

Sometimes, to avoid a long or awkward sentence, you might want to use two sentences for the thesis statement:

> In fact, good writing skills are essential to the successful practice of accounting. During a typical business day, an accountant may write to clients, managers, agencies, or colleagues.

Conclusion

The conclusion should provide the reader with a sense of closure—a feeling that the essay is complete, and that the train of thought has come to a logical end. You can give your writing closure by repeating the main idea, usually in some variation of the thesis statement. You may also want to end with a forceful statement that will stay in the reader's mind, thus giving the discussion a more lasting impact. For a strong ending, you can use several techniques, many of which resemble those used in the introduction:

- Show a broad application of the ideas suggested in the discussion.
- End with an authoritative direct quotation that reinforces your position.
- Challenge the reader.
- Echo the attention-getting sentences. For example, if you began by posing a question in the introduction, you can answer it explicitly in the conclusion.

If you're writing an essay on an exam, a concluding paragraph might not be necessary, but it's important that the discussion seem finished. The essay will seem complete if you've developed your thesis statement fully.

Sample Essay

The following is an assignment given in an accounting class. The answer in Figure 3–1 illustrates some of the principles of good organization and development.

> *Assignment.* The International Accounting Standards Board (IASB) is responsible for the development of a set of international accounting standards. Explain why the development of international accounting standards may be important.

FIGURE 3–1   Example of an Essay

The Importance of International Accounting Standards

The need for international accounting standards has received great attention for many years. This attention is due to the expanding globalization of business and capital markets. When different countries have different business regulations and use different accounting methods, the increased complexity of conducting business and raising capital across national borders presents major challenges. By analogy, consider how difficult the reporting process in our own country would be if each of the 50 states employed different business regulations and a different set of accounting standards. Clearly, in such a case our capital markets as reflected by the activities of the New York Stock Exchange (NYSE) and NASDAQ could not operate as efficiently or robustly as they now do. Indeed, many believe the need for international accounting standards has become more important in recent years.

If investors in international capital markets must make investment choices among corporations that use different accounting standards, competing investment opportunities become less comparable and much more risky. The result is likely to be that fewer investors will undertake the effort or assume the risk of investing in foreign corporations or in corporations that have extensive foreign holdings. Consequently, fewer corporations may list their securities on a foreign exchange. Ultimately, such difficulties could seriously impede the expansion of international capital markets and the development of more healthy international economies.

The International Accounting Standards Board (IASB) has been responsible for setting international standards since 2001. Together with its predecessor, the International Accounting Standards Committee (IASC), these two organizations have issued numerous International Accounting Standards (IASs) and International Financial Reporting Standards (IFRSs). Through its efforts the IASB hopes to achieve convergence of international financial reporting standards.

Most international accounting organizations, securities exchanges, and governments support this effort to harmonize standards. Several of the world's securities exchanges either permit or require compliance with IASs and IFRSs by their registrants. The International Organization of Securities Commissions (IOSCO) and the Organization for Economic Cooperation and Development (OECD) cooperate with the IASB in its development of international financial reporting standards. The European Union has accepted the international standards issued by the IASC and the IASB for its member countries.

Although the prospect for uniform financial reporting standards among all countries is not realistic, reducing differences through the concept of harmonization is clearly a worthwhile goal.

Discussion Papers

As noted above, discussion papers resemble essays in structure and organization, except that discussion papers are usually much longer than essays. A discussion paper is typically an in-depth treatment of an accounting topic and often requires extensive research. Discussion papers are usually concerned with broad, theoretical topics under consideration by the accounting profession, as opposed to the concrete issues faced by a particular client or business entity. They may be organized to resemble a lengthy essay, or they may be formatted as a formal report, technical memo, or other business document. Whatever the format, a discussion paper uses principles of coherent organization that are similar to those for an essay: introduction, including summary of main ideas; body that develops those ideas; and conclusion. Chapter 11 discusses discussion papers more fully.

Organizing Business Documents

Most documents typical of business, such as letters, memos, and reports, will be organized with a complex deductive structure such as that discussed in the previous section. That is, they will have a three-part structure, with the main topics or idea(s) stated in the introduction of the document. The documents will develop those ideas with body paragraphs that provide direct and indirect support, and they will end with a conclusion.Later chapters in this book discuss writing business documents in more detail.

TEST YOURSELF

Is the following paragraph coherent? If not, revise it to improve its organization, using some of these techniques:

- Write a strong topic sentence stating the paragraph's main idea.
- Use transitional devices to show the relation between sentences.
- Eliminate sentences that don't fit.
- Divide long, disunified paragraphs into shorter, unified ones.
- Rearrange sentences by grouping ideas together (add sentences if necessary).

Accountants used to enter data into spreadsheets by hand. Accountants performed calculations by hand, and they had adding machines. Much of the work accountants did in the past was tedious and time consuming. Computers have drastically changed the practice of accounting. If accountants made errors, accountants would have to erase the mistakes with chemicals that would dissolve the ink. These chemicals could stain their clothes and sometimes irritate their skin and make their desks messy.

TEST YOURSELF: ANSWER

This paragraph needs revision. Here is one possibility:

> Computers have drastically changed the practice of accounting in the past few decades. In the past, accountants performed calculations by hand, or perhaps with the help of adding machines. They entered data into spreadsheets by hand; if they made errors in their entries, they would have to erase the mistakes with chemicals that dissolved the ink, or they would have to enter the data again from the beginning. These examples suggest that much of the work accountants did in the past was tedious and time consuming.

EXERCISES

Exercise 3–1 [General]

Look online for Web sites sponsored by an accounting organization or publication, such as the AICPA or *Accounting Today*. Look for short discussions published on those sites. Analyze these discussions, using the following questions:

- What is the main idea of the article?
- How does the author develop the main idea? That is, what are the supporting ideas?
- How long are paragraphs?
- How does the author develop the paragraphs? Can you find illustrations, examples, appeals to authority, or definitions?
- What transitions connect the ideas in the article?
- Is the article interesting to read? Does it seem relevant to its intended audience?

Present the findings from your analysis in a class discussion. Chapter 16 discusses how to make oral presentations.

Exercise 3–2 [General]

Look for an editorial in print or online editions of *The Wall Street Journal* or other financial publication. Analyze the editorial according to the characteristics of a longer discussion presented in this chapter. Consider the following questions:

- What is the main idea of the article?
- How does the author develop the main idea? That is, what are the supporting ideas?
- How long are paragraphs?
- How does the author develop the paragraphs? Can you find illustrations, examples, appeals to authority, or definitions?

- What transitions does the author use?
- Is the article interesting to read? Does it seem relevant to its intended audience?

Present the findings from your analysis in a class discussion. Chapter 16 discusses how to make oral presentations.

Exercise 3–3 [Financial]

Write a discussion on one of the following topics using the techniques covered in this and earlier chapters. Your answer might range from one to six paragraphs or more, depending on the topic.

1. Discuss how to test for impairment of intangible assets with indefinite lives under FASB standards.
2. Discuss the role of The International Integrated Reporting Council (IIRC) in the future development of corporate reporting.
3. Define *fair value accounting* and discuss the pros and cons of its use.
4. Explain the difference between revenues and gains.
5. Discuss the importance of convergence in the context of establishing International Financial Reporting Standards (IFRSs) as well as the pros and cons of adopting IFRSs in the United States.

Exercise 3–4 [Systems]

Write about one of the following topics using the techniques covered in this and earlier chapters. Your answer might range from one to six paragraphs or more, depending on the topic.

1. Explain normalization and semantic data modeling approaches to database design.
2. A database can view data in either a physical view or a logical view. Explain each of these views and when each may be useful.
3. Explain what COBIT is and the benefits of its use.
4. Explain the Systems Development Life Cycle, which describes the design and implementation of an information system. What role do accountants play?

Exercise 3–5 [Managerial]

Write about one of the following topics using the techniques covered in this and earlier chapters. Your answer might range from one to six paragraphs or more, depending on the topic.

1. Discuss the purpose of the IMA (The Association of Accountants and Financial Professionals in Business), which was formally known as the Institute of Management Accountants.

2. Discuss the Certified Global Management Accountant (CGMA) certification process, including what the CGMA is and what the benefits are of acquiring the designation.
3. Discuss why ethics is important in managerial accounting.

Exercise 3–6 [Auditing/Current Professional Issues]

Write about one of the following topics using the techniques covered in this and earlier chapters. Your answer might range from one to six paragraphs or more, depending on the topic.

1. Discuss the pros and cons of requiring audit firm rotation and shareholder ratification of audit firms.
2. Discuss the role of the National Peer Review Committee (NPRC), which was formally known as the Center for Public Company Audit Firms Peer Review Program (CPCAFPRP).
3. Discuss what the consequences may be if the Public Company Accounting Oversight Board (PCAOB) finds significant performance deficiencies during its inspection of an audit firm.

Exercise 3–7 [Tax]

Write about one of the following topics using the techniques covered in this and earlier chapters. Your purpose is to provide a very general explanation to readers who have never heard of these terms or topics. Your answer might range from one to six paragraphs or more, depending on the topic.

1. Discuss the concepts of *dependency exemption* and *personal exemption* as they apply to the income tax of individuals.
2. Discuss the concept of *constructive receipt* as it applies to the income tax of individuals.
3. Discuss the American Opportunity Tax Credit and the Lifetime Learning Credit, including the requirements of these credits.
4. For individual tax purposes, why is the distinction between deductions *for* adjusted gross income and deductions *from* adjusted gross income important?
5. Discuss the Foreign Account Tax Compliance Act (FATCA). Include an explanation of its requirements and a discussion of its objectives.

A Sense of Style: Writing with Conciseness and Clarity

4

Learning Objectives

After studying this chapter, you should be able to

4.1 Write concise sentences.

4.2 Write clear sentences: appropriate jargon, precise word choices, unambiguous modifiers and pronouns.

4.3 Write readable sentences: voice, variety, tone.

So far we've looked at writing mainly as an organizational task: planning the structure and contents of the paper so that it achieves its purpose in a way readers will find meaningful. We have stressed the quality of coherence: writing that is easy to follow, with main ideas that stand out. Chapters 2 and 3 looked at writing in terms of large units—the document as a whole as well as sections and paragraphs.

We turn now to a more detailed level of effective writing. This chapter looks at word choices and sentence structures that contribute to a vigorous and readable writing style. In this discussion of style, we emphasize two other important qualities of effective writing: conciseness and clarity (two of the writing tips listed in Figure 1–1 in Chapter 1).

CONCISENESS

LO4.1 **Write concise sentences.**

Readers prefer concise writing so they can find the information they need quickly and easily. Chapter 3 showed how to make your writing more concise by eliminating digressions and irrelevant detail. In general, concise writing contains no unnecessary elements—no extra words, phrases, sentences, or paragraphs.

Unnecessary Words

The easiest way to make every word count is to see how many words you can cross out of your writing, often with only a simple revision of the sentence. These examples show how sentences can be revised to eliminate unnecessary words:

WORDY: Participants in the audit of Flip's Frog Ponds, Inc., found a large number of weaknesses in the way the lily pond inventory is accounted for. [25 words]

CONCISE: The auditors found many weaknesses in the lily pad inventory accounting of Flip's Frog Ponds, Inc. [16 words]

WORDY: It is my understanding that a good number of our new employees are using their company email accounts for communicating with their friends and family. [25 words]

CONCISE: Many of our new employees are using company email accounts for personal communication. [13 words]

WORDY: We hope the entire staff will help us in our attempts to spend less money on energy. [17 words]

CONCISE: We hope the entire staff will help us reduce energy costs. [11 words]

WORDY: Forecasts for profits for the coming year range all the way from $300,000 to upwards of $500,000. [17 words]

CONCISE: Next year's profit forecasts range from $300,000 to $500,000. [9 words]

WORDY: To stay informed on the latest information, accountants must read a great number of published materials about accounting. [18 words]

CONCISE: To stay current, accountants read many accounting publications. [8 words]

Watch out for *there is* and *there are*. They can usually be eliminated. *The fact that, which is, who is,* and *which are* can sometimes be left out as well:

WORDY: There are several strategic planning strategies that we can use to reduce our income taxes. [15 words]

CONCISE: We can reduce our income taxes through strategic planning. [9 words]

WORDY: I would like to call your attention to the fact that we have a staff meeting scheduled for next Wednesday. [20 words]

CONCISE: Remember our staff meeting scheduled for next Wednesday. [8 words]

or (even better)

Remember next Wednesday's staff meeting. [5 words]

Simplicity

Another way to make your writing concise is to write as simply as possible. Sometimes writers get into the habit of using big words and long, complicated sentences. Such writing is hard to read.

SEC Commissioner Cynthia A. Glassman has offered this example of a footnote disclosure that is almost impossible to understand:[1]

> Any interest collections on the loans remaining after payments of interest on the notes and the company's expenses will be available to cover any losses on the loans that are not covered by the insurance policies.

Glassman has suggested this translation into simpler wording:

> After we pay our expenses and interest on the notes, we will use any remaining funds to cover uninsured losses.

For an example of simple, clear writing, review the narrative description of a payroll processing system shown in Figure 1–2 (page 6). Notice how the choice of familiar, simple words makes the narrative easy to understand. The narrative's sentences, which are mostly short and always clear, also contribute to the document's effectiveness.

Good writers use short, everyday words as much as possible. For example, they may write *use* instead of *utilize* and *help* instead of *assistance*. Shorter, familiar words are easier to read and make writing more forceful.

Table 4–1 shows two columns of words. Column B lists short, familiar words; Column A lists longer, more difficult words that are often substituted for the everyday words in Column B. The table also shows how single words (*because*) can often replace phrases (*for the*

TABLE 4–1 Simplifying Word Choices

As a rule, use the words and phrases in Column B rather than those in Column A.

Column A	Column B
above-mentioned firms	these firms
absolutely essential	essential
activate	begin
advise	tell
aggregate	total
along the lines of	like
anticipate	expect
as per your request	as you requested
assist	help
at all times	always
at this point in time	now
at this time	now
attempt	try

(cont.)

TABLE 4–1 (*Cont.*)

Column A	Column B
commence	begin
communicate	write, tell
completely eliminated	eliminated
comprise	include
consider	think
constitute	are, is
discontinue	stop
disutility	uselessness
due to the fact that	because
during the time that	while
earliest convenience	promptly, soon
effort	work
enclosed herewith	enclosed
enclosed please find	enclosed is
endeavor	try
exercise care	be careful
facilitate	ease, simplify
failed to	didn't
few in number	few
for the purpose of	for
for the reason that	since, because
from the point of view that	for
furnish	send, give
i.e.	that is
implement	carry out
in advance of	before
in all cases	always
in many cases	often
in most cases	usually
in behalf of	for
in connection with	about
in terms of	in
in the amount of	of, for
in the case of	if
in the event that (of)	if
in the nature of	like
in the neighborhood of	about
in this case	here
indicate	show, point out
initiate	begin
in view of the fact that	because
inasmuch as	since
investigate	study
it has come to my attention	Ms. Jones has just told me; I have just learned
it is felt	I feel; we feel
it is our understanding that	we understand that
it should be noted that	(omit)
maintain	keep
maintain cost control	control cost
make an analysis of	analyze
make a purchase	buy

(*cont.*)

TABLE 4–1   (*Cont.*)

Column A	Column B
make application to	apply
make contact with	see, meet
maximum	most, largest
minimum	least, smallest
modification	change
obtain	get
on the order of	about
on the part of	by
optimum	best
past history	history
per annum	annually, per year
period of time	time, period
pertaining to	about, for
philosophy	plan, idea
please be advised that	(omit)
prepare an analysis	analyze
presently	now
prior to	before
procure	get, buy
provide	give
provide continuous indication	indicate continuously
pursuant to your inquiry	as you requested
range all the way from	range from
regarding	about
relative to	about
represent	be, is, are
require	need
so as to	to
subsequent to	after, later
substantial	large, big
sufficient	enough
terminate	end, stop
the major part of	most of
the manner in which	how
the undersigned; the writer	I, me
thereon, thereof, thereto, therefrom	(omit)
this is to acknowledge	thank you for; I have received
this is to inform you that	
we shall send	we'll send
through the use of	by, with
transpire	happen
true facts	facts
under separate cover	separately
until such time as	until
utilize	use
vital	important
with a view to	to
with reference to	about
with regard to	about
with respect to	on, for, of, about
with the object to	to
with the result that	so that

reason that). As a general rule, use the words and phrases in Column B rather than those in Column A. Some of the terms in Column A can be omitted (such as *it should be noted that*).

Another way to achieve a simple, readable style is to use short sentences. Short sentences are particularly important when you are explaining complicated ideas. The average sentence should be about 15 words long. Note that 15 words is an *average*. Some sentences are longer, some shorter. In fact, it's a good idea to vary sentence lengths so that the writing doesn't become monotonous. Sentence variation will be discussed again later in this chapter.

If you find that you have written a sentence that is too long, first eliminate unnecessary words and phrases, as described above. If the sentence is still too long, try dividing it into two or more shorter sentences. You will need to revise the new sentences slightly so that they are clear and correct. Here is an example:

> The auditors planned the audit after reviewing the files from previous years' audits, and they also reviewed additional documentation provided by the client's controller.

Revision (long sentence divided):

> The auditors planned the audit after reviewing prior years' audit files. In addition, they reviewed other documentation provided by the client's controller.

or

Revision (long sentence condensed):

> The auditors planned the audit after reviewing prior years' audit files and other documentation provided by the client's controller.

Verbs and Nouns

Another way to make your writing more concise, as well as clearer and more readable, is to use active verbs and descriptive nouns, rather than lots of adverbs and adjectives. See how this sentence can be improved:

WORDY: There will be many positive advantages to our business if we make investments in the latest state-of-the-art technology. [21 words]

CONCISE: Investment in state-of-the-art technology will cut costs of production. [12 words]

One common cause of wordy writing is hidden verbs. For example,

> *came to a conclusion that* instead of *concluded*
> *causes a misstatement of/* instead of *misstates*
> *makes an analysis of* instead of *analyzes*
> *will serve as an explanation of* instead of *will explain*

What are the hidden verbs in the following sentences?

> The auditors came to the conclusion that the financial statements were not complete.

> Johnson made reference to the new tax laws to support his recommendation.

In the first sentence, the hidden verb is *concluded*; in the second sentence, it is *referred*. The revised sentences are a little less wordy, a little more forceful:

> The auditors concluded that the company's financial statements were incomplete.

> Johnson referred to the new tax laws to support his recommendation.

Finally, avoid sentence introductions that weaken the sentence idea:

WORDY: It has come to my attention that we need additional staff for this audit. [14 words]

CONCISE: We need additional staff for this audit. [7 words]

WORDY: Enclosed please find our invoice for $400. [7 words]
CONCISE: Our invoice for $400 is enclosed. [6 words]

WORDY: This is to acknowledge receipt of your letter of June 1. [11 words]

CONCISE: Thank you for your letter of June 1. [8 words]

In summary, clear, readable writing contains no unnecessary words and is written as simply as possible. Be concise—your writing will be more forceful.

CLARITY

LO4.2   Write clear sentences: appropriate jargon, precise word choices, unambiguous modifiers and pronouns.

Unless you write clearly, your readers will not understand what you are saying. One way to write with clarity is to be concise, so that important ideas are not buried in unnecessary words and details. Writing as simply as possible will also help you achieve clarity because you'll be using words the reader knows and feels comfortable with.

Other techniques for improving the clarity of your writing include the careful use of jargon and precise, concrete word choices.

Jargon

Jargon is the specialized language or technical terminology of a group of people. We all recognize accounting jargon: words and phrases such as *amortization, accrual, debit, GAAP*, and *deferred income taxes*.

One kind of jargon is acronyms: words composed of the first letter of a group of words, such as *FASB, ASR, GAAP, CMA, CGMA,* and *LIFO*. To introduce an acronym, write out the words of the acronym, with the acronym in parentheses:

> Some companies account for inventory using the last-in, first-out (LIFO) method.

> A management accountant may now achieve either the Certified Management Accountant (CMA) designation or the Chartered Global Management Accountant (CGMA) designation.

After you have identified the acronym, you can use the acronym alone throughout the rest of the document. If you're sure that the readers will be familiar with an acronym, and if you're writing an informal document, it's usually acceptable to use the acronym without writing it out.

Unless you use acronyms and other forms of jargon carefully, they will detract from the clarity of your writing. Two guidelines can help you decide when to use jargon and when to look for other words. The first is to remember your readers' needs and to use language they will understand. Another accountant will probably understand what you mean by *straight-line depreciation*, but managers or clients who have not studied accounting may not. Be careful when using jargon even with your accounting colleagues. Would everyone with a degree in accounting know what you mean by *back-flush costing*?

The second guideline for the use of jargon is to keep your word choices as simple as possible. Avoid jargon when ordinary language will say what you mean. For example, why say "the bottom line" if you mean net income or loss?

Jargon may be unavoidable when you need to communicate technical information as efficiently as possible, but remember the needs of your readers. Define or explain any technical terminology with which they may not be familiar.

Precise Meaning

Precision is one of the most important elements of clear writing. Word choices must be accurate and sentences must be constructed so that their meaning is clear. Precision is particularly important in accountants' writing because accountants are often legally responsible for the accuracy of what they write. Moreover, the technical nature of accounting makes precise writing a necessity. Consider this sentence:

UNCLEAR: The major drawback of the current value method is verifiability.

REVISED: The major drawback of the current value method is *the lack of* verifiability.

The revision certainly improves the precision and intelligibility of the sentence!

Word Choices

Imprecise writing has several causes. One culprit is poor diction, or the inaccurate use of words:

> The major *setback* of the old system is that it is inefficient. [Poor diction. The writer meant *drawback*.]

> The advantage of measurements in terms of market values is that the values reflect *what the item is worth*. [What is the precise meaning of the italicized phrase? *Worth* is vague.]

In these examples, the diction problems are italicized:

POOR DICTION: These financial statements *upset* two accounting standards.

REVISED: These financial statements violate two accounting standards.

POOR DICTION: The users of our financial statements may see the decline in our revenues and become *worrisome*.

REVISED: The users of our financial statements may see the decline in our revenues and become worried.

POOR DICTION: Our advertising expense, which is 1% of total sales, is a *negligent* amount.

REVISED: Our advertising expense, which is 1% of total sales, is a negligible amount.

Unclear, awkward writing can also result from the misuse of words ending in -*ing*:

AWKWARD AND UNCLEAR: We do not have all the data, therefore failing to complete the analysis.

REVISED: We do not have all the data, so we can't complete the analysis.

AWKWARD AND UNCLEAR: In finding out this information, we will have to be thorough in our asking of questions of the concerned parties.

REVISED: To find out this information, we must thoroughly question the concerned parties.

AWKWARD AND UNCLEAR: When purchasing bonds at a discount, the investment cost is less than the face value of the investment.

REVISED: When bonds sell at a discount, the investment cost is less than the face value of the investment.

Faulty Modifiers

Another type of imprecise writing is misplaced and dangling modifiers. With a misplaced modifier, the modifying word or phrase is not placed next to the sentence element it modifies. The result is a confusing sentence:

> Process cost systems are often used by businesses that produce goods for general distribution *such as oil refineries and dairies*. [The italicized phrase appears to modify *goods*, but it really modifies *businesses*.]

> Process cost systems are often used by businesses such as oil refineries and dairies, which produce goods for general distribution.

Consider another sentence with a misplaced modifier:

> This technique identifies tax returns for audits with a high probability of error.

Revised:

> To identify tax returns for audit, this technique flags returns that have a high probability of error.

Dangling modifiers, which usually come at the beginning of a sentence, do not actually modify any word in the sentence. Usually the word modified is implied rather than stated directly. Look at this sentence:

> After buying the bonds, the market price will fluctuate.

This sentence illogically suggests that the buyer of the bonds is "the market price." The writer probably meant something like this:

> After we buy the bonds, the market price will fluctuate.

Pronoun Reference

Faulty pronoun reference can also cause writing to be ambiguous and confusing:

> The regulations governing the hospitality industry have changed substantially since we opened the hotel last year. Because of this, we have hired a consultant to help us with it.

The meaning of the second sentence is unclear. What is the problem? What kind of help will the consultant provide? *This* and *it* are confusing; their references are vague. Here is one possible revision:

> The regulations governing the hospitality industry have changed substantially since we opened the hotel last year. Because of these changes, we have hired a consultant to oversee the application of the new regulations to our business.

Faulty pronoun reference can be labeled *vague, ambiguous,* or *broad.* These terms all mean that the writer doesn't make clear what the pronoun refers to. The pronoun *this* is particularly troublesome:

FAULTY REFERENCE: The use of generally accepted accounting principles does not always produce the true finan-
cial position of a company. *This* is a problem for
the FASB.

REVISED: The use of generally accepted accounting principles does not always produce the true financial position of a company. This weakness in the
principles is a problem for the FASB.

A good rule is to never use *this* by itself. Add a noun or phrase to define what *this* is.

Another pronoun that can cause reference problems is *it:*

FAULTY REFERENCE: The inventory valuation method can correspond
to the physical flow of goods, but *it* is not necessary.

REVISED: The inventory valuation method can correspond
to the physical flow of goods, but this correspondence is not necessary.

Misplaced and dangling modifiers and faulty pronoun reference are grammatical errors, which are discussed further in Chapter 5. However, writing can be grammatically correct and still be imprecise. Consider this sentence:

UNCLEAR: Your writing is not clear because your readers can't understand it.

REVISED: Readers can't understand what you write because your
writing isn't clear.

The revision certainly makes a difference in our ability to understand the sentence.

The ability to write precisely is often a function of careful reading and thinking. For example, an accounting professor assigned his Accounting Theory students two papers for the quarter. He then wrote the following statement on the board:

An Accounting Theory student who completes the course requirements for this class will write a total of two papers this semester. True or false?

The careful thinkers in the class realized that the statement might not be true. The students could write papers for other classes as well. Therefore, some students could write more than two papers for the semester.

Learn to analyze carefully what you read and what you write. Then write so that your meanings are clear and precise.

Concrete, Specific Wording

Chapter 3 discussed using concrete facts, details, and examples to develop paragraphs. Concrete, specific writing adds clarity to your documents and makes them much more interesting.

Concrete writing can be best explained by defining its opposite: abstract writing. Abstract writing is vague, general, or theoretical. Abstract writing is hard to understand because it's not illustrated by particular, material objects. Concrete writing, on the other hand, is vivid and specific; it brings a picture into the reader's mind.

Illustrations of abstract and concrete writing styles make them easier to understand:

ABSTRACT: Historical cost is important in accounting. It is easy for accountants to use, and it is often seen in the financial statements. Historical cost has some disadvantages, but it has its good points, too.

CONCRETE: Historical cost is the amount of money paid for an object when it was purchased. For example, if a truck was purchased in 2018 for $60,000, then $60,000 is the truck's historical cost. An argument in favor of the use of historical cost to value assets is that such values are usually easy to determine from invoices and other records of the original purchase.

However, in times of inflation the historical cost of an asset may not indicate its true value. For example, an acre of land bought in 1990 for $50,000 might be worth several times that amount today, but it would still be recorded in the owner's books and on the balance sheet at its historical cost. Thus, one disadvantage of historical cost accounting is that it often undervalues assets.

By giving more detailed information and specific, concrete examples of historical cost, the second example makes this concept easier to understand and more interesting to read.

In the following examples, vague, abstract sentences are replaced by more concrete writing:

VAGUE: Accountants should write well.

REVISED: Accountants need to write clear, concise letters to their clients and other business associates. [This sentence replaces the vague *well* with two characteristics of effective writing: *clear* and *concise*. The revision also gives an example of one type of accountants' writing: letters to clients and associates.]

VAGUE: The financial statements are interesting.

REVISED: Flip's financial statements for 2018 may encourage investors. The earnings statement, for example, shows a net gain of $2,346,121.

The example just given illustrates a particularly effective technique you can use to make your writing concrete: Illustrate your ideas with specific details about the situation you're discussing. That is, if you're writing about Flip's financial statements, as in the example above, add relevant details to clarify what you mean.

See how specific wording improves the clarity of these sentences:

VAGUE: Action on the stock market today was interesting.
CLEAR: The Dow rose 351 points today.

VAGUE: This liability should appear on the income statement because of materiality.
CLEAR: This liability should appear on the income statement because the amount, $55,000, is material.

Finally, remember your readers' interests when you select the details to include in your writing; choose the details they will find meaningful and relevant. Which of the following two sentences would you prefer to read in a letter from your tax accountant?

Your tax situation this year poses some interesting possibilities.

If you can document your business expenses this year with the necessary receipts, you may be eligible for a refund of at least $5,500.

READABLE WRITING

LO4.3 Write readable sentences: voice, variety, tone.

If your writing is interesting to read, it will almost always be clear. Lively, natural sentences hold readers' attention and keep them involved in what you are saying, so they have an easier time understanding your ideas.

This section of the chapter is devoted to several techniques that will make your sentences readable and clear: using active voice, varying vocabulary and sentences, and writing with an appropriate tone.

Passive and Active Voice

This technique for achieving a good writing style might seem technical, but it will become clear after a few definitions and examples. Your writing will be clearer if you use active voice for most sentences.

In the active voice, the subject of the sentence performs the action described by the verb.

ACTIVE: Most corporations issue financial statements at least once a year.

Passive voice, on the other hand, describes an action done to somebody or something by another agent. The agent is not always named in the sentence.

PASSIVE: Financial statements are issued (by most corporations) at least once a year.

This formula will help you identify passive voice verbs:

Passive voice   = | a form of the verb *to be* | + | the past participle of another verb (usually ending in -*ed*) |

forms of the verb *to be*:   **typical past participles:**

is, are, were, was, been,   *accrued, received, used,*

being, be, am   *computed, given, kept*

Sometimes passive verb phrases also contain a form of *to have* (*has, have, had, having*) or an auxiliary (*will, should, would, must,* and so on), but passive voice always contains a *to be* form plus a past participle.

Active voice sentences are often clearer than passive voice sentences. Consider these examples:

PASSIVE: It is predicted that the stock's price will double. [In this example, most readers would want to know who made the prediction.]

ACTIVE: Jim Samuel predicted that the stock's price will double.

PASSIVE: The gasoline tax was raised by 50%.

ACTIVE: The state legislature raised the gasoline tax by 50%.

Unfortunately, writers of "officialese," especially in government, business, and research, have so badly overused passive voice that we tend to accept it as standard style. Passive voice is seldom effective—it lacks the forcefulness and clarity of active voice. Compare the following pairs of sentences:

PASSIVE: Deliberate understatement of assets and stockholders' equity with the intention of misleading interested parties is prohibited.

ACTIVE: SEC regulations prohibit deliberate misstatement of assets and stockholders' equity with the intention of misleading investors.

PASSIVE: A determination has been made that the statements are in violation of GAAP.

ACTIVE: The auditors have determined that the statements are in violation of GAAP.

Good writers avoid using passive voice in most situations. They ask themselves two questions: What is the action (verb)? Who or what is doing it (subject)?

One word of warning: Avoid substituting a weak active verb for passive voice. Be particularly careful of colorless verbs such as *to exist* and *to occur*. The following sentences are written in active voice, but the sentences are weak:

> Capitalization of option costs on land subsequently purchased should occur.
>
> FIFO bases itself on the assumption that the first inventory acquired is the first inventory sold.

Use descriptive, vigorous verbs to substitute for weak verbs:

> We must capitalize option costs on land that we subsequently purchased.
>
> The assumption that underlies FIFO is that the first inventory acquired is the first inventory sold.

When to Use Passive Voice

Although it's usually better to write in active voice, passive voice is sometimes preferable. For example, the two sentences in the preceding example could be effectively written in passive voice:

> Option costs on land that we subsequently purchased should be capitalized.
>
> FIFO is based on the assumption that the first inventory acquired is the first inventory sold.

Here's another example of an effective sentence written in passive voice:

> Our system has been hacked.

rather than:

> Some person or persons unknown have hacked our system.

Finally, passive voice may enable you to be tactful when you must write bad news or some sort of criticism:

> These figures were not calculated correctly.

This sentence doesn't say who is at fault for the erroneous calculation; here, passive voice may be the most diplomatic way to identify the problem without assigning blame.

We talk more about writing tactfully later in the chapter.

Variety and Rhythm

Another way to make your writing natural and more readable is to add variety. Vary vocabulary, sentence lengths, and sentence structures. Read the writing aloud to hear how it sounds.

The purpose of sentence variety is to avoid monotony —a sing-song, awkward repetition of the same sentence rhythms or overuse of a word or phrase. Read the following paragraph aloud:

> Financial analysts use ratios to analyze financial statements. Ratios show a company's liquidity. The current ratio shows the ratio of current assets to current liabilities. Ratios also show a company's solvency. The equity ratio is an example of a solvency ratio. It shows the ratio of owners' equity to total assets. Ratios also show profitability. The return-on-investment ratio is an example. It shows the ratio of net earnings to owners' equity.

This paragraph does not sound pleasing. In fact, it could easily lull the reader to sleep. The sentences are too similar in length and structure and the word *ratio* is repeated too often. Let's try again:

> Ratios based on financial statements can reveal valuable information about a company to investors, creditors, and other interested parties. Liquidity ratios show whether a company can pay its debts. The quick ratio, for example, is a good indication of debt-paying ability for companies with slow inventory turnover. Ratios can also indicate a company's solvency; the equity ratio, for instance, shows the percentage of owners' equity to total assets. Investors in bonds use this figure to evaluate the safety of a potential investment. Finally, ratios can give a measure of a company's profitability, which is of special interest to potential investors. The earnings-per-share ratio is probably the most popular of the profitability ratios.

Another cause of monotonous sentences is too many prepositional phrases, particularly when several are linked together. Look at the following sentence. Prepositions are in bold type; the rest of the phrase is underlined:

> The communication **of** information **about** the income **of** a corporation will provide **to** potential investors **in** the corporation help **in** the making **of** their investment decision.

This sentence contains seven prepositional phrases, several of which are linked together. A good rule is to avoid more than two or three prepositional phrases in a sentence. The sentence can be revised as follows:

> Information about a corporation's income will help investors make sound decisions.

Here is a partial list of prepositions:

about	after	as	at
because of	before	between	by
during	for	from	in
in front of	in regard to	like	near
of	on	over	through
to	together with	under	until
up	with		

Variety is an important element of readable writing because it gives sentences and paragraphs a pleasing rhythm. Read your paragraphs aloud. If you notice a word or phrase repeated too often, look for a synonym. If the sentences sound choppy and monotonous, vary their structures and lengths. Often a change in the way sentences begin improves the rhythm of the paragraph. Add an occasional short sentence and an occasional longer one (but be sure longer sentences are still easy to understand). Avoid using too many prepositional phrases. You don't want to bore your readers, and varied sentences are one way to keep your writing lively.

Tone

The tone of a document reflects the writer's attitude toward the topic or the readers. Tone might also be described as the effect the writing has on the reader or the impression the document makes. A letter can have a formal or informal tone; it can be personal or impersonal. It can be apologetic, cold, humorous, threatening, arrogant, respectful, or friendly.

Choosing the best tone for a document depends, in part, on who the reader will be. If you are writing to a colleague who is also a good friend, you can be much more informal than if you are writing to someone you don't know well. Be particularly careful to show respect to those who are much older than you are or those in higher positions of authority.

One way to decide on the proper tone of a document you are writing is to imagine that you are in a conversation with your reader. How formal would you be? How would you show that you were interested in your reader's point of view and concerns? No matter how formal (or casual) you decide to make your tone, always be courteous. Treat your correspondent with tact, politeness, and respect. Avoid abruptness, arrogance, condescension, or any other form of rudeness. Remember that the choice of tone may involve ethical considerations: Treat others as you wish to be treated.

Here are some examples of poor tone:

Tax planning is a complicated subject, so I have tried to simplify it for you. [This sentence is condescending; it implies that the reader is not very bright.]

I acknowledge receipt of your letter and beg to thank you. [Too formal and artificial.]

Send me that report immediately. I can't understand why it has taken you so long to prepare it. [In certain situations you might *think* this way, but it's better to write with tact and courtesy.]

For all but the most formal documents, such as some contracts, the use of personal pronouns (*you, I, we*) contributes to a warm, personal tone. Keep the first person singular pronouns (*I, me, my, mine*) to a minimum; focus instead on the reader with second person (*you, your, yours*) or, in some cases, first person plural (*we, us, our, ours*).

A personal tone, including personal pronouns, is especially effective when the message you are conveying is good news or neutral information. When you must write bad news or criticize someone, it's better to be impersonal in order to be tactful. Passive voice can also make a sentence more tactful:

TACTLESS: You failed to sign your income tax return.
  BETTER: Please sign your return on the line indicated.

Another guideline for an effective tone is to stress the positive. Emphasize what can be done rather than what cannot:

NEGATIVE: Because you were late in sending us your tax information, we cannot complete your tax return by April 15.
POSITIVE: Now that we have the information on your taxes, we can complete your tax return. We will request an extension of the deadline so that you will not be fined for a late filing.

Finally, be honest and sincere; avoid exaggeration and flattery. This sentence doesn't sound credible:

Working with you on this audit has shown me what a superb accountant you are.

In the final analysis, the guidelines for an effective writing tone are the same as those for good relationships. Learn to view a situation from the other person's point of view and communicate in a way that shows empathy and respect.

TEST YOURSELF

Revise the following sentences so that they are written in a more effective style, using the techniques covered in this chapter. Answers are provided below.

1. After reading the following paragraphs, a recommendation will suggest a way we can reduce the cost of purchase.
2. Complete information was wanted by management on the new project that had been proposed by the engineers.
3. The important issue to address in this company's situation is that of the expression of an opinion of the going concern.
4. To determine what information to include in our report for 2018, we will make an analysis of the users' needs.
5. I have attempted to explain the three proposed alternatives for recording the cost of the machinery.
6. This recommendation can easily be implemented by our clients.

7. The main problem of this company is to minimize the amount of taxes for 2018.
8. It is our recommendation that Byron Corporation choose to value the property at $95,000.
9. The letter discussed the alternative ways to finance the purchase of the new equipment. Its purpose was ...
10. This information was prepared by our research department.

TEST YOURSELF: ANSWERS

(Note: Some of the errors in the previous sentences can be corrected in more than one way; this key shows only one possible correction. If you recognize the error, you probably understand how to correct it.)

1. The following paragraphs explain how we can reduce the cost of the purchase.
2. Management wanted complete information on the new project that the engineers had proposed.
3. We must determine whether this company is a going concern.
4. To determine what to include in our 2018 report, we will analyze users' needs.
5. I have explained the three proposals for recording the cost of the machinery.
6. Our clients can easily implement this recommendation.
7. This company's main problem is to minimize taxes for 2018.
8. We recommend that Byron Corporation value the property at $95,000.
9. The letter discussed the alternative ways to finance the purchase of the new equipment. The purpose of the letter was ...
10. Our research department prepared this information.

EXERCISES

Exercise 4–1 [General]

Revise the following sentences so that they are written as simply and concisely as possible. Be alert for hidden verbs.

1. These procedures will provide for an improved control of inventory.
2. The history of Elliot Industry's performance, which is marginal at best, may be an indication of solvency problems that will occur in the future.
3. A number of problems have come to light that may make it necessary for us to issue an opinion that is other than unqualified.
4. I have attempted to explain the three proposed alternatives for recording the cost of the land that has been purchased.

5. It is my recommendation that New York Corporation choose to value the asset at $95,000.
6. As you are no doubt aware, in the economic environment of today, having these services available from a firm with experience is indispensable and quite valuable.
7. I am in need of improved writing skills.
8. In conclusion, I would like to state that I feel this seminar is an excellent opportunity.
9. There are several benefits that can come from attending the seminar.
10. I hope this memo will exhibit the reasons why the conference will be beneficial.
11. The benefits of this educational program will avail themselves to the corporation via language and letters which are fresh, accurate, and clear.
12. Per the discussion held with you during our recent visit, there are several control objectives within the above-mentioned cycles that need to have techniques established or refined to ensure that these objectives are met.
13. These techniques will provide for an increased understanding of the problem.
14. Enclosed please find the information you will need to make an analysis of our inventory control.
15. We hope to begin production of our new product line before the end of this year.
16. Utilization of linear models alone may lead to unnecessary limitations as to inferences that one may be able to draw from the data.
17. When executing the purchase of land, there are a number of costs incurred.
18. This method provides proper matching of expenses to revenues.

Exercise 4–2 [General]

Review the lists of simplified word choices in Table 4-1. Then, without looking at the list again, write a shorter and/or simpler version of the following words and phrases.

Original: **Simplify to:**
in all cases   always

1. exercise care
2. enclosed please find
3. facilitate
4. initiate
5. prior to
6. so as to

7. the major part of
8. make a purchase
9. make an analysis of
10. for the purpose of
11. in the amount of
12. optimum
13. maintain cost control
14. the writer
15. this is to acknowledge

Exercise 4-3 [General]

Identify the jargon in the following sentences.

1. We'll have to research the regs and rules that apply to this problem.
2. Negative cash flows may affect our position with our creditors.
3. We can issue convertible debt to improve our equity position.
4. The FASB and the SEC, as well as the AICPA, are organizations that concern the profession of accounting.
5. GAAP requires a different treatment of inventory costs.
6. The project's NPV was negative, so it was rejected.
7. My CPA advised me to file a Schedule C with my return.
8. Because of her income this year, she will be able to recapture.
9. Our auditors must follow all requirements of the PCAOB.
10. Credit Cash for $200.

Exercise 4-4 [General]

The meaning of the following sentences is not clear. Revise the sentences so that they are unambiguous and precise.

1. The new regulations will exasperate the difficulty of reporting income.
2. The unexpected retirement of six auditors created a heavier workload for the remaining staff, causing them to miss several deadlines. This is a problem.
3. After calculating the tax effects, the selling price of the property seemed more reasonable.
4. The branch office will be located at a new cite.
5. The stock's price dropped by a negligent amount.
6. This product is unique. Only two manufacturers produce it.
7. The HB Transportation Company's improved position is due to decreasing fuel prices and the company's response in increasing prices.
8. Expense recognition states that once a cost expires, we should recognize expense.
9. This policy is based on a logical rational.
10. These financial statements upset two accounting standards.

Exercise 4–5 [General]

The following sentences are abstract or vague. Revise them, using facts, details, or examples to make them more concrete. You may need to replace one vague sentence with several concrete sentences, or even a short paragraph. Alternatively, you could introduce a short paragraph with an abstraction and then develop the idea with more concrete, specific sentences. Feel free to invent details that make the ideas more specific.

1. Internal control is important.
2. Sometimes firms keep two sets of records.
3. We must record this asset at its true value. (Hint: what is "true value"?)
4. The audit did not satisfy me.
5. The firm sold the asset for its cost. (Hint: what cost?)
6. Accounting for leases is tricky.
7. The nature of this asset requires us to capitalize it.
8. The accountant in charge of accounts receivable is not doing his job.
9. These stocks look like a good buy.
10. Accountants must use good judgment.

Exercise 4–6 [General]

Identify the passive-voice constructions in the following sentences and revise them to active voice. Be careful not to substitute weak active verbs for passive voice. For some sentences you may need to invent a subject for the active verb.

Example:

PASSIVE: That pension plan could have been adopted.
ACTIVE: We (or the firm, our client, Everest Corporation, etc.) could have adopted that pension plan.

1. This information was prepared by our research department.
2. No audit work on Flip Flop's internal control was performed by our firm.
3. Each month our net income is reduced by accrued expenses.
4. These disclosures are required for external reporting.
5. This procedure can easily be implemented.
6. The option kept the land available until a decision was reached.
7. Although our computer was purchased last year, it is already obsolete.
8. At the seminar guidelines will be provided for lease accounting.
9. It is recommended that finished parts inventories be physically controlled.
10. The prior years' audit files were reviewed.

Exercise 4–7 [General]

Identify the prepositional phrases in the following sentences. Where too many phrases are linked together, revise the sentence.

Example:

The problem of our client will be solved through the selection of one of the accounting methods presented.

Prepositional phrases identified:

The problem **of** <u>our client</u> will be solved **through** <u>the selection</u> **of** <u>one</u> **of** <u>the accounting methods</u> presented.

Revised:

One of the accounting methods should solve our client's problem.

1. The effects of the ruling by the IRS will affect the reported income of Gargantuan Corporation.
2. The manager of the department called a meeting for 9:00 a.m. to discuss problems with the proposed budget.
3. An accrual of expenses reports a more accurate picture of the operations of the current business period of the company.
4. Improvements of the efficiency of production will change the forecast for income in the year to come.
5. The main problem of the staff is the determination of the cost at which to record the purchase.
6. The effect on our audit report of the sale of the bonds is twofold.
7. The income tax return for Steve Warren was filed on April 10.
8. The calculation of the present values of the principal of the bonds and their cash flows will reveal our risk.
9. The amortization of the discount of the bond will allow us to realize the cash flows of the bond at an even rate throughout the life of the bond.
10. The determination of the net income of the company will pose no problems for the accountants in our department.

Exercise 4–8 [General]

Read this paragraph aloud and notice how monotonous it sounds. Then revise it so that sentence lengths and structures are more varied. Note also when a word or phrase is repeated too often.

Regional Coach Lines (RCL) runs bus service between several cities in three states. RCL also carries freight for several regional businesses. RCL's financial statements have reported poor profits for several years. Poor profits were caused by increased costs of operations including fuel costs, labor costs, and other costs. Increased costs caused RCL to increase passenger fares and freight prices. These increases caused passenger and freight volume to decrease drastically. Therefore, 2018 was a disastrous year for RCL. Preliminary information shows RCL is on the verge of bankruptcy.

Exercise 4–9 [General]

Revise the following sentences so that they are more effective, based on the guidelines discussed in this chapter.

1. An audit program has been designed by us for use in future audits of Lotus Vineyard.
2. A qualified opinion was issued on the 2018 financial statements.
3. Two weeks of vacation will be taken by new employees.
4. The completion of the project by the due date of next week will challenge the accountants in the department.
5. Wordiness is the problem that makes my writing less effective than it ought to be.
6. This memo provides an explanation of our policies on the use of company email.
7. The auditors came to the conclusion that additional procedures should be performed by them on inventory.
8. There are several benefits that can come from investing in new equipment.
9. Expense recognition states that once a cost expires, we should recognize expense.
10. The option kept the land available until a decision was reached about whether to buy it.

NOTES

1. Cynthia A. Glassman, "Speech by SEC Commissioner: Remarks at the Plain Language Association International's Fifth International Conference," Securities and Exchange Commission, 2005. www.sec.gov/news/speech/spch110405cag.htm (21 December 2016).

CHAPTER

Standard English: Grammar, Punctuation, and Spelling

5

Learning Objectives

After studying this chapter, you should be able to

5.1 Eliminate major sentence errors from your writing: fragments, comma splices, and fused sentences.

5.2 Use verbs correctly, including effective tense, mood, and agreement.

5.3 Use pronouns correctly so that agreement, reference, and gender are clear and appropriate.

5.4 Avoid problems with modifiers.

5.5 Write with parallel grammatical structure.

5.6 Use punctuation according to conventional usage: apostrophes, commas, colons, and semicolons.

5.7 Incorporate direct quotations into your writing, following conventions of standard usage.

5.8 Avoid problems with spelling.

One way to improve the clarity of your writing is to use Standard English, the language used daily by people in business, government, and other professions. Standard English is defined as language that is widely used by educated people in both formal and informal settings, including generally accepted conventions of spelling, grammar, and vocabulary.

In addition to improving the clarity of what you write, using Standard English will help you produce professional, polished documents, which is the final tip for writers given in Figure 1–1 in Chapter 1. A mastery of Standard English tells the reader much about you as a person and as a professional. Your use of correct grammar says that you are an educated person who understands and appreciates the proper use of language.

A grammatically correct document, free of mechanical and typographical errors, also shows that you know the importance of detail and are willing to spend the time necessary to prepare an accurate, precise document. Careful attention to detail is an important skill for an accountant, whether the detail is verbal or quantitative.

This chapter presents some of the most common errors in grammar, punctuation, and spelling. Because only a few principles can be covered in this short space, you should consult an English handbook for more complete coverage. This discussion focuses on areas that typically give accountants the most trouble.

MAJOR SENTENCE ERRORS

LO 5.1 Eliminate major sentence errors from your writing: fragments, comma splices, and fused sentences.

Major sentence errors include three kinds of problems: fragments, comma splices, and fused (or run-on) sentences. These errors are distracting to readers and may seriously interfere with their ability to understand the meaning of a sentence.

Fragments

A sentence fragment is just what its name suggests: part of a sentence. Recall that every sentence needs two essential elements, a subject and a verb (or predicate). In sentence fragments, at least one of these elements may be missing. A sentence fragment may also be recognized because it expresses an incomplete thought. Here are some examples:

To account for the transfer of stock correctly.

For example, all the employees who are eligible for retirement. [The subject is *employees*. In the clause that modifies the subject, the verb *are* is related to the pronoun *who*, but the predicate for the sentence is missing.]

The problem being increased production costs. [*Being* is a present participle;* it cannot be substituted for a complete verb such as *is* or *was*.]

Although our new system makes billing much faster. [This dependent clause has a subject and verb, but it cannot stand alone as a sentence because it is introduced by a subordinate conjunction, *although*.]

Comma Splices

The second major sentence error is comma splices, which occur when independent clauses are linked by a comma alone. An independent clause is a group of words with a subject and a verb; it can stand alone

---

*Consult a grammar handbook for explanations of technical grammatical terms such as this.

as a sentence. These two independent clauses are punctuated as separate sentences:

> Increases in assets are recorded as debits on the left side of a T-account. Decreases are recorded as credits on the right side.

Sometimes writers want to combine two independent clauses into one sentence. This can be done correctly in several ways:

1. Put a semicolon (;) between the clauses.

   > Increases in assets are recorded as debits on the left side of a T-account; decreases are recorded as credits on the right side.

2. Combine the clauses with a coordinating conjunction (*and, but, for, or, nor, yet, so*).

   > Increases in assets are recorded as debits on the left side of a T-account, and decreases are recorded as credits on the right side.

3. Combine the clauses with a semicolon, a conjunctive adverb, and a comma. (Conjunctive adverbs include *however, therefore, thus, consequently, that is, for example, nevertheless, also, furthermore, indeed, instead, still.*)

   > Increases in assets are recorded as debits on the left side of a T-account; however, decreases are recorded as credits on the right side.

Study the following comma splices. The independent clauses are joined by a comma alone:

COMMA SPLICE:	Accounting firms realize the importance of effective writing, they may offer training to improve employees' skills.
REVISED:	Accounting firms realize the importance of effective writing, so they may offer training to improve employees' skills.

or

Because accounting firms realize the importance of effective writing, they may offer training to improve employees' skills. [This revision changes the first independent clause into a dependent clause.]

COMMA SPLICE:	We must not only improve our internal control system, we must also review our procedures for accounts receivable.
REVISED:	We must not only improve our internal control system; we must also review our procedures for accounts receivable.

or

(to make the sentence more concise)
We must improve our internal control system and review our accounts receivable procedures.

COMMA SPLICE: These transactions were not recorded correctly, they were not recorded in the proper accounts.

REVISED: These transactions were not recorded correctly; they were not recorded in the proper accounts.

or

(to make the sentence more concise)
These transactions were not recorded in the proper accounts.

Fused Sentences

Fused sentences, which are also called run-on sentences, occur when two independent clauses are joined without any punctuation at all:

FUSED SENTENCE: Generally accepted accounting principles are not laws passed by Congress however, the AICPA's code of professional ethics requires accountants to follow GAAP.

REVISED: Generally accepted accounting principles are not laws passed by Congress. However, the AICPA's code of professional ethics requires accountants to follow GAAP.

FUSED SENTENCE: The manager sent a memo to all new employees she wanted them to have complete information about the company's sick leave policy.

REVISED: The manager sent a memo to all new employees because she wanted them to have complete information about the company's sick leave policy.

PROBLEMS WITH VERBS

LO 5.2   Use verbs correctly, including effective tense, mood, and agreement.

The correct use of verbs is a complicated matter in any language, as you will appreciate if you have ever studied a language other than English. For writers whose first language is English, the correct use of verbs usually presents few problems.

Verb problems do sometimes occur, however, even in the writing of fluent speakers of English. We will now look briefly at some of those problems.

Tense and Mood

The *tense* of a verb reflects the time of the action described by the verb:

PAST TENSE:	The company *increased* its investment in R&D last year.
PRESENT TENSE:	The company *is increasing* its investment in R&D this year.

or

Is the company *increasing* its investment in R&D this year?

or

The company *increases* its investment in R&D every year.

FUTURE TENSE:	The company *will increase* its investment in R&D next year.

Usually the choice of tense is logical and gives writers few problems.

The *mood* of a verb, however, is a little more confusing than its tense. Three moods are possible: indicative (states a fact or asks a question), imperative (a command or request), and subjunctive (a condition contrary to fact). The subjunctive mood causes the most trouble, although we often use it without realizing it:

If I *were* you, I would revise that report. [condition contrary to fact]

The most common use of the subjunctive is to follow certain verbs such as *recommend, suggest,* and *require*:

I recommend that we *hire* Jill Edmonds.

I suggest that he *contact* the sales representative immediately to discuss the lost orders.

The IRS requires that our client *include* that income in this year's return.

One common problem is an unnecessary shift in tense or mood:

TENSE SHIFT:	The president *approached* the podium and then *announces* the good news. [Shift from past to present tense.]
REVISED:	The president *approached* the podium and then *announced* the good news.
MOOD SHIFT:	If we *changed* our credit policy, we *will attract* more customers. [Shift from subjunctive to indicative.]
REVISED:	If we *changed* our credit policy, we *would attract* more customers.

or

If we *change* our credit policy, we *will attract* more customers.

Subject-Verb Agreement

Another major problem with verbs is subject-verb agreement. A verb should agree with its subject in number. That is, singular subjects take singular verbs; plural subjects take plural verbs. Note that singular verbs in the present tense usually end in *s*:

> The IT *specialist checks* the system every week.

> Two IT *specialists check* the system every week.

Some irregular verbs (*to be, to have*, etc.) look different, but you will probably recognize the singular and plural forms:

> That *stock is* a good investment.

> Those *stocks are* risky.

> The Drastic Measures *Corporation has* five frantic accountants on its staff.

> Some *corporations have* enough accountants to handle the workload efficiently.

There are a few difficulties with this rule. First, some singular subjects are often thought of as plural. For example, *each, every, either, neither, one, everybody*, and *anyone* take singular verbs:

> *Each* of the divisions *is* responsible for maintaining accounting records.

Second, sometimes phrases coming between the subject and the verb make agreement tricky:

> The *procedure* used today by most large companies with large inventories *is explained* in this article.

Finally, two or more subjects joined by *and* take a plural verb. When subjects are joined by *or*, the verb agrees with the subject closest to it:

> Neither the *president nor the supervisors understand* the new policies.

> *Ellen Atkins and John Simmons are* partners.

> Either *Ellen Atkins or John Simmons is* the partner-in-charge.

PROBLEMS WITH PRONOUNS: AGREEMENT, REFERENCE, AND GENDER

LO 5.3   Use pronouns correctly, so that agreement, reference, and gender are clear and appropriate.

Two common problems with pronouns are agreement and reference. Understanding agreement is easy: A pronoun must agree with its antecedent (the word it stands for). Thus, singular antecedents take singular pronouns and plural antecedents take plural pronouns:

Susan took *her* check to the bank.

The *employees* were pleased with *their* raises.

This rule usually gives trouble only with particular words. Note that *company, corporation, firm, management*, and *board* are singular; therefore, they take singular pronouns:

The *company* moved *its* main office to Atlanta. (Not *company . . . their.*)

The *Board* of Directors discussed earnings projections in *its* quarterly meeting. [Not *Board . . . their.*]

Management issued *its* quarterly report. [But: The *managers* issued *their* report.]

The second problem with pronouns is vague, ambiguous, or broad reference. The pronouns that give the most trouble are *this, that, which,* and *it*. This problem was discussed in Chapter 4, but here are some additional examples for you to consider:

FAULTY REFERENCE:	Although our bottling machines were purchased last year, this year's revenue depends on them. *This* associates the true cost with this year's revenues.
REVISED (ONE POSSIBILITY):	Although our bottling machines were purchased last year, this year's revenue depends on them. To associate the true cost of the machines with this year's revenue, we must apply the matching principle.
FAULTY REFERENCE:	Adjusting entries are needed to show that expenses have been incurred, but not paid. *This* is a very important step.
REVISED:	Adjusting entries are needed to show that expenses have been incurred, but not paid. Making these adjusting entries is a very important step.

Although agreement and reference cause writers the most problems with pronouns, occasionally other questions arise.

One question is the use of first and second person, which some people have been taught to avoid. In the discussion of tone in Chapter 4 we saw how using these personal pronouns can often contribute to an effective writing style for many informal documents. Personal pronouns are not usually appropriate in formal documents, such as some reports and contracts.

A few other cautions apply in the use of personal pronouns. First, use first person singular pronouns (*I, me, my*, and *mine*) sparingly to avoid writing that sounds self-centered. The second problem to avoid is using *you* in a broad sense to mean people in general, or as a substitute for another pronoun:

INCORRECT: I don't want to file my income tax return late because the IRS will fine *you*.

REVISED: I don't want to file my income tax return late because the IRS will fine *me*.

Pronouns and Gender

English has no singular personal pronouns that refer to an antecedent that could be either masculine or feminine. Until about a generation ago, the masculine pronouns (*he, him, his*) were understood to stand for either gender:

Every auditor should submit his reports on time.

Sentences like this one were common even though the pronoun's antecedent (in this case, *auditor*) could be either male or female.

Most people today believe that this older pronoun usage is no longer appropriate. They prefer to use pronouns that are gender neutral, unless, of course, the antecedent is clearly male or female:

The *controller* of Marvelous Corporation was pleased with *his* company's financial statements. [The controller is a man.]

or

The *controller* of Marvelous Corporation was pleased with *her* company's financial statements. [The controller is a woman.]

When the pronoun's antecedent is not clearly male or female, many people write sentences like these:

Every *auditor* should submit *his or her* reports on time.

Every *auditor* should submit *his/her* reports on time.

Unfortunately, constructions such as *he or she* and *he/she* can be awkward, especially if several occur in the same sentence:

Every auditor should submit *his or her* reports on time to fulfill *his or her* professional obligations.

What's the solution? The best approach for most sentences is to use plural nouns and pronouns so that the language will be inclusive:

Auditors should submit *their* reports on time to fulfill *their* professional obligations.

For some sentences, however, you can't use plurals. In these situations, some writers use gendered pronouns arbitrarily and switch often; sometimes they use a feminine pronoun and sometimes a masculine one. Whatever approach you use to avoid gender bias in your use of pronouns, keep these guidelines in mind:

- Most of today's business publications prefer gender-neutral writing, including a careful use of pronouns. If you use the older style, your writing will seem outdated.
- Some of your readers will be annoyed by a choice of pronouns that seems to be gender-biased.

PROBLEMS WITH MODIFIERS

LO 5.4 Avoid problems with modifiers.

Chapter 4 discussed the two main problems that can occur with modifiers: misplaced modifiers, which occur when the modifier is not placed next to the word it describes, and dangling modifiers, which do not modify any word in the sentence:

MISPLACED MODIFIER:	We only found one problem with the audit. [*Only* is misplaced. It should be next to the word or phrase it modifies.]
REVISED:	We found only one problem with the audit.
DANGLING MODIFIER:	When preparing financial statements, GAAP must be adhered to.
REVISED:	When preparing financial statements, we must adhere to GAAP.

The best guideline for using modifiers correctly is to place them next to the word or phrase they describe. For a further discussion of problems with modifiers and additional examples, see Chapter 4.

PARALLEL STRUCTURE

LO 5.5 Write with parallel grammatical structure.

Parallel sentence elements are those that are grammatically equal (such as verb phrases, noun phrases, dependent clauses, and sentences). When these items appear in a list or a compound structure, they should be balanced, or parallel. Noun phrases should not be matched with clauses, for example, nor should sentences be matched with phrases. One-word nouns and noun phrases are considered parallel, however, and can be combined in a list or compound structure.

These examples illustrate problems with parallel structure:

STRUCTURE NOT PARALLEL: During the meeting management will explain the purpose of the new policy, when it will go into effect, and its advantages. [This sentence combines a noun phrase, a dependent clause, and another noun phrase.]

REVISED: During the meeting management will explain the purpose of the new policy, its implementation date, and its advantages.

STRUCTURE NOT PARALLEL: We recommend the following procedures:

- Hire a consultant to help us determine our needs. [verb phrase]
- Investigate alternative makes and models of equipment. [verb phrase]
- We should then set up a pilot program to assess retraining needs for employees who will use the new equipment. [sentence]

REVISED: We recommend the following procedures:

- Hire a consultant to help us determine our needs. [verb phrase]
- Investigate alternative makes and models of equipment. [verb phrase]
- Set up a pilot program to assess retraining needs for employees who will use the new equipment. [verb phrase]

PUNCTUATION

LO 5.6 Use punctuation according to conventional usage: apostrophes, commas, colons, and semicolons.

An important component of Standard English is the correct use of punctuation marks. The following discussion clarifies the use of apostrophes and plurals, commas, colons, and semicolons.

Apostrophes and Plurals

The rules for apostrophes and plurals are quite simple, but many people get them confused. Most plurals are formed by adding either *s* or *es* to the end of a word. If you are unsure of a plural spelling, consult a dictionary.

With one exception, apostrophes are never used to form plurals. Apostrophes are used to show possession. For singular words the form is *'s*. For plural words the apostrophe comes after the *s*:

Singular	**Plural**
client's file	clients' files
statement's format	users' needs
business's budget	businesses' budgets

A common mistake is *stockholder's equity*. When stockholder(s) is plural (it usually is), the apostrophe comes after the *s*: *stockholders' equity*.

The plural-apostrophe rule has one exception. The plurals of letters, numerals, or acronyms can be formed with *'s*. Either choice in the following sentences is correct:

Most CPAs [or CPA's] are familiar with these regulations.

Cross your *t*'s and dot your *i*'s. [Or: Cross your *t*s and dot your *i*s.]

I can't read these figures because the *1*'s and *7*'s look alike. [Or: *1*s and *7*s.]

Often a phrase requiring an apostrophe can be rewritten using *of* or its equivalent:

the president's letter [the letter of the president]
June's income [the income for June]
a week's work [the work of a week]
the year's total [the total for the year]

Either of these possessive forms is correct, but remember the caution given in Chapter 4 about using too many prepositional phrases in a sentence. The result can be awkward or wordy.

And note these possessive plurals:

two companies' statements
five months' income
three weeks' work
prior years' statements
ten years' total

Ten years' total might also be written *ten-year total*, but analyze the difference in meaning between *ten-year total* and *ten years' totals*.

Finally, some writers confuse *it's* with *its*. *It's* is a contraction of *it is*; *its* is the possessive pronoun:

It's time to hire new accountants.

The firm was proud of its new hires.

Commas

Commas are important because they can make sentences easier to understand. Lack of a comma makes the meaning of this sentence ambiguous:

> I wouldn't worry because you appear to have a thriving business.

Adding a comma clears up the confusion:

> I wouldn't worry, because you appear to have a thriving business.

Comma Guide Sheet

This guide sheet will help you determine when to use (or not use) commas.

Use Commas:

1. Before *and, but, or, not, for, so,* and *yet* when these words come between independent clauses:

   > We sent Mr. Hernandez an invoice for our services, and he mailed a check the next day.

   > Our competitors increased their advertising, but our customers remained loyal.

2. Following an introductory adverbial clause:

   > If we purchase this program, we will be able to generate our reports more quickly.

   > Because production costs have increased, we will be forced to raise our prices.

3. Following transitional expressions and long introductory phrases:

   > In a letter addressed to its corporate clients, the firm explained the changes in the services it would offer.

   > To improve the service to our Atlanta customers, we are adding three new sales representatives. However, we still need four more representatives.

4. To separate items in a series (including coordinate adjectives):

   > Accounting students must be intelligent, dedicated, and conscientious.

   > Jenny Tran, Sam Clark, and Raul Ramirez announced they would retire next year.

5. To set off nonrestrictive clauses and phrases (compare to rule 4 under the heading *DO NOT USE COMMAS*):

   > The SEC, which is an agency of the federal government, is concerned with the independence of auditors.

The annual report, which was issued in March, contained shocking news for investors.

6. To set off contrasted elements:

Treasury stock is a contra-capital account, not an asset.

We want to lower our prices, not raise them.

7. To set off parenthetical elements:

Changes in accounting methods, however, must be disclosed in financial statements.

"Our goal," he said, "is to dominate the market."

Do Not Use Commas:

1. To separate the subject from the verb or the verb from its complement:

Incorrect:
Some international mutual funds, have shown high returns.

Correct:
Some international mutual funds have shown high returns.

Incorrect:
We must correctly record, these entries.

Correct:
We must correctly record these entries.

2. To separate compound verbs or objects:

Incorrect:
She wrote angry letters to her CPA, and to her attorney.

Correct:
She wrote angry letters to her CPA and to her attorney.

But note this usage:
She wrote angry letters to her CPA, her attorney, and the Chamber of Commerce. [Commas are correct in this sentence because they separate the items in a series. See rule 4 under the heading *USE COMMAS.*]

3. To set off words and short phrases that are not parenthetical:

Incorrect:
Financial transactions are recorded, in journals, in chronological order.

Correct:
Financial transactions are recorded in journals in chronological order.

4. To set off restrictive clauses, phrases, or appositives (compare to rule 5 under the heading *USE COMMAS*):

Incorrect:

An advantage, of computerized tax programs, is the accuracy of the returns.

Correct:

An advantage of computerized tax programs is the accuracy of the returns.

5. Before the first item or after the last item of a series (including coordinate adjectives):

Incorrect:

Some asset accounts are noncurrent, such as, land, buildings, and equipment.

[The faulty comma is the one before *land.*]

Correct:

Some asset accounts are noncurrent, such as land, buildings, and equipment.

Colons and Semicolons

The rules for colons (:) are few and easy to master, although sometimes writers use them incorrectly. Used correctly—and sparingly—colons can be effective because they draw the readers' attention to the material that follows the colon.

Colons can be used in the following situations:

1. To introduce a series:

    Three people spoke at the meeting: Elaine Brodie, CEO of Halifax Industries; John Mitchell, President of Oxford Inc.; and Billie Martin, CEO of Gigantic Corporation.

2. To introduce a direct quotation, especially a long quotation that is set off from the main body of the text:

    The senior partner issued the following instruction: "All audit workpapers should include concise, well-organized memos summarizing any problem revealed by the audit."

3. To emphasize a summary or explanation:

    Our study of Sebastian Enterprises has revealed one primary problem: Unless management hires new researchers to develop technical innovations, Sebastian will lose its position of market dominance.

Note: When the summary or explanation following the colon is a complete sentence, as in this example, it is correct to capitalize the first letter of the sentence, or to use a lower case letter:

Our study of Sebastian Enterprises has revealed one primary problem: unless management hires new researchers to develop technical innovations, Sebastian will lose its position of market dominance.

4. Following the salutation in a business letter:

Dear Ms. Wade:

When a colon introduces a series, an explanation, or a summary, the clause that precedes the colon should be a complete statement:

We have sent engagement letters to the following clients: B and B Conglomerates, Abigail's Catnip Boutique, and Sharkey's Aquarium Supplies.

not

We have sent engagement letters to: B and B Conglomerates, Abigail's Catnip Boutique, and Sharkey's Aquarium Supplies.

Semicolons (;) are used for only two situations: between independent clauses (see discussion of comma splices on page 81–83) and between items in a series, if the items themselves have internal commas:

Promotions were announced for Ann Moore, regional vice president; Larry Yeo, sales manager; and John Green, internal control manager.

DIRECT QUOTATIONS

LO 5.7 Incorporate direct quotations into your writing, following conventions of standard usage.

The punctuation of direct quotations depends on their length. Short quotations (fewer than five typed lines) are usually run in with the text and enclosed with quotation marks. Longer quotations are set off from the text—indented 1 inch from the left margin—with no quotation marks. Direct quotations should be formally introduced; a colon may separate the introduction from the quoted material. Study the following examples:

According to the FASB, "*Accounting Standards Codification*™ is the source of authoritative generally accepted accounting principles (GAAP) recognized by the FASB to be applied to nongovernmental entities."[1]

The FASB has issued the following statement about codification:

The FASB *Accounting Standards Codification*™ is the source of authoritative generally accepted accounting principles (GAAP) recognized by the FASB to be applied to nongovernmental entities. The Codification is effective for interim and annual periods ending after September 15, 2009. All previous level (a)-(d) US GAAP standards issued by a standard setter are superseded. Level (a)-(d) US GAAP refers to the previous accounting hierarchy. All other accounting literature not included in the Codification will be considered nonauthoritative.[2]

A direct quotation requires a citation identifying its source. It's also better to identify briefly the source of a quotation within the text itself, as the preceding examples illustrate. If a quotation comes from an individual, use his or her complete name the first time you quote from this person. You may also need to give the title or position of the person you are quoting, or otherwise explain that person's credentials. Study the following examples:

> According to Richard Smith, an executive officer of the Fairways Corporation, "The industry faces an exciting challenge in meeting foreign competition."

> Elaine Howard, who supervised the market research for the new product, provided this assessment of its sales potential: "Within five months from the product's introduction into the market, we expect sales to approach 500,000 units."

Notice the placement of punctuation in relation to quotation marks:

- Periods and commas should be placed inside the quotation marks:

> Allison said, "Our audit is complete."

> "Our audit is complete," Allison said.

- Semi-colons should be placed outside the quotation marks:

> Allison said, "Our audit is complete"; a further examination of the files, however, revealed that additional work was necessary.

- Placement of a question mark will vary, depending on whether the question mark is part of the original quotation:

> Allison said, "How much additional work is there?"

> Did Allison say, "I'm sick and tired of this audit"?

One final remark: Some writers may depend too heavily on direct quotation. It's usually better to paraphrase—to express someone else's ideas in your own words—unless precise quotation would be an advantage. As a rule, no more than 10% of a paper should be direct quotation. To be most effective, quotations should be used sparingly, and then only for authoritative support or dramatic effect.

Chapter 8, which discusses accounting research, gives more information on the use of sources, including direct quotations and paraphrases.

SPELLING

LO 5.8 Avoid problems with spelling.

Finished, revised writing should be entirely free of misspelled words. When you work at a word processor, use a spell checker to catch misspelled words and typographical errors. Note that a spell checker will not distinguish between homonyms such as *affect* and *effect* or *their* and *there*; nor will it check the spelling of most proper nouns, such as names. You may find it helpful to consult a dictionary when you aren't sure about a word's spelling.

Spelling: Always check every word!

The following short list contains words commonly misspelled or misused by accountants:

accrual, accrued
advise/advice
affect/effect
cost/costs, consist/consists, risk/risks
led, misled
occurred, occurring, occurrence
principal/principle
receivable, receive
separate, separately

The italicized words in the following sentences are often confused:

Please *advise* the customers to put the invoice number on their checks. [*Advise* is a verb.]
The *advice* we received was quite helpful. [*Advice* is a noun.]

This change in accounting policy will not *affect* the financial statements. [*Affect* is usually a verb; in the social and cognitive sciences, it can be used as a noun meaning *emotion* or *mood*.]
This change in accounting policy will have no *effect* on the financial statements. [*Effect* is usually a noun. Rarely, *effect* is a verb meaning to cause to happen.]

The replacement *cost* for the equipment is more than we had estimated. [*Cost* is singular.]
The *costs* to repair the equipment will affect the budget. [*Costs* is plural, but when you say the word aloud, you may not hear the final *s*.]

Investment in this stock carries a *risk*.
Investment in these stocks may carry several *risks*.

The ambiguous footnote may *mislead* investors. [*Mislead* is present or future tense.]
This ambiguous footnote *misled* investors. [*Misled* is past tense.]

How should we record the *principal* of this loan? [The *principal* is the face amount of the loan.]

This procedure does not follow generally accepted accounting *principles*. [*Principles* are rules.]

The *principal* reason for the investment is to generate income. [*Principal* means most important.]

HELP FROM THE COMPUTER

Some writers check their text for grammatical errors by using grammar-check software that is included in some word processing programs. These grammar-check programs can help you identify some problems with grammar, including errors with verbs, pronouns, and punctuation. These computer aids may not catch all your grammatical errors, however, and they may flag as an error a usage that is actually correct.

Using a spell-checker is another matter. As we've pointed out many times, a spell-checker is a tremendous help in correcting spelling and typographical errors.

A final word: Be sure to proofread the final hard copy of your document for errors you may have missed earlier. Computers aren't foolproof; sometimes what appears on the screen doesn't look the same on a printed page. Moreover, the auto-correct feature in some word processing programs may substitute an erroneous word into a sentence. Any errors, including those caused by the computer or printer, make work look sloppy and the writer seem careless. Effective writing should look professional: correct, neat, and polished.

TEST YOURSELF

Identify and correct the errors in the following exercises, using the guidelines discussed in this chapter. Answers are provided below.

1. Ms. Eliot, the controller, argued that these expenditures do not provide future benefits, thus, she expensed them.
2. Each candidate must demonstrate their ability to write well.
3. One provision of the new policies are causing confusion for the auditors.
4. New SEC requirements for handling this kind of transaction forces accountants to change the way they perform some procedures.
5. Although, the reason for our decreased sales is not obvious.
6. Many types of users rely on financial statement information, for example, investors may use the information to decide whether to purchase stock in the company.
7. If we change our marketing strategy, we would attract more customers.

8. We might suggest to the controller that he consider the FASB's Accounting Standards Codification® Topic 805 which deals with accounting standards for business combinations.
9. A statement with supplementary disclosures provide additional information to investors.
10. To increase the revenues from its new muffin products the Muffet Muffin Company introduced an advertising campaign in New York Chicago and Los Angeles.

TEST YOURSELF: ANSWERS

(Note: Some of the errors can be corrected in more than one way. For most sentences, this key shows only one possible correction. If you recognize the error, you probably understand how to correct it.)

1. Comma splice. Correction:
   Ms. Eliot, the controller, argued that these expenditures do not provide future benefits; thus, she expensed them.
2. Pronoun agreement. Correction:
   Candidates must demonstrate their ability to write well.
3. Subject-verb agreement. Correction:
   One provision of the new policies is causing confusion for the auditors. (The verb should agree with *provision*.)
4. Subject-verb agreement. Correction:
   New SEC requirements for handling this kind of transaction force accountants to change the way they perform some procedures. [The verb should agree with the subject *requirements*.]
5. Sentence fragment. Correction:
   However, the reason for our decreased sales is not obvious.
6. Comma splice. Correction:
   Many types of users rely on financial statement information. For example, investors may use the information to decide whether to purchase stock in the company.
   [Alternate: Many . . . information; for example, . . .]
7. Mood shift. Correction:
   If we changed our marketing strategy, we would attract more customers.
   or
   If we change our marketing strategy, we will attract more customers. [The original sentence contained a shift in mood from indicative to subjunctive. Either mood is correct here; the key is to be consistent.]
8. Comma error. Correction:
   We might suggest to the controller that he consider the FASB's Accounting Standards Codification® Topic 805, which deals with accounting standards for business combinations. [In this example,

we assume we know the controller, who is a man. If we know the controller is a woman, the pronoun should be changed to *she*.]

9. Subject-verb agreement. Correction:
A statement with supplementary disclosures provides additional information to investors. [The verb should agree with *statement*.]

10. Punctuation errors. Correction:
To increase the revenues from its new muffin products, the Muffet Muffin Company introduced an advertising campaign in New York, Chicago, and Los Angeles.

EXERCISES

Exercise 5–1 [General]

Join these independent clauses together in three ways.

under variable costing a company's sales will influence income
under absorption costing both sales and production will affect income.

Exercise 5–2 [General]

Identify and correct fragments, comma splices, or fused sentences. Some sentences are correct.

1. The reason for our low inventory turnover being that this is our slow season.
2. To improve our profits; therefore, we reduced expenses.
3. The proposal was unclear, so the Board requested additional information.
4. Tax season is our busiest time of the year everyone works long hours.
5. After the president announced the new policy, employees became worried.
6. Although, the new equipment has improved our rate of production.
7. Accountants do not depreciate land, therefore, we cannot allocate land costs on a systematic and rational basis.
8. Accountants write many letters as part of their professional responsibilities, for example, they may write letters to the IRS.
9. Two managers postponed their vacations, and thus we were able to handle the emergency.
10. Although we increased our advertising, sales did not improve.

Exercise 5–3 [General]

Some of these sentences have verb errors, either subject-verb agreement or shifts in tense or mood. Identify these errors and correct the sentences.

1. We will depreciate this asset over ten years. First, however, determine its salvage value.
2. If we hired a consultant, we will be able to design a new system.
3. Neither the president nor the supervisors understand the new policy.
4. One problem we found in our reviews of the records were that revenues were not always recorded in the proper period.
5. A statement with supplementary disclosures provide additional information to investors.
6. The physical flow of goods generally follow the FIFO pattern.
7. Each of these statements is prepared according to GAAP.
8. We reviewed the client's system of internal control; then we will recommend ways to improve it.
9. The future benefits provided by the bond is partly due to its high interest rate.
10. Problems with understanding the new computer system is frustrating everyone.

Exercise 5–4 [General]

Correct any pronoun errors you find in the following sentences.

1. The trouble with our new system is that you have so much trouble understanding it.
2. Hamilton Exports, Inc., increased their advertising this year.
3. The FASB deals with research and development costs in its Accounting Standards Codification® Topic 730.
4. Management is interested in improving the revenue figures for their report to the stockholders.
5. Each accountant is required to complete his report on time.
6. The Smallwood Corporation has greatly increased it's advertising expense.
7. A switch to LIFO usually results in a lower income tax liability and a lower inventory figure on the balance sheet; this would be important to our company.
8. The Board of Directors will hold its next meeting in July.
9. Every corporation coming under SEC regulations must follow certain procedures in preparing their financial statements.
10. Three new procedures were used to improve the responsibility of Nancy Copeland.

Exercise 5–5 [General]

Revise the following sentence for parallel grammatical structure:

This committee will study the problem, a recommendation for correcting it, and they will oversee the correction procedures.

Exercise 5–6 [General]

a. Complete the following chart.

Singular	Singular Possessive	Plural Possessive
statement		
company		
business		
cost		
risk		
CPA		
year		
industry		

b. Use the words from the chart to fill in these sentences. The singular form of the correct word is given in the parentheses.

1. (CPA) _____ must be able to write effectively.
2. (business) Investors examine a _____ statements to determine its financial condition.
3. (cost) Record all these _____ in the proper accounts.
4. (statement) Which of the _____ requires footnote disclosure?
5. (cost) What is the replacement _____ of this machine?
6. (risk) Investors in these bonds must accept certain _____.
7. (industry) Research and development are crucial in many _____.
8. (year) We should see a profit in two _____ time.
9. (company) The Board of Directors considered the _____ pension plan.
10. (statement) We are making changes in the two _____ totals.

Exercise 5–7 [General]

Punctuate the following sentences correctly.

1. The Board of Directors met December 12, 2018 in Charlotte North Carolina.
2. Before we issue an opinion on these financial statements we must be sure that this transaction was recorded correctly.
3. The biggest problem in our firm however is obsolete inventories.
4. The firm hired two new auditors thus the work will be finished on time.
5. For example Elixir Products should consider the FASB's Accounting Standards Codification® Topic 840 which deals with leases.

6. The auditors revealed several problems in Thompson Company's financial records such as its depreciation policy its handling of bad debts and its inventory accounting.
7. The presidents letter contained the following warning "If our revenues don't increase soon the plant may be forced to close"
8. "We're planning a new sales strategy" the manager wrote in reply.
9. We have decided not to invest in the Allied bonds at this time instead we are considering Blackstone's common stocks.
10. The contract was signed by the president, the controller and the attorney.

Exercise 5–8 [General]

Identify and correct any misspelled words in the following list. Look up any words you are unsure of; not all of these words were included in the chapter.

1. its (the possessive pronoun)
2. recieve
3. occured
4. seperate
5. accural
6. advice (the verb)
7. existance
8. principle (the rule)
9. cost (plural)
10. mislead (past tense)
11. advise (the noun)
12. effect (the noun)
13. thier
14. intrest
15. trail balance
16. its (the contraction of *it is*)

Exercise 5–9 [General]

Revise the following sentences, as needed, using the guidelines covered in this chapter.

1. The letter was dated May 8 2018 and mailed from Boston Massachusetts.
2. The guidelines will explain who is eligible for the benefits, costs, and how to apply.
3. We have assigned more auditors to this project thus we hope to complete the report on time.
4. The report was signed by the controller the internal auditor and the vice president.
5. Neither Susan nor Lisa are on the committee.

6. This is the employee's parking lot.
7. Either the president or the attorneys is expecting a challenge.
8. The benefits of this health insurance policy is obvious to employees.
9. We review the client's system of internal control. Then we will recommend ways to improve it.
10. Three new procedures were used to improve the internal control system. This was the responsibility of Hugh Tran.

Exercise 5–10 [General]

Revise the memo in Figure 5–1 below using the guidelines you've studied in this and other chapters. Your goal will be to produce a more effective memo.

FIGURE 5–1   Memo to Accompany Exercise 5–10

To: Miss Elaine Jacobs
From: Jonathan Brooks
Subject: Banquet for Veteran Employees
Date: March 12 2018

How are you doing? I am fine.

I have been asked by the Human Resources Department to organize a banquet for employees who have been with our firm ten years or more we are considering scheduling the event for May 8 which will be a convenient time for most people. Each of the honorees have already agreed that the date will work with his schedules. Being that you have experience in setting up events for our department. We hope you will take charge of the arrangement with the caterer the florist and the printer for the program. All these cost covered by the Human Resources Department. In the past, we give special gifts to the honorees, therefore they has something tangible as a reward for their service. Please ask somebody to look into this, coordinate with Human Resources about the amount of money we can spend on each persons' gift. How many honoree's we have will effect the amount we can spend on each gift. We want to ensure that each honoree realizes how much the firm appreciate's his service. Please let me know if you can do this. Also can you suggest names of other people who might be willing to work on a committee for this banquet. I'm too busy with more important work to spend much time on this project.

NOTES

1. Financial Accounting Standards Board, "Notice to Constituents About the Codification," *Accounting Standards Codification*® (v 4.1), (Stamford, Conn: FASB, April 30, 2010), 4.

2. Ibid.

CHAPTER

Format for Clarity:
Document Design

6

Learning Objectives

After studying this chapter, you should be able to

6.1 Design documents that are attractive and readable.

6.2 Design documents that look professional: paper and print quality, white space, and neat appearance.

6.3 Format documents to emphasize main ideas and divisions of the discussion: headings, set-off lists, and pagination.

6.4 Design graphic illustrations that support the information provided in a document.

How a document looks at first glance can make a big difference in how the reader reacts to it. An attractive document generally gets a positive response, but one that is not pleasing to the eye may never be read. A good design does more for the readers than appeal to them visually. A well-planned format also contributes to the clarity of documents by making them easier to read. Good design also helps a document look polished and professional after final revision, which is the seventh tip for effective writing (refer to Figure 1–1 in Chapter 1).

This chapter looks at techniques of document design that you can use to make everything you write look more appealing. These techniques can be used for any kind of document, including letters, memos, reports, and even email. We consider the choice of paper and font and the use of white space. We also show how techniques of formatting, such as headings, lists, and graphic illustrations, can make your documents clearer and more readable. Most of these formatting techniques apply to both electronic and paper documents. Later chapters cover the conventions and formats specific to particular kinds of documents, such as the standard parts of letters, memos, and reports. Chapter 12 discusses formatting techniques for electronic communication.

GOOD DESIGN: ATTRACTIVE AND READABLE

LO6.1   Design documents that are attractive and readable.

To illustrate the difference good design can make in the appearance and readability of a document, study the example in Figures 6–1 through 6–3, which are three versions of the same memo. Figures 6–1 shows straight text, with no divisions for paragraphs, headings, or other features of good document design. Figures 6–2 divides the text into readable para- graphs with a little more white space, and Figure 6–3 uses addit white space, headings, and a set-off list. Which version of the m do you think is most effective? Does the version in Figure 6–3 su formatting techniques you can use in your own writing?

FIGURE 6–1   Memo for Comparison (see Figures 6–2 and 6–3)

TO: Paul J. Streer, Partner

FROM: Billie Sanders

DATE: April 17, 2018

SUBJECT: Tax implications of Robert Burke's prospective joint purchase of rental real estate.

Our client, Robert Burke, has expressed concern about the tax implications of a venture he is considering, a joint purchase of real estate with Anne Simmons. The issue that must be considered is wheth- er Mr. Burke will be subject to a deduction limitation because the prop- erty will be used as a residence by Ms. Simmons. The conclusion is that because the rental agreement is a shared equity financing agreement, Mr. Burke will not be subject to a deduction limitation. On January 1, 2019, Ms. Simmons and Mr. Burke plan to purchase rental real estate, which Ms. Simmons will occupy as her residence. They will enter into an agreement whereby Mr. Burke will provide the down payment and one-half of the monthly mortgage payment. Ms. Simmons will pay the remaining portion of the monthly mortgage, monthly rental payments to Mr. Burke, and the monthly operating costs of the home. They will split the property taxes evenly. Mr. Burke will receive one-half of the appreciation value of the home upon its sale and has the option to demand that his interest in the property be paid to him after five years. The issue to be settled is whether Mr. Burke is subject to the deduction limitation in 280A(c)(5) because the rental property was used as a resi- dence by the taxpayer. The agreement between Ms. Simmons and Mr. Burke qualifies as a shared equity financing agreement under 280A(d) (3)(C). Because the agreement can be classified as such, 280A(c)(5) will not apply and cannot limit the deductions attributable to the rental of Mr. Burke's share of the property to the gross income derived from the rental. This conclusion was also reached by the IRS in Private Letter

FIGURE 6–1 *(Contd.)*

Ruling 8410038. To override the limitation of 280A(c)(5), the shared equity financing agreement must meet certain requirements: (1) under 280A(d)(3)(D), both Ms. Simmons and Mr. Burke must have a qualified ownership interest in the property (an undivided interest for more than fifty years in the entire property) and (2) the rent Ms. Simmons pays to Mr. Burke must be the fair rental at the time the agreement is entered, taking into account Ms. Simmons' qualified interest. Because Mr. Burke will be allowed the deductions and Ms. Simmons will not (except for expenses allowable even if the dwelling were not rented), payment of expenses should be the responsibility of Mr. Burke. The agreement can contain a provision that compensates Mr. Burke for this additional encumbrance. If those expenses were paid by Ms. Simmons, the deduction would go unused. The joint purchase Mr. Burke proposes to enter into is sound. The agreement will not have unfavorable tax implications for him if he is careful to follow these recommendations.

FIGURE 6–2 Memo for Comparison (see Figures 6–1 and 6–3)

TO: Paul J. Streer, Partner

FROM: Billie Sanders

DATE: April 17, 2018

SUBJECT: Tax implications of Robert Burke's prospective joint purchase of rental real estate.

Our client, Robert Burke, has expressed concern about the tax implications of a venture he is considering, a joint purchase of real estate with Anne Simmons. The issue that must be considered is whether Mr. Burke will be subject to a deduction limitation because the property will be used as a residence by Ms. Simmons. The conclusion is that because the rental agreement is a shared equity financing agreement, Mr. Burke will not be subject to a deduction limitation.

On January 1, 2019, Ms. Simmons and Mr. Burke plan to purchase rental real estate, which Ms. Simmons will occupy as her residence. They will enter into an agreement whereby Mr. Burke will provide the down payment and one-half of the monthly mortgage payment. Ms. Simmons will pay the remaining portion of the monthly mortgage, monthly rental payments to Mr. Burke, and the monthly operating costs of the home. They will split the property taxes evenly. Mr. Burke will receive one-half of the appreciation value of the home upon its sale and has the option to demand that his interest in the property be paid to him after five years.

The issue to be settled is whether Mr. Burke is subject to the deduction limitation in 280A(c)(5) because the rental property was used as a residence by the taxpayer.

FIGURE 6–2   *(Contd.)*

The agreement between Ms. Simmons and Mr. Burke qualifies as a shared equity financing agreement under 280A(d)(3)(C). Because the agreement can be classified as such, 280A(c)(5) will not apply and cannot limit the deductions attributable to the rental of Mr. Burke's share of the property to the gross income derived from the rental. This conclusion was also reached by the IRS in Private Letter Ruling 8410038.

To override the limitation of 280A(c)(5), the shared equity financing agreement must meet certain requirements: (1) under 280A(d) (3)(D), both Ms. Simmons and Mr. Burke must have a qualified ownership interest in the property (an undivided interest for more than fifty years in the entire property) and (2) the rent Ms. Simmons pays to Mr. Burke must be the fair rental at the time the agreement is entered, taking into account Ms. Simmons' qualified interest.

Because Mr. Burke will be allowed the deductions and Ms. Simmons will not (except for expenses allowable even if the dwelling were not rented), payment of expenses should be the responsibility of Mr. Burke. The agreement can contain a provision that compensates Mr. Burke for this additional encumbrance. If those expenses were paid by Ms. Simmons, the deduction would go unused.

The joint purchase Mr. Burke proposes to enter into is sound. The agreement will not have unfavorable tax implications for him if he is careful to follow these recommendations.

FIGURE 6–3   Memo for Comparison (see Figures 6–1 and 6–2)

TO: Paul J. Streer, Partner

FROM: Billie Sanders

DATE: April 17, 2018

SUBJECT: Tax implications of Robert Burke's prospective joint purchase of rental real estate.

Our client, Robert Burke, has expressed concern about the tax implications of a venture he is considering, a joint purchase of real estate with Anne Simmons. The issue that must be considered is whether Mr. Burke will be subject to a deduction limitation because the property will be used as a residence by Ms. Simmons. The conclusion is that because the rental agreement is a shared equity financing agreement, Mr. Burke will not be subject to a deduction limitation.

FIGURE 6–3 (*Contd.*)

Client's Situation
On January 1, 2019, Ms. Simmons and Mr. Burke plan to purchase rental real estate, which Ms. Simmons will occupy as her residence. They will enter into an agreement whereby Mr. Burke will provide the down payment and one-half of the monthly mortgage payment. Ms. Simmons will pay the remaining portion of the monthly mortgage, monthly rental payments to Mr. Burke, and the monthly operating costs of the home. They will split the property taxes evenly. Mr. Burke will receive one-half of the appreciation value of the home upon its sale and has the option to demand that his interest in the property be paid to him after five years.

Tax Issue
The issue to be settled is whether Mr. Burke is subject to the deduction limitation in 280A(c)(5) because the rental property was used as a residence by the taxpayer.

Tax Implications
The agreement between Ms. Simmons and Mr. Burke qualifies as a shared equity financing agreement under 280A(d)(3)(C). Because the agreement can be classified as such, 280A(c)(5) will not apply and cannot limit the deductions attributable to the rental of Mr. Burke's share of the property to the gross income derived from the rental. This conclusion was also reached by the IRS in Private Letter Ruling 8410038.

Recommendations
To override the limitation of 280A(c)(5), the shared equity financing agreement must meet certain requirements:

(1) Under 280A(d)(3)(D), both Ms. Simmons and Mr. Burke must have a qualified ownership interest in the property (an undivided interest for more than fifty years in the entire property).
(2) The rent Ms. Simmons pays to Mr. Burke must be the fair rental at the time the agreement is entered, taking into account Ms. Simmons' qualified interest.

Because Mr. Burke will be allowed the deductions and Ms. Simmons will not (except for expenses allowable even if the dwelling were not rented), payment of expenses should be the responsibility of Mr. Burke. The agreement can contain a provision that compensates Mr. Burke for this additional encumbrance. If those expenses were paid by Ms. Simmons, the deduction would go unused.
The joint purchase Mr. Burke proposes to enter into is sound. The agreement will not have unfavorable tax implications for him if he is careful to follow these recommendations.

A PROFESSIONAL APPEARANCE

LO6.2   **Design documents that look professional: print quality, white space, and neat appearance.**

If you already have a job, you may find models of well-designed documents written by people with whom you work. In fact, your employer may expect all documents to be written a certain way—in a standard format, for example, and on the company's letterhead and standard stock paper. You'll seem more professional if you learn your employer's expectations for document design and adhere to them.

Often, whether you're on the job or still in school, you'll have some leeway in how you design documents. The remainder of this chapter looks at techniques you can use to give your documents a professional appearance. For print documents, choose high-quality material—the best paper and the best print. Plan your pages so that they have an attractive use of margins and white space, and be sure they are perfectly neat.

Paper and Print

If you're already employed, you might not have any choice about the paper; you'll probably use your company's letterhead stationery and standard stock for all your documents. If you are still a student, select a paper that makes a good impression. For the final copy of a paper you submit for a grade, your instructor may prefer that you use 8½ × 11-inch paper of a high-quality bond, about 24-pound weight, in white or off-white.

Print the paper on a good printer that gives a professional appearance. Choose a 12-point type size and a standard font such as Times New Roman throughout your document. Type sizes and fonts should be easy to read, and they should not draw attention to themselves, so be conservative in your choices. Never use unusual fonts for business documents.

White Space and Margins

White space is the part of a page that does not have any print. White space includes margins, the space between sections, and the space around graphic illustrations.

A document with visual appeal will have a good balance between print and white space. White space also makes a document easier to read. The space between sections, for example, helps the reader see the paper's structure.

There are no hard-and-fast rules for margin widths or the number of lines between sections. As a general guideline, plan a 1-inch margin for the sides and bottoms of your papers. The top of the first page should have a 2-inch margin; subsequent pages should have a 1-inch margin at the top.

Leave an extra line space between the sections of your document. A double-spaced page, for example, would have three lines between sections.

For any document that is single-spaced, be sure to double-space between paragraphs.

Neatness Counts!

Sloppiness in a document is unprofessional and careless. Your computer's spell checker will help you to find errors and make corrections with ease. (Remember, spell checkers don't distinguish between homonyms like *bear* and *bare*. Chapter 5 discusses this problem more fully.) For printed documents, always proofread the final hard copy as well, because it's possible for errors to appear on the printed page that don't show up on a computer screen.

FORMATTING

LO6.3   Format documents to emphasize main ideas and divisions of the discussion: headings, set-off lists, and pagination.

Some writers think of their document's format only in terms of straight text: page after page of print unbroken by headings or other divisions. If you look at almost any professional publication, including this handbook, you'll see how various formatting devices, such as headings, lists, and set-off material, make pages more attractive and easier to read.

Headings

For any document longer than about half a page, you can use headings to divide the paper into sections. Headings make a paper less intimidating to readers because the divisions break up the text into smaller chunks. Headings give readers a chance to pause and reflect on what they've read.

Headings also help readers by showing them the paper's structure and the topics it covers. In fact, many readers preview the contents of a document by skimming through to read the headings. For this reason, headings should be worded so that they indicate the contents of the section to follow. Sometimes headings suggest the main idea of the section, but they should clearly identify the topic discussed. If you look through this book, you'll see how the headings suggest the chapters' contents.

Headings can be broken down into several levels of division. Some headings indicate major sections of a paper and others indicate minor divisions. In other words, a paper can have both headings and sub-headings. In this chapter, for example, "A Professional Appearance" indicates a major section of the chapter; "Paper and Print" marks the beginning of a subtopic, because it's just one aspect of a document's appearance. Generally, a short document needs only one heading level, but this rule can vary depending on what you are writing.

The style of the heading (how the heading is placed and printed on the page) varies with the levels of division. Some styles indicate major headings; other styles indicate subheadings. As an example, the major headings might be printed in a boldface font in all capital letters at the left margin, and subheadings might be indented, boldfaced, with only the initial letter of each main word capitalized, as follows:

FIRST LEVEL: BOLD FONT, LEFT MARGIN, ALL CAPS
    Second Level: Bold Font, Initial Letters Capitalized, Indented
    Third Level: Indented, Italicized

This book uses the following system of headings:

FIRST LEVEL: BOLD FONT, LEFT MARGIN, ALL CAPS
Second Level: Bold Font, Left Margin, Initial Letters Capitalized
    Third Level: Indented, Italicized
    FOURTH LEVEL: INDENTED, BOLD ALL SMALL CAPS FONT

Here is another example of heading styles and the corresponding levels of division:

        FIRST LEVEL: CENTERED, ALL CAPS, BOLDFACED
Second Level: Left Margin, Boldfaced
    Third Level: Indented, Italicized

If you use fewer than three levels, you can use any combination of headings, as long as they are in descending order. For example, you might use second-level headings for main topics and third-level head-ings for subtopics. If you are using only one level of headings, any style is acceptable.

When you write the headings for your paper, it's usually preferable to have all the headings of a certain level grammatically parallel: Nouns and noun phrases, such as the headings in Figure 6–3, are common for headings. Verb phrases can also be an effective choice if you're enumerating the steps in a process, or a series of actions someone will perform. For example, a memo written to summarize work done on an audit might use these verb phrases as headings for the body of the memo, which describes the steps of the inventory audit process:

    Observing clients' inventory taking
    Making test counts
    Identifying obsolete and damaged goods
    Observing cutoff controls

Chapter 5 discusses parallel grammatical structure more fully.

It's possible to overuse headings. You should not normally use a heading for every paragraph, for example.

Lists and Set-Off Material

Another formatting technique that can make a document easier to read is set-off material, especially lists. Mark each item on the list with a number, a bullet, or some other marker. Double-space before and after the list. The items can be single-spaced or double-spaced.

Here is an example using bullets:

Your firm should update its systems in these areas:

- Budgets
- Payrolls
- Fixed assets
- Accounts payable
- Accounts receivable

Set-off lists not only improve the paper's appearance by providing more white space, but they also make the paper more readable. The following example presents the same information as straight text and in a list format. Which arrangement do you prefer?

The meeting will discuss the new vacation policy. First, we'll explain who is eligible for extended vacation leave. Next, we'll discuss when the policy will take effect. Finally, we'll discuss how to get vacation requests approved.

The meeting will discuss the new vacation policy:

- Eligibility for extended leave
- Effective date
- Approval process

Remember that set-off lists should be written with parallel grammatical structure (see pages 88–89). The set-off list in the previous example uses noun phrases.

Occasionally, you'll use set-off material for other purposes besides lists. Long direct quotations are set off, and on rare occasions you might set off a sentence or two for emphasis. Chapter 8 discusses the use of direct quotations.

Pagination

The next formatting technique is a simple one, but it's overlooked surprisingly often. For every document longer than one page, be sure to include page numbers. They can be placed at either the top or the bottom of the page, be centered, or be placed in the upper right corner. Begin numbering on page 2.

GRAPHIC ILLUSTRATIONS

LO6.4 Design graphic illustrations that support the information provided in a document.

Graphic illustrations—such as tables, graphs, and flowcharts—can make a document more interesting and informative. They enable you to summarize a great deal of information quickly and help readers identify and remember important ideas.

Tables are an efficient way to summarize numerical data in rows and columns. When you use a table, label the rows and columns, indicate the units of measure you are reporting, and align the figures. Table 6–1, which shows the consolidated statements of income of The Northeastern Beverage Company and Subsidiaries, is an example of a table.

TABLE 6–1   The Northeastern Beverage Company and Subsidiaries Consolidated Statements of Income

	Year ended December 31		
	2017	2016	2015
(In millions except per share data)			
NET OPERATING REVENUES	**$41,879**	$38.563	$34,121
Cost of goods sold	**12,173**	11,924	9,945
GROSS PROFIT	**29,706**	26,639	24,176
Selling, general, and administrative expenses	**15,674**	12,949	11,811
Other operating charges	**401**	357	332
OPERATING INCOME	**13,631**	13,333	12,033
Interest Income	**163**	302	283
Interest Expense	**315**	408	413
Equity income (loss) – net	**666**	15	27
Other income (loss) – net	**39**	31	(4)
INCOME BEFORE INCOME TAXES	**14,184**	13,273	11,926
Income taxes	**3,429**	2,761	2,173
CONSOLIDATED NET INCOME	**$10,755**	$10,512	$9,753
Less: Net income attributable to Noncontrolling interests	**98**	76	61
NET INCOME ATTRIBUTABLE TO SHAREOWNERS OF THE NORTHEASTERN BEVERAGE COMPANY	**$10,657**	$10,436	$9,692
BASIC INCOME PER SHARE	**$3.02**	$3.01	$2.87
DILUTED NET INCOME PER SHARE	**$3.00**	$2.99	$2.85
AVERAGE SHARES OUTSTANDING	**3,528**	3,472	3,381
Effect of dilutive securities	**26**	19	17
AVERAGE SHARES OUTSTANDING ASSUMING DILUTION	**3,554**	3,491	3,398

Refer to Notes to Consolidated Financial Statements.

A pie chart shows how a whole is divided into parts, just as a pie is divided into slices. When you use a pie chart, label the wedges and show what percentages of the whole they represent. The pie chart in Figure 6–4 shows The Northeastern Beverage Company's case volume by state for 2017. The circle represents the total volume, and the slices show the percentages of that total for each state.

Graphs, which can take several forms, are useful for comparisons. Two of the most common types of graphs are bar graphs and line graphs. Bar graphs compare quantities or amounts. The bar graph in Figure 6–5 shows total revenue for Southeastern Sporting Goods.

A line graph, which also compares quantities, is helpful for showing trends. A line graph may have a single line or multiple lines. The line graph in Figure 6–6 compares revenue, expense, and net income trends for Sebastian Corporation over nine years.

Another type of graphic illustration is a flowchart, which shows the steps in a process or procedure. If you use a flowchart in your documents, use boxes or other shapes to show activities or outcomes; label each box or shape and arrange them so that the process flows from left to right and from the top to the bottom of the page. Use arrows to show the direction of the flow. Figure 6–7 shows a typical example.

Systems analyses often include very sophisticated flowcharts to show how a system works, with established symbols and formats to represent different components of the system.

If you include graphic illustrations in the documents you write, whether flowcharts, graphs, or tables, you should follow certain guidelines. Be sure to number the graphic illustrations and give them descriptive titles. Tables should be called Tables (such as Table 6–1), and graphs

---

FIGURE 6–4   The Northeastern Beverage Company Case Volume by State

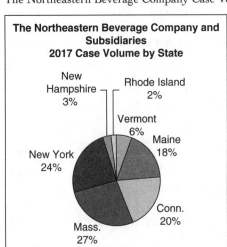

FIGURE 6–5   Southeastern Sporting Goods Total Revenue

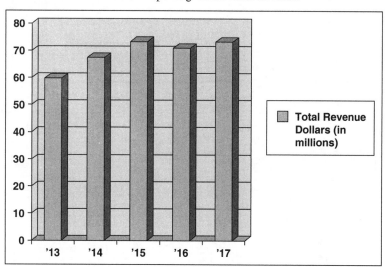

FIGURE 6–6   Sebastian Corporation Revenue, Expense, and Net Income

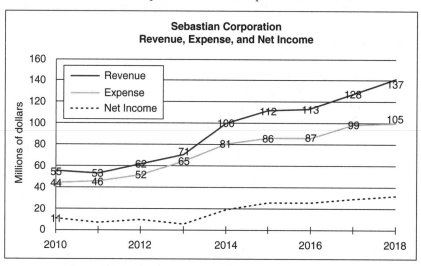

and flowcharts should be called Figures (such as Figure 6–7). Graphic illustrations should be labeled sufficiently so that they are self-explanatory, but they should also be discussed in the text of the document. This discussion should refer to the illustration by description, name, and number. The discussion should precede the illustration. The illustrations can be placed either in the body of the document, close to the place in the text where they are discussed, or in an appendix.

Finally, if you use a graphic illustration from another source, identify the source fully at the bottom of the illustration.

FIGURE 6–7   Net Present Value Process in Capital Budgeting

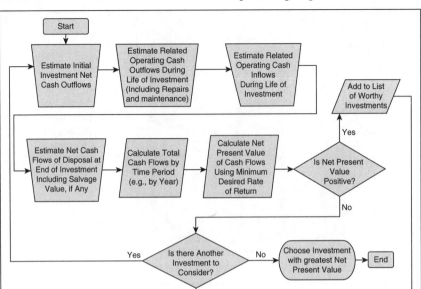

EXERCISES

Exercise 6–1 [General]

Assume you are the president of your school's chapter of Beta Alpha Psi (the national accounting honorary society). The chapter wishes to request funding from the school's Dean of Student Affairs for a job fair, and you have been asked to write a letter to the dean making the request. What topics should the letter include? What tone is appropriate for a letter to the dean? Write the letter, using effective document dean making the request. Chapter 9 discusses letters. Invent any information necessary to complete this assignment.

Exercise 6–2 [General]

Select three companies in the same industry with the same fiscal year-end. Construct both bar and line graphs that compare their price/earnings ratios at the end of each of the last five fiscal years.

Exercise 6–3 [Tax]

A client, Carter Fowlkes, owns a second home which he has been unable to sell for quite awhile. He has struck upon the idea of granting the local fire department rights to use it for training, including the right to destroy it by fire or other means, if that would prove beneficial to the department. He would then like to deduct the value of the structure on his income tax return. When the fire department is finished with the structure, Mr. Fowlkes would build something else on the property. Your client has asked you to explain what effects this transaction will have on his income taxes. Write a letter to Mr. Fowlkes responding to his inquiry, using the principles of effective document design discussed in this chapter. Chapter 9 discusses letter writing. Invent any information necessary to complete this assignment."

Exercise 6–4 [Tax]

In December 2017, one of your clients, Tim Huffman, donated a valuable piece of art to a local charity to be auctioned at its annual fundraising auction. When Mr. Huffman donated the art, it was appraised for $20,000. However, at the auction held on January 20, 2018, it sold for $35,000. Mr. Huffman claims that the appraisal was obviously wrong and that the value of what he donated was obviously $35,000. Consequently, he wants to deduct $35,000 on his 2017 tax return. Write a letter to Mr. Huffman discussing the tax implications of the appraisal and subsequent sale of the art he donated. Use the principles of effective document design discussed in this chapter. Chapter 9 discusses letter writing. Invent any information necessary to complete this assignment.

Exercise 6–5 [Auditing]

Assume you are an auditing partner in a regional CPA firm. Write a memo to all audit staff members explaining how subsequent events may or may not affect a compilation and review engagement. Chapter 10 discusses memo writing. Your memo should illustrate effective document design using the techniques discussed in this chapter. Invent any information necessary to complete this assignment.

Exercise 6–6 [Auditing/Ethics]

As a member of the ethics standards team of your CPA firm, you have been asked to write a memo to all audit staff discussing the importance of ethics in auditing in general, and of compliance with Rule 501 of the AICPA's *Code of Professional Ethics* in particular. Write the memo, paying attention to good document design. Chapter 10 discusses memo writing. Invent any information necessary to complete this assignment.

Exercise 6–7 [Systems]

You are a systems consultant. One of your clients, Susan Reid of Reid Manufacturing, wants to enter e-commerce. Write a letter to her explaining some of the control and accounting issues involved in e-commerce. Your letter should demonstrate effective document design. Chapter 9 discusses letters. Invent any information necessary to complete this assignment.

Exercise 6–8 [Systems]

You are a systems consultant. One of your clients, Ben Hill of Hill Manufacturing, is concerned about protecting his company from fraud. He has recently learned that there is fraud detection software available and has asked you whether or not he should be using such software and what it might do for his company. Write a letter to Mr. Hill responding to his request. Your letter should demonstrate effective document design. Chapter 9 discusses letters. Invent any information necessary to complete this assignment.

Exercise 6–9 [International/Managerial/Current Professional Issues]

The International Integrated Reporting Council (IIRC) (http://www.theiirc.org/) believes the current framework of corporate reporting that emphasizes financial statements is not sufficient to answer the question of what the value of the entity is. In the IIRC's view, additional information concerning corporate strategy, governance, performance, and prospects should be reported along with financial statements in an "International Integrated Reporting Framework."

Write a briefing memo to the managing partner of your accounting firm defining and elaborating upon this effort of the IIRC as well as evaluating its desirability. Use the techniques of document design discussed in this chapter. Chapter 10 discusses briefing memos. Invent any information necessary to complete this assignment.

Exercise 6–10 [Current Professional Issues/Auditing]

You are a partner in a regional CPA firm, Shield, McClune, & Butterfield. You are convinced that your firm should consider expanding its client services by getting into the field of fraud and forensic accounting. You have decided to prepare a memo to all partners of the firm explaining what this field involves, its opportunities, and the pros and cons of establishing expertise it. Prepare the memo. Memos are discussed in Chapter 10. Invent any information necessary to complete this assignment.

CHAPTER

Thinking on The Job: Higher Order Thinking Skills

Learning Objectives

After studying this chapter, you should be able to

7.1 Discuss higher order thinking skills and the importance of these skills to the successful practice of accounting.

7.2 Summarize the steps used to solve accounting problems.

7.3 Explain the two approaches to constructing an argument: inductive and deductive reasoning.

7.4 Recognize and avoid logical fallacies.

7.5 Explain how higher order thinking skills can be used to resolve ethical dilemmas.

W e noted earlier that the ability to think clearly is an essential qualification for a professional accountant, and these cognitive skills are becoming even more important as the profession changes. In fact, professional certification exams, including the CPA, CGMA, and CMA exams, now expect candidates to demonstrate their mastery of higher order thinking skills. This chapter will delve into these thinking skills more closely by discussing concepts and definitions related to higher order thinking, reinforced by examples and exercises. Chapter 8, *Accounting Research,* will develop this discussion further with more technical and advanced accounting applications.

THE IMPORTANCE OF THINKING SKILLS

LO7.1 **Discuss higher order thinking skills and the importance of these skills to the successful practice of accounting.**

As we have seen, higher order thinking skills are essential to the successful practice of accounting. Among these higher order skills, the

AICPA includes "critical thinking, problem solving and analytical ability, as well a professional skepticism."[1] Some sources that explore cognitive abilities use *critical thinking* as a synonym for *higher order thinking skills,* while the AICPA describes *critical thinking* as one component of the broader category of *higher order thinking skills.* In spite of such differences in terminology, however, the underlying skills and concepts are very similar. Thus, if you've taken a course entitled Critical Thinking, you have a good start in acquiring the cognitive skills in demand within the accounting profession. These skills include analysis, evaluation, problem solving, and professional skepticism. You must be able to recognize issues, identify errors in reasoning, challenge assumptions, and apply professional judgment.[2] You will also be expected to draw valid conclusions and support them fully when you address issues and search for answers to problems.

We might also describe higher order thinking as fair, open-minded thinking that asks appropriate questions and considers all relevant information before reaching a conclusion. Careful thinkers consider problems from multiple points of view before reaching a decision, and they avoid errors in reasoning, which are called logical fallacies. They also use precise, clear language to construct unambiguous arguments that readers can understand and, in turn, evaluate fairly. In other words, effective thinkers analyze issues, conduct the necessary research, and evaluate alternative solutions. They then communicate their findings responsibly. Thus, careful thinking is inseparable from effective communication and can even be considered a component of professional ethics.

THINKING TO SOLVE PROBLEMS

LO7.2 Summarize the steps used to solve accounting problems.

As a practicing professional, you will sometimes be asked to solve problems for your firm, your clients, or the organization for which you work. Often part of the problem-solving process will be to construct an argument in support of the solution you recommend. Solving a problem and constructing an argument to support your recommendation both entail a process. Here is a summary of this process:

1. Identify the key issues.
2. Anticipate alternative solutions and different points of view.
3. Research all sides of the issue, using authoritative sources.
4. Weigh the evidence for all points of view, and build support for your position.
5. Identify and respond to counterarguments.
6. Communicate your conclusions.

Sometimes as you follow the steps in the process, you may discover that you need to return to earlier steps. As you research the issues, for example, you may discover additional issues or other possible solutions to the problem.

To illustrate the process, consider this hypothetical scenario. You are an accountant employed by a medium-size accounting firm. The firm has 20 accountants on its staff, in addition to technical and clerical support staff. The firm has had its offices in a grand old office building in the downtown heart of the city for the past 60 years. However, the owners of the building have decided to convert the building to residential condominiums, forcing your firm to relocate. You have been asked to recommend the best alternative for the new office. After researching the alternatives, you will present your recommendation in a briefing memo to the firm's partners. How do you form and communicate your recommendation? The process listed previously will help you as you construct an argument to support your conclusions.

A word of caution is in order here: Remember that it's always important to consider the expectations of your readers and the purpose of the document you are writing. What are the expectations of the partners who asked you to investigate the relocation problem? Do they expect you to identify the one best site for the firm, or have they asked you to recommend several viable locations, giving the advantages and disadvantages of each choice? In the latter case, the partners themselves would make the final selection, based on the information you have provided in a briefing memo. You would have narrowed the field, then, through your analysis and research. For the purposes of this hypothetical example, assume that the partners have asked you to evaluate the alternatives and recommend the best site. They will expect you to document the thoroughness with which you investigated the alternatives and the reasons for your conclusions.

1. *Identify key issues.*   The first step in constructing an argument is to identify the key issues. In the situation just described, the most important issues might be, first, where in the city the new office should be located, and second, whether the firm should lease office space, purchase an office condominium, purchase its own building, or construct its own building. Each of these major issues should be further analyzed. You should consider the availability and costs of suitable space, the suitability of potential sites for the firm's business, and the accounting implications of the decision to lease, purchase, or construct.

2. *Anticipate alternative solutions and different points of view.* Before you reach your conclusions, identify all the reasonable alternatives. With preliminary research, you'll gather information about the obvious choices. You also need to identify the preferences of other people involved in the decision and take account of

their knowledge, experience, assumptions, and biases. It's especially important to consider the views of those who will make the final decision, in this case the firm's partners. For example, before you suggest leasing, purchasing, or constructing in this scenario, find out if the partners are willing to consider all three possibilities. You should also determine which sections of the city they believe to be viable locations for the firm. Are they determined to maintain the firm's office in the center of the city, or would they consider moving to a midtown or suburban location?

3. *Research all sides of the issue, using authoritative sources.* After you have identified the alternative solutions to your problem, you can research the possibilities, including sources for both accounting and non-accounting information. Consider your firm's needs and how alternative sites would accommodate those needs. Is the location convenient to the firm's employees and clients, and is the location suitable for business? Is adequate parking and/or public transportation available for the firm's employees and clients? What other businesses are located in this area? Would proposed buildings require renovation? What are the costs, in both time and money, of these renovations, as well as other moving costs? All these decisions involve accounting considerations, which you also must research. What are the accounting and tax implications of the decision to lease, purchase, or construct? Refer to specific GAAP and tax provisions for these scenarios. (For more information on documenting authoritative accounting sources, see Chapter 8.)

4. *Weigh the evidence for all points of view, and build support for your position.* After you've completed your research, the solution may be obvious. In this example, assume that you have identified the best site for the firm's relocation after considering all alternatives, and you are now ready to summarize your conclusions. Organize the support for your conclusions in an outline: the key issues, the recommendations, and the reasons to support your recommendations, from most to least important.

5. *Identify and respond to counterarguments.* In this office relocation example, some of the partners may have initial preferences for a particular location, or they may raise objections to the site you've selected. You should identify in advance the reasons why some of the partners might disagree with your conclusions. That is, you must identify the counterarguments (arguments against your recommendations). You must also decide how you will respond to these objections—whether you will agree with them (concede the counterarguments) or argue against them (refute the counterarguments).

The response to a counterargument may be a combination of concession and refutation. For instance, one of the partners in this example may object to your recommendations because the site you've chosen requires extensive, costly renovation. You might concede that those costs will be high, but also point out that over time the costs will be more than made up because the cost of the new lease (or purchase) will be considerably lower than the cost of the firm's current lease.

Sometimes people constructing an argument believe that presenting all sides of the argument will weaken their position. Just the opposite is the case, however. By presenting all sides, you'll create the impression that you are a responsible person who has carefully considered all sides of an issue before reaching a conclusion. Thus, people will find you credible and fair, and they will take your argument seriously.

6. *Communicate your conclusions.* In this step, you present your conclusions and your arguments, along with your responses to any counterarguments. You may present your conclusions orally, perhaps in a meeting, or in a written document such as a memo, letter, or report. In this example, you'll write a briefing memo as the partners have requested.

REACHING SOUND CONCLUSIONS: TWO APPROACHES TO LOGIC

LO7.3   Explain the two approaches to constructing an argument: inductive and deductive reasoning.

To solve problems, you will often construct an argument, such as the process outlined in the scenario above. Another way to think about problem solving is as an exercise of logic, which is defined as the practice of careful reasoning and as such is an important component of higher order thinking skills. The science of logic is often divided into inductive and deductive reasoning, as discussed in Chapter 3. In this chapter, we discuss these forms of reasoning further, as well as some of the more commonly made errors in reasoning, which are called fallacies.

Inductive Reasoning

The process used to construct an argument in the office relocation scenario discussed above demonstrates one form of inductive reasoning: gathering evidence, and then reaching a conclusion. More formally, inductive reasoning is defined as reaching conclusions about the entirety of something (the whole) from a study of representative examples (parts of that whole). The scientific method of research is one example of inductive reasoning: observing samples, gathering data, and drawing tentative conclusions, or hypotheses, which are then further tested for verification. Some variations of inductive reasoning include making comparisons (drawing analogies), analyzing causes, conducting surveys, referring to authoritative sources, and citing statistics. In short, inductive reasoning begins with specific facts and from these facts derives general conclusions or principles.

Deductive Reasoning

With inductive reasoning, you gather specific information and then reach a general conclusion. With deductive reasoning, you apply reasoning in the opposite direction; you begin with one or more general assumptions or premises and arrive at a specific conclusion. Consider these examples:

> All accounting majors at this university must take a course in tax accounting.
>
> Jenny is an accounting major at this university.
>
> Therefore, Jenny must take a course in tax accounting.

Deductive reasoning is often stated in the form of a syllogism. A *syllogism* consists of a major premise, a minor premise, and a conclusion. The premises are the assumptions upon which the conclusion is based. In the preceding example, the first line is the major assumption or premise, the second line is the minor premise, and the third line is the conclusion.

Here's another example of a syllogism:

MAJOR PREMISE: Asset account balances increase with debits.
MINOR PREMISE: The asset account was debited.
CONCLUSION: The asset account balance increased.

To reach sound conclusions using deductive reasoning, you must be sure your arguments are both valid and sound. These terms—*valid* and *sound*—will become clearer with examples. First, a valid argument is one in which the conclusion has been correctly drawn from the premises. Study the following examples:

Example 1: Valid argument:

MAJOR PREMISE: All the students in this class have passed the placement test.
MINOR PREMISE: Robert is a student in this class.
CONCLUSION: Therefore, Robert has passed the placement test.

Example 2: Invalid argument:

MAJOR PREMISE: All the students in this class have passed the placement test.
MINOR PREMISE: Robert has passed the placement test.
CONCLUSION: Therefore, Robert is a student in this class.

In the valid argument in Example 1, the conclusion has been correctly drawn from the premises, unlike the invalid argument in Example 2. In Example 2, even though Robert has passed the placement test, he might not be a student in the class for any number of reasons. He might have taken the class in an earlier semester, postponed the class until a later semester, be enrolled in a different section of the class, changed his major, or transferred to another school.

Let's look at two more examples. Example 3 is a valid argument—the conclusion has been correctly drawn from the premises—but Example 4 is invalid:

Example 3: Valid argument:

MAJOR PREMISE: All publicly held companies must construct financial statements following GAAP.
MINOR PREMISE: Brite Company is a publicly held company
CONCLUSION: Therefore, Brite Company must construct its financial statements following GAAP.

Example 4: Invalid argument:

MAJOR PREMISE: All publicly held companies must construct financial statements following GAAP.
MINOR PREMISE: Brite Company constructs its financial statements following GAAP.
CONCLUSION: Brite Company is a publicly held company.

Many companies that are not publicly held also construct financial statements following GAAP. Thus, Brite Company might not be publicly held.

Deductive reasoning must be *sound*, as well as valid, for the conclusions to be true. Sound reasoning requires not only that (a) the conclusion has been correctly drawn from the premises, but also (b) that the premises are themselves true. For a sound conclusion, both the major and minor premises must be true. For instance, in the preceding Example 1, the conclusion would not be sound if either the major or minor premise is not true: (1) some students in the class have not passed the placement test, or (2) Robert is not a student in the class.

Recall that the ability to challenge the truth of assumptions is one of the higher order thinking skills identified by the AICPA as essential to the practice of accounting and evaluated on the CPA exam.

Sometimes the use of a syllogism will help you spot errors in reasoning. Consider the following example:

The SEC has filed charges against The Gigantic National Corporation for cheating its former employees out of their pension benefits. Larry Womack, the CEO, issues this statement to the press: "The buck stops here. As CEO, I must accept responsibility for the fraud uncovered by the SEC. A few unscrupulous middle managers have violated company policy and the law by authorizing and carrying out this fraud. Those responsible will be identified, and will no longer work for this corporation. I deplore what has happened, but I will not resign."

What is wrong with the reasoning expressed in Mr. Womack's statement? We can analyze his argument in the form of a syllogism such as this one:

MAJOR PREMISE: The person(s) responsible for the fraud will no longer work for this corporation.
MINOR PREMISE: I am responsible for the fraud. (Recall the CEO's assertion: "I must accept responsibility for the fraud uncovered by the SEC.")
CONCLUSION: I will not resign.

You can see that the conclusion in this case does not follow logically from the major and minor premises. This argument is invalid. Put another way, the CEO has contradicted himself.

FALLACIES: ERRORS IN REASONING

LO7.4   Recognize and avoid logical fallacies.

To reach sound conclusions, you must be careful to avoid errors in reasoning. That is, you must learn to recognize and avoid fallacies in the arguments you make or those made by others. Some common fallacies that you should avoid are listed here along with examples of each:

- *Fallacies involving language*   Using ambiguous word choices (vague or undefined), loaded language, labels, and slogans

    Anyone who favors the passage of this legislation is unpatriotic.

    (What does *unpatriotic* mean in this case? This word, as it is used here, is vague and loaded. That is, it may generate an emotional response unrelated to critical thinking about the legislation in question.)

- *Fallacies involving appeals to emotion*   Appealing to fear, pity, anger, or prejudice

    If we change our pension plan, widows and orphans will suffer.

    (This argument illustrates an appeal to pity. Of course, decision-makers should consider the effects of the proposed change on pension recipients, but other factors should also be evaluated. It might be, for example, that the company will go bankrupt if it doesn't change its pension plan.)

- *Fallacy of appeal to tradition*   Arguing for something only because it's customary

  We shouldn't promote Joanne Risling to a partner position. Her degree is from a private university. It's tradition that our partners graduate from the state university.

- *Fallacy of false authority*   Using authorities that are unidentified, irrelevant, or lacking proper credentials

  Experts agree that all accounting firms should be involved in social media.

  (Who are these experts?)

  We should invest in this stock, because all our friends are buying it.

  (This statement illustrates a type of false authority called the bandwagon fallacy: "Get on the bandwagon and do what everybody else is doing.")

- *Ad hominem fallacy*   Attacking opponents' character, rather than their arguments

  Don't listen to what he's saying. He's an idiot.

- *Post hoc fallacy*   Assuming that because one circumstance happens before another, the first circumstance is the cause of the second

  After we hired Stan Sterling, our company's profits increased. Clearly Stan is the reason for our increased profitability.

  (Hiring Stan may indeed have affected the company's profits; however, we need more information before reaching this conclusion. What is Stan's position? What other factors, such as changes in the market, might be responsible for the growth in profits?)

- *Hasty generalization fallacy:*   Using poor or inadequate sampling techniques

  Professor Brown is a poor teacher. I know this because my roommate took his tax accounting course and complained about it every day.

- *Either/or fallacy (false dilemma):*   Assuming there are only two choices, when there may be several

  You're either for me or against me.

  (I may support you as a general rule, but disagree with you on this particular point.)

  Either we adopt this measure, or we face bankruptcy.

  (We might adopt a different measure and avoid bankruptcy.)

- *Slippery slope fallacy*   Arguing that if one event occurs, a series of undesirable events will inevitably occur as a result

  If we provide cell phones to our sales staff, the next thing you know they'll demand their own tablet computers, then company cars, and then chauffeurs to drive those cars. They'll then want unlimited expense accounts for trips to Las Vegas. The company will go bankrupt.

Earlier, we defined careful thinking as fair, open-minded thinking that asks appropriate questions and considers all relevant information before reaching a conclusion. Although there is no formula for becoming a careful thinker, if you keep in mind the factors we have discussed in this chapter, your thinking will be much more responsible, enabling you to be a more effective communicator.

HIGHER ORDER THINKING AND ETHICAL DILEMMAS

LO7.5 Explain how higher order thinking skills can be used to resolve ethical dilemmas.

In Chapter 1 we discussed the importance of ethics in the practice of accounting. Accountants find guidance for making ethical decisions in legal requirements, codes of ethics (such as the AICPA's Code of Professional Ethics or the IMA's Statement of Ethical Professional Practice), and their personal ethical values. Often what constitutes ethical behavior is obvious, but sometimes accountants face complex situations for which the ethical solution is not immediately clear. Careful thinking can help resolve these ethical dilemmas.

The process for resolving ethical dilemmas resembles the steps you take to solve problems and make a strong argument, as discussed earlier in this chapter. Indeed, identifying and defending a course of action as the most ethical among several alternatives is itself a kind of argument, even if one you have only with yourself. When you are faced with a situation that requires you to make an ethical decision, follow these steps:

1. Obtain all the facts relevant to the situation.
2. Identify all the ethical issues.
3. Determine who will be affected by the way these issues are resolved. Consider both individuals and groups, such as shareholders, employees, and the general public.
4. Identify alternative solutions to the issues, including arguments that might be used to support each alternative.
5. Analyze how the individuals and groups identified in step 3 would be affected by the alternative solutions.
6. Consider guidelines for ethical decisions, such as applicable legal requirements, codes of ethics, and your own ethical values. Be careful to avoid logical fallacies in your thinking.
7. Decide on the appropriate action and, when necessary, communicate your decision to the appropriate parties. If the situation is potentially contentious, be prepared to provide the reasons for your decision. When you write or speak to someone about the ethical issues, be especially tactful, courteous, and respectful to all parties concerned.

As you can see, resolving ethical dilemmas depends on higher order thinking, as well as effective communication.

EXERCISES

Exercise 7–1 [General]

The following statements contain mistakes in reasoning (fallacies). Which fallacies are illustrated here? (Some statements may illustrate more than one fallacy.)

1. Ever since she changed accountants, the profits in her business have increased. Clearly the new accountant knows how to cook the books.
2. Give them an inch and they'll take a mile.
3. Either we redesign all our accounting information systems or we might as well close down the business.
4. Don't listen to him. He's just a nerdy, detail-obsessed accountant.
5. Three out of four accountants agree: *The Daily Balance Sheet* is the best source of financial news.
6. We don't need more public transportation in our city. Everyone in my office agrees they'd rather drive their own cars.
7. We've used Biddy and Bully as our firm's legal firm for four generations. Even though their work has become unsatisfactory, I wouldn't want to change firms.
8. We shouldn't hire Jim Blankenship. He's from Hick City, and everybody knows people from there are just a bunch of ignorant buffoons.

Exercise 7–2 [General]

Some administrators in your school have proposed a change in grading policy for major level courses, that is, beyond the principles or introductory level. They propose that instructors be required to grade courses on a Pass/Fail basis only. What would be the advantages and disadvantages of this proposed policy? Consider both sides of this question, and analyze the pros and cons of the proposal. Then write a letter to the editor of your school's newspaper, or the local newspaper where your school is located, in which you summarize your findings. Chapter 9 discusses letters.

Exercise 7–3 [General]

Look for illustrations of the fallacies discussed in this chapter in print media, on radio or television, on social media, or in the conversations you hear. Quote or paraphrase the passage that illustrates the fallacy, giving a citation of the source. Then identify the fallacy and explain the error in reasoning the passage demonstrates. Chapter 8 discusses how to document sources.

Exercise 7–4 [Financial/Ethics]

You are a staff accountant at Outrageous Corporation. The controller of the company, Howard Eino, is concerned that profits reported in the annual report will not meet those forecast at the beginning of the year. He has asked you to decrease the amount of annual depreciation charged on certain equipment by revising the estimated life. When you tell Mr. Eino that revision of useful life solely to "manage" profit is not appropriate, he responds by saying, "Oh, everybody does it." You realize that if you fail to do what your boss wants, you may receive an unfavorable annual performance evaluation. How will you resolve this dilemma?

After analyzing and researching this problem, write a memo to Mr. Eino that explains your position. Write the memo in a respectful, courteous tone, while supporting your position clearly. Chapter 10 discusses memos.

Exercise 7–5 [Financial/Theory]

Some people would argue that historical costs should no longer be used in accounting because they are not relevant. Others argue that departing from historical cost introduces too much subjectivity into accounting. Write a briefing memo for Elizabeth Jansen, the managing partner of your firm. Ms. Jansen will use the memo to prepare a presentation on this topic for the local chapter of a professional accounting organization. Provide a defense of both points of view and explain why the FASB has chosen to depart from historical cost in many of its accounting standards.

To prepare for this assignment, you may wish to review Chapter 10, which discusses briefing memos.

Exercise 7–6 [Auditing/Theory]

Some have suggested eliminating the provision of Rule 203 of the AICPA's professional ethics that permits non-conformance with GAAP if, in the opinion of the CPA, following GAAP would result in misleading financial statements. Thoroughly discuss the pros and cons of eliminating this provision of Rule 203 and summarize these arguments in a briefing memo to the managing partner of your CPA firm, Elaine Morgan. Chapter 10 discusses briefing memos.

Exercise 7–7 [Tax]

Prepare an oral presentation that addresses the purpose, structure, and recent activities of the IRS Oversight Board. Include a discussion of its strategy to reduce the "tax gap," that is, to reduce the amount of uncollected taxes. Your presentation should demonstrate your understanding of higher order thinking skills. Assume the audience for your presentation is accounting students in your class. Chapter 16 discusses oral presentations.

Exercise 7–8 [Systems]

Write a brief article for your accounting honorary society's Web page about the kinds of issues that must be considered when designing an accounting information system. Your purpose is to generate interest among the students in taking an accounting information systems course. Your article should demonstrate your understanding of higher order thinking skills. Chapter 15, which discusses writing for publication, will help you prepare your article.

Exercise 7–9 [Managerial]

Your accounting honorary society's Web page is running a series of articles about various careers in accounting that accounting students might choose. You have been asked to write an article about the advantages of a career in management accounting. Write the article with the purpose of persuading students to seek a career in management accounting without discouraging them from considering other career choices. Your article should demonstrate your understanding of higher order thinking skills. Chapter 15 discusses writing for publication.

Exercise 7–10 [Professional Issues]

You are a partner in a medium-size CPA firm. You are convinced that the issue of sustainability, that is, sustainable business practices, offers a good opportunity for your firm to expand its services to clients. Write a memo to your partners explaining the sustainability challenge and opportunity for your firm. Your memo should demonstrate your understanding of higher order thinking skills. Memos are discussed in Chapter 10.

NOTES

1. American Institute of Certified Public Accountants, Exposure Draft, *Maintaining the Relevance of the Uniform CPA Examination*. (New York; AICPA, September 1, 2015), p. 3. Available at https://www.aicpa.org/BecomeACPA/CPAExam/nextexam/DownloadableDocuments/Next-CPA-Exam-Exposure-Draft-20150901.pdf (26 December 2016).

2. Ibid. p.8.

CHAPTER

Accounting Research

8

Learning Objectives

After studying this chapter, you should be able to

8.1 Identify the main sources for accounting information.

8.2 Take notes and document sources used in your research.

8.3 Explain how higher order thinking skills help in accounting research.

8.4 Summarize the steps in the financial accounting research process and apply this process to your assignments.

Accountants and business services professionals often do research to solve technical accounting or tax problems or to gather information on some general topic of interest, such as the feasibility of offering a new service to their clients. This chapter discusses how to conduct research and write a research paper, report, documented discussion paper, or technical memorandum.

The first part of the chapter discusses basic guidelines for all research, including using electronic and printed sources of information, taking and using notes, using direct quotations and paraphrases, and documenting your sources. The remainder of the chapter focuses on specific steps in the technical accounting research process, including determining relevant facts, identifying key issues, researching the literature, considering alternative solutions, and communicating results. These steps in the research process are similar to the guidelines given in Chapter 7 for solving problems, constructing an argument, and resolving ethical dilemmas, all of which require higher order thinking skills.

ACCOUNTING RESEARCH: SOURCES FOR INFORMATION

LO8.1   Identify the main sources for accounting information.

If your project requires research, chances are you already know something about the topic you will research. If you don't, you may need to do some initial reading so that you have a basic familiarity with your subject. After you have a general idea of what your topic involves, you're ready to begin your research in more depth.

Good research requires deliberation, care, and diligence. You should look at all possible sources of information so that you don't overlook something important.

Plan Your Research

Often it's a good idea to write out a research plan before you begin your research. In the plan you can list sources of information with which you're already familiar, as well as references you can consult that will guide you to additional resources. For example, let's assume your research topic is "forensic services" and that you are aware that the AICPA has published a report on this topic. You also realize that professional journals have published articles on forensic services. Initially, your research plan might list the following:

- Check the AICPA Web site to see if the report on forensic services is posted. You can also check the Web site for other information on forensic services or links to such information.
- Check the *Journal of Accountancy* and other professional journals for past articles. These articles may be available online, or you may have to locate printed copies of the journals.
- Do a keyword search of any electronic literature indexes available at the library or online for articles or reports from the past few years.
- Do a topical and keyword search of the Web.
- Search an online database service (see Appendix 8–B to this chapter).
- Search other sources of accounting and financial information on the Internet (see Appendix 8–A to this chapter).

As you follow your research plan, modify it to include other additional resources you find. Thus, you may add references to specific articles, reports, Web sites, indexes, or searchable databases. As you come across specific sources, such as published articles and reports, look at the bibliographical, footnote, or endnote references and hyperlinks they may contain. These will often lead you to useful material you may not otherwise find.

As you conduct your research, keep track of what you have done by checking off the steps listed in your plan. If your research includes a keyword search of an electronic index or database, keep a log of the keywords and keyword combinations you have used in your search and the results they have obtained. Keeping good records will increase the efficiency of your research because you can avoid duplicating searches; at the same time, you can critique the search process you have followed to determine what you may have missed or how to refine the process. Keeping records of your sources will also help you write the citations for your final document.

FASB Accounting Standards Codification®

Several years ago the Financial Accounting Standards Board (FASB) released a codification system for Generally Accepted Accounting Principles (GAAP) called the *FASB Accounting Standards Codification*® ("ASC" or "Codification" for short). The FASB refers to the Codification as "the single source of authoritative nongovernmental U.S. Generally Accepted Accounting Principles (U.S. GAAP)." The Codification supersedes all non-Securities and Exchange Commission (non-SEC) standards. The FASB issues all authoritative U.S. GAAP in the form of "Accounting Standards Updates" (ASUs).[1] ASUs are used to revise the Codification and are not by themselves considered to be authoritative.[2]

The FASB's Codification affects the way you cite accounting standards for papers you prepare for any accounting writing you may complete. The Codification uses a system of Topic numbers, Subtopic numbers, Section numbers, and Paragraph numbers. So, for example, the definition of goodwill may be found in Topic 350 ("Intangibles—Goodwill and Other"), Subtopic 20 ("Goodwill"), Section 05 ("Overview and Background"), Paragraph 01, and would be cited as "FASB ASC par. 350-20-05-01."

The Codification is available in both printed and electronic form. (See Appendix 8-B "Online Database Services," pp. 153–154, for more information on this source.)

Electronic Sources of Information

Electronic sources of information include the Internet and online databases (including the electronic version of the *FASB Accounting Standards Codification*®). The quantity and availability of these electronic sources, along with how quickly and easily they can be searched, should place them high on your list of resources for most research.

The Internet

One step in your research plan should be to search the Internet for material related to your topic. Search engines such as Google enable you to locate documents ("pages") on the Web. Tailor the search to your needs by using keywords or phrases associated with your research topic.

The Internet may lead you to publications available at your library or to documents that you can download. Read the material you find on the Internet carefully and take accurate notes of your findings, including complete references to the sources you are using. A later section of this chapter discusses note taking and how to properly indicate references in more detail. Print out useful material you find unless the length of a particular source makes this impractical, in which case you should save it on your computer, a disk, an external drive, or a CD. When you save this material, be sure to record the Web address (Uniform Resource Locator or URL).

Appendix 8–A at the end of this chapter shows some of the better Web sites available on the Internet that offer information related to accounting and finance as well as links to other useful sites.

Online Databases

Many information databases are available online. The FASB Accounting Standards and AICPA Professional Standards are available in this manner.

The *FASB Accounting Standards Codification® Research System* covers accounting literature issued by several standard setters. FASB publications included are Statements, Interpretations, Technical Bulletins, Staff Positions, Staff Implementation Guides, and Statement 138 Examples. Abstracts and Topic D of the Emerging Issues Task Force are included, as are Derivatives Implementation Group Issues, Accounting Principles Board Opinions, Accounting Research Bulletins, and Accounting Interpretations. AICPA Statements of Position, Audit and Accounting Guides, Practice Bulletins, and Technical Inquiry Service issuances are also available here along with authoritative SEC and SEC staff material.

CCH's Accounting Research Manager® contains a wide range of useful data including primary source data from all major accounting standard setting bodies.

The *CCH® Tax Research NetWork™* or CCH's *Standard Federal Tax Reporter*, which are available in print or accessible electronically through CCH's *IntelliConnect®*, can be indispensable for tax research. Thomson Reuters' *Checkpoint* is another good online data-base for tax research.[3]

Many other databases are available online. Appendix 8–B lists many of the most useful computerized references and databases available for accounting and finance research together with their web addresses.

Printed Sources of Information

Although electronic media can provide excellent sources for your research, some important information may not be available in electronic form. Printed information sources will require conventional library research. Even if your library doesn't have specialized electronic databases, it most likely has a general database that lists articles published in accounting periodicals. You'll access this database by a keyword search.

One print source of information about technical accounting topics is official accounting standards. As we indicated earlier, the *FASB Accounting Standards Codification®* is available in printed as well as electronic form. You can also study printed versions of government regulations or laws to find out how to handle a client's technical problem.

Appendix 8–C lists some of the popular printed sources of accounting information. The library probably has other helpful references as well, such as indexes of major newspapers.

A librarian can help you find references that will help you to prepare your paper.

NOTES AND DOCUMENTATION

LO8.2 Take notes and document sources used in your research.

After you have located a useful source, take notes on what you read. You may decide to take notes on a computer, which can help you write your notes and organize them at the same time. Any good word processing or database program can be used to take notes. Or you may prefer to write notes by hand.

If you take notes on a computer, you'll need two computer files— one for the bibliography (the list of sources you used) and another for your notes. (If you take notes by hand, you can use two sets of cards—4×6-inch cards for your notes and 3×5-inch cards for your bibliography.)

Be sure to include in the *bibliography file* all the information you will need for the bibliography (see the section on documentation later in this chapter). The following are examples of entries you might make in your bibliography file:

1. Financial Accounting Standards Board (FASB). *Accounting Standards Codification®*, Topic 350, "Intangibles—Goodwill and Other." Stamford, Conn.: FASB 2017.

2. Financial Accounting Standards Board (FASB). *Objectives of Financial Reporting by Business Enterprises, Statement of Financial Accounting Concepts No. 1.* Stamford, Conn.: FASB 1978.

Give each of your sources a number. The number will save time when you take notes from that source and later when you draft your paper. The sources just illustrated are numbered *1* and *2*.

The *note file* contains the information you will actually use in your paper. Notice the parts of this note file entry:

II. A. 1. – Goodwill definition
[1] Subtopic 20, Sect. 05, Par. 01

"An asset representing the future economic benefits arising from other assets acquired in a business combination or an acquisition by a not-for-profit entity that are not individually identified and separately recognized."

The first line of the note file entry gives an outline code (II. A. 1.) that corresponds with the section in your outline where the note fits, and a short description of what the note is about. The second line gives the number of the source for this note as contained in your bibliography file and the page or paragraph numbers where this information was found—[1] Subtopic 20, Sect. 05, Par. 01. The note itself is taken from the source and is the material you will use in your paper.

Direct Quotation and Paraphrase

You can take notes in two ways: as a direct quotation (the exact words from the source) or as a paraphrase (your own words and sentence structures). If you take notes as direct quotations, you can decide later whether to use a direct quotation or paraphrase in your paper. However, if you're sure you won't need a direct quotation in your paper and you take the time to paraphrase as you research, you'll save time when writing the draft. Remember that no more than about 10 percent of most papers should be direct quotation.

Here's a good way to paraphrase. Read a section from your source—perhaps several short paragraphs. Then look away and try to remember the important ideas. Write them down. Then look back to check your notes for accuracy.

If you take notes as quotations, use quotation marks so you'll know later that these are someone else's words. Copy the quotation exactly, including capitalization and punctuation. Direct quotations must be accurate in every way; paraphrases must be your own words and sentence structures, not just a slight variation of your source.

Plagiarism

It's essential to give credit for material you borrow from someone else, whether you paraphrase or quote directly, and whether you've used electronic or printed sources. You must also give credit for visual materials, as well as language and ideas. If you don't give credit, you'll be guilty of plagiarism. *The Prentice Hall Guide for College Writers* contains the following discussion of plagiarism:

> Plagiarism occurs when you use the language, ideas, or visual materials from another person or text without acknowledging the source—even if you do this unintentionally. . . . Do not use language, ideas, or graphics from any essay, text, or visual image that you find online, in the library, or from commercial sources without acknowledging the source.[4]

Plagiarism can thus involve the unacknowledged (undocumented) use of someone else's ideas, opinions, research, or graphics—not just the use of someone's exact words.

The key to avoiding plagiarism is to document your sources adequately with either internal documentation or notes (see the section on documentation). In actual practice, sometimes you might not know whether you should identify the source of information you want to use in your paper. The difficulty arises because information that is considered common knowledge in a given field need not be documented. Obviously, the problem is to decide what is common knowledge. One guideline says that if you can find the same information in three different sources, that information is considered common knowledge and therefore needs no documentation.

There are many gray areas when it comes to issues of plagiarism. Perhaps the safest rule is to document your sources whenever there is any question of possible plagiarism. That is, when in doubt, document.

Remember: plagiarism is theft of another person's words or ideas. In some situations, it's punishable by law. If you plagiarize at school, the repercussions may be very serious: You may fail the assignment, fail the course, or be expelled, depending on your school's policies. Plagiarism on the job may lead to termination.

Organizing Your Notes and Ideas

As you are taking notes, you will probably form some idea of the major divisions of the paper. That is, you should be getting a rough idea of its outline, which you can now begin to construct. Stop and evaluate the outline from time to time. Are you covering all the important areas of your topic? Is the outline getting too long? Should you narrow the topic? Are some sections of the outline irrelevant to the topic? Answering these questions will guide you as you continue your research.

Writing Your Research Report or Memo

When your research is complete, you are ready to begin writing your report or memo. Your first step should be to refine your outline. Be sure that your topic is completely covered and that the ideas are arranged in the most effective order. Think about the introduction and conclusion to your paper, as well as any other relevant parts. Do you want to include charts, tables, or graphs?

Next, arrange your notes in the order of the outline and write the appropriate outline code beside each note.

With a completed outline and an orderly arrangement of your notes, you're ready to begin writing.

Integrating Notes into Your Writing

The draft of a research paper is written just like that of any other kind of writing, except you are incorporating notes taken from your sources into your own ideas. If you have already paraphrased the notes, your task is much easier. Include in your draft an indication of where your notes came from. In the final version of your paper, these references will be footnotes, endnotes, or parenthetical citations. In the draft, you can indicate your sources with a parenthetical notation like this: *([1] p. 403)*. The numbers come from your notes and refer to the source and page or paragraph number of each note.

Revising

After you have completed the draft, revise it to perfect the organization, development, style, grammar, and spelling. You might also ask a colleague to review your paper and suggest ways it can be improved.

Documentation

As noted earlier, any information you get from a source other than your own knowledge must be documented; that is, you must say where you got the information. Even if you are using your own knowledge, it may be useful to add documentation to bolster the authority of your ideas. Styles for documentation vary, but we'll look at two of the most common: internal documentation and notes.[5] The format we illustrate for both styles is consistent with *The Chicago Manual of Style*[6] and Kate L. Turabian's *A Manual for Writers of Term Papers, Theses, and Dissertations*[7] or, in the case of electronic citations, Walker and Taylor's *The Columbia Guide to Online Style.*[8]

Internal Documentation

Many writers prefer to use internal documentation, which places abbreviated information about sources within the text, using parentheses ( ) or brackets [ ], followed by a list of references at the end of the paper. What goes within the parentheses or brackets depends on the kind of source you are using. Appendix 8–D at the end of this chapter gives sample citations and reference list entries for sources typically used by accounting professionals.

You should introduce quotations or paraphrases within the text itself, such as in this example:

> According to the *FASB Accounting Standards Codification®*, current assets are "cash and other assets or resources commonly identified as those that are reasonably expected to be realized in cash or sold or consumed during the normal operating cycle of the business" (FASB ASC, par. 210-10-45-01).

Note that the end punctuation for the quotation, in this case the period, comes after the parentheses. The numbers shown in this citation refer to Codification Topic (210), Subtopic (10), Section (45), and Paragraph (01). This is the standard way of citing the Codification. If readers check the reference list at the end of the paper, they will find:

> Financial Accounting Standards Board (FASB), 2017. *Accounting Standards Codification®*. Stamford, Conn.: FASB.

Here's one reminder about the use of technical sources. Consider whether the readers of your paper will be familiar with the literature cited. If they won't be, you should identify the source more fully and briefly explain its significance.

Endnotes or Footnotes

The other style of documentation in wide use is endnotes or footnotes. The difference between these two note forms is that footnotes come at the bottom of the page where the references occur, whereas endnotes come at the end of the paper. Most authorities consider endnotes acceptable. If you prefer footnotes, your word processor should be able to place footnotes on the right pages, in the acceptable format. With either endnotes or footnotes, you have the option of adding a bibliography at the end of your paper, listing your sources in alphabetical order.

Appendix 8–E at the end of this chapter gives examples of notes and bibliographical entries for typical accounting sources.

As with internal documentation, you should introduce your paraphrased or quoted material:

> According to an article in *The Wall Street Journal*, many accounting firms find the poor writing skills of their new employees to be a serious problem.[9]

The introduction to this paraphrase tells generally where the information came from; the note and bibliographical entry give complete information about the source.

Citing Electronic Sources

You will probably need to cite material that you have found online. An acceptable form of citation for documents available from electronic sources usually resembles the pattern of citations for hard-copy sources, but you need to provide additional information so that your readers can find the file or document online. You should also note the date you accessed the document, because the document may be modified or even removed from online availability after you have accessed it. For the same reason, it's also a good idea to save a copy of the document you are citing.

Examples of citations for electronic sources are illustrated in Appendices 8–C and 8–D at the end of this chapter.

HIGHER ORDER THINKING AND TECHNICAL ACCOUNTING RESEARCH

LO8.3   Explain how higher order thinking skills help in accounting research.

In Chapter 7 we discussed higher order thinking skills in general. In this section, we examine their importance and application to accounting research.

One noted author has defined technical accounting research this way:

> . . . [technical accounting] research . . . is a <u>process</u>, and its result is a defensible solution to the problem or issue at hand. By process we mean a systematic routine of identifying the problem or issue, specifying alternative plausible solutions, conducting an inquiry into the propriety of the alternatives, evaluating the authoritative literature found, making a choice among the alternatives, and communicating the results. Since the solution must be defensible, the accounting professional must be certain that the search of the professional literature is exhaustive and the reasoning employed in determining the solution is sound.[10]

Notice the importance of higher order thinking skills to the process of accounting research: identifying the issues or problems; identifying alternative solutions; evaluating the best solution; and communicating the recommended solution, giving reasons for its preference.

Technical accounting research is most often done in either financial or tax accounting. The following discussion, which focuses on financial accounting, will give you an idea of the complexity of this kind of research, as well as a strategy you can use when faced with a difficult accounting problem.

FINANCIAL ACCOUNTING RESEARCH: A PROCESS

LO8.4   Summarize the steps in the financial accounting research process and apply this process to your assignments.

Research in financial accounting is often necessary (particularly in larger accounting firms and industry) because financial transactions may not always be directly covered by generally accepted accounting principles (GAAP). In other words, you may not always find guidance in published accounting standards that fits a particular transaction or that fairly represents the conditions under which the transaction occurred. When this situation occurs, you must devise an accounting solution that can be defended based on accounting theory and logic found elsewhere in generally accepted accounting principles. The following section suggests a procedure you can use for this research.

Steps in the Financial Accounting Research Process

Financial accounting research involves the following steps:

1. Determine all the relevant facts.
2. Identify all the issues involved.
3. Research the issues in the accounting literature.
4. Identify alternative solutions and arguments for and against each.
5. Evaluate alternative solutions and choose the one that can be best defended.
6. Communicate the results of your research to interested parties.

Note that these steps are similar to those presented in Chapter 7, but applied more directly to financial accounting research. Let's discuss these steps one at a time.

Determine All the Relevant Facts

Determining the relevant facts is often fairly straightforward. If you realize that research is necessary, you're probably already aware of most facts of the transaction. Be sure you have *all* the facts before you begin your research. Do you fully understand the transaction and the conditions under which it was made? If the transaction is supported by a contract or other documents, examine them thoroughly. Are there any hidden contingencies, liabilities, or unperformed duties on the part of any participants? What motivated the parties to make the transaction?

Identify All the Issues Involved

Sometimes identifying the issues can be one of the more difficult steps in the accounting research process. It's not uncommon for facts (or a lack of facts), terminology, and researcher bias to obscure some issues rather than clarify them. Ethical issues may also become apparent as you gather additional information and consider alternative solutions. Attention to critical thinking will help you ensure that all the issues are identified.

Consider the case of a custom machine parts manufacturer that routinely manufactures more parts than its customers order, expenses the cost of these extra parts as part of cost of goods sold, and physically holds the parts in inventory at a carrying value of zero. If a customer later has an emergency need for another part or two, the parts can be delivered immediately; however, this almost never happens, and the additional revenue from the sale of these extra parts is of no consequence. The question is whether the manufacturer's method of accounting for this situation is appropriate. What are the issues?

A quick reading of the facts presented may suggest that the issue is whether the cost of manufacturing the extra parts is properly accounted for by expensing it as part of cost of goods sold and carrying the inventory at zero, or whether the cost of the extra parts should be attributed to the inventory. Certainly the questions of inventory valuation and accounting for cost of goods sold will be answered by our research and the conclusions we draw from it. However, the central issue is best stated quite differently.

The basic issue in this case is the nature of the expenditure involved in producing the extra parts. That is, which one of the elements discussed in *Statement of Financial Accounting Concepts No. 6* best describes the expenditure? Does the expenditure result in an asset (not necessarily the physical parts)? This is the question to start with because definitions of the other elements depend on the definition of an asset. If an asset has resulted from the expenditure, the type of asset is still in question: Is it inventory, goodwill, or some other intangible asset? If an asset has not been the result, has an expense been incurred? If so, is it appropriate to include it as part of cost of goods sold, or is it some other type of expense? If an expense has not been incurred, the expenditure must be accounted for as a loss.

Research the Issues in the Accounting Literature

After you have identified the issues, the next step is to research the accounting literature to gather all relevant material. If the issues involve theoretical questions, as most probably will, you should consult relevant parts of the *Statements of Financial Accounting Concepts*. Certainly you should review the *FASB Accounting Standards Codification*® to identify generally accepted accounting principles (GAAP) bearing directly or indirectly on the issues.

Sometimes you may find useful information in GAAP covering an unrelated area. For example, if an issue involves revenue recognition of an entity in the software industry, GAAP covering the music industry or some industry even further removed from the software industry may contain logic or guidance that could serve as a basis for a solution.

It's possible that your research may take you beyond the materials just discussed. Regulations of the Securities and Exchange Commission (SEC), regulations of other federal agencies, accounting books, and articles in accounting journals all may prove useful. SEC regulations may be controlling if the entity involved falls under SEC jurisdiction. Online databases such as those listed in Appendix 8–B are good sources for much of this material.

Identify Alternative Solutions and Arguments For and Against Each

If you're engaged in technical accounting research, you're probably dealing with issues for which there are no established solutions. You must identify all alternative solutions, determine the best solution, and defend that solution against all others.

Evaluate Alternative Solutions and Choose the One That Can Be Best Defended
In the end, you must be able to present a well-reasoned defense of your accounting method. Although accounting is not law (except as governed by the SEC), just as a lawyer may prepare a well-reasoned defense of an issue using legal precedent and logic, an accountant doing technical accounting research must use similar skills to defend a proposed solution to an accounting issue. Indeed, it's possible that the solution you choose may have to be defended in a court during some legal proceeding.

If you anticipate that your readers will oppose your recommended treatment, or prefer an alternative, your written document should anticipate and answer such objections. You should explain the reasons that support your recommendation, as well as why alternatives are not acceptable.

Communicate the Results of Your Research to Interested Parties
You will usually communicate the results of your research in a report, letter, or memo, and occasionally you may report orally as well. However you report your research, incorporate all the elements of effective communication discussed in this book. Audience analysis, precision, clarity, and logical development are particularly important.

EXERCISES

Exercise 8–1 [General]

Choose one of the following topics and narrow it if necessary. Write a documented discussion paper on your topic, using the steps discussed in this chapter. Chapter 11 provides additional information on discussion papers.

- Congressional attempts to affect the accounting standard setting process
- The future of Extendable Business Reporting Language (XBRL) and how it might be used to support the development of other comprehensive bases of accounting (OCBOA) outside of GAAP
- The Public Company Accounting Oversight Board (PCAOB)
- The Chartered Global Management Accountant (CGMA) designation now offered cooperatively through a joint venture of the AICPA and the CIMA
- The International Auditing and Assurance Standards Board (IAASB) and its role in establishing International Standards on Auditing (ISAs)
- The use of fair value measurements in Generally Accepted Accounting Principles
- The future of "integrated reporting" and the possible expansion of the attest function
- The role of judgment in the application of accounting standards and whether that role should be reduced or expanded

Exercise 8–2 [Managerial/Systems]

The controller of your company, Mr. Dennis Patterson, has asked you to write a briefing memo discussing the Committee of Sponsoring Organizations' (COSO) Internal Control—Integrated Framework. Mr. Patterson wants to know how the Board of Directors and higher level management might use this framework to better design the company's system of internal control. Write the memo, inventing any facts that may be necessary. Chapter 10 discusses briefing documents.

Exercise 8–3 [Financial/Theory]

Harmon Industries manufactures and sells industrial machinery around the world. The company is heavily dependent upon contracts with transatlantic and transpacific shipping companies to deliver its products. Because fuel prices are unpredictable, several of the shipping companies Harmon uses have included a clause in their contracts allowing them to impose a fuel supplement if the price of West Texas Intermediate fuel exceeds a stipulated price per barrel. Although the price of fuel is not expected to increase anytime soon, Harmon's controller, Trent Johnson, is concerned about how he will account for the supplement if it is ever imposed. Typically, contracts state that the supplement may be imposed on June 30 each year to cover the shipping company's fuel purchases during the preceding 12 months. The amount of the surcharge levied on any one shipper, like Harmon, would be based on a formula that takes into account the number of shipments and tonnage shipped by that shipper during the period. Based on Harmon's projections, such a levy could result in several millions of dollars of additional expense.

Harmon has a fiscal year-end of December 31. Mr. Johnson has asked you, a member of his accounting staff, to research the problem of accounting for any fuel supplement that might be imposed. He has asked you to look into these questions:

- Should the supplement be treated as an expense of the period in which it is imposed, or should it be apportioned between the current and preceding periods in some manner?
- How should the supplement be reported (classified) in the financial statements?
- What type of risk disclosure (if any) should be included in the financial statements?

Mr. Johnson has asked you to look into all accounting and reporting aspects of the situation and not just his list of questions. If he has left anything significant out of his list, you should cover that as well.

Write a report to Mr. Johnson responding to his concerns. Chapter 12 discusses reports.

Exercise 8–4 [Managerial/Financial]

In early 2016, Boeing came under scrutiny by the SEC for the way it accounted for expected sales and costs of its 787 Dreamliner and 747 jumbo jet aircraft using a GAAP permitted method known as program accounting. Write an article for your business school's newspaper describing this accounting method, the pros and cons of its use, and why the SEC was so concerned about the manner in which Boeing used it. Chapter 15 discusses writing for publication.

Exercise 8–5 [Financial/Theory]

American Petroleum Company (AP Oil) owns and operates deep-water drilling rigs in international waters off the coast of Euromania, a Western European country. Several months ago it experienced a disastrous explosion and fire at one of its rigs that resulted in a monumental oil spill, which has yet to be contained. The spill is expected to have dire effects on hundreds of miles of the Euromanian coastline, putting untold thousands of people in fishing, tourist, and supporting industries out of work. Since the disaster occurred in international waters, the ability of the Euromanian courts to impose liability judgments against AP is probably limited to its ability to seize whatever AP assets are located within its jurisdiction. These assets are carried on AP's books at $20 billion. In addition, Euromanian law limits liability in such cases to a maximum of €107 million ($112 million). However, due to a feeling of ethical obligation and in an effort to salvage the good name of the company, AP's Board of Directors has agreed to honor all damage claims in an unlimited fashion. It is estimated that the value of such claims could reach €93 billion ($97 billion).

Your firm has served as the auditors for AP for several years. AP's Board of Directors has requested that your firm prepare a report for the Board discussing how its decision should be reflected in AP's financial statements under U.S. GAAP. Your supervisor, Charles Brogan, has asked you to research the technical issues involved and prepare a briefing memo for him recommending how the issues should be handled; he will subsequently prepare the report for AP. He has told you not to be concerned with the issue of foreign currency translation, as that is well understood by AP. Prepare the memo for Mr. Brogan. Chapter 10 discusses briefing documents.

Exercise 8–6 [Financial/Theory]

Your client, Smooth Brew Company, has just purchased a brewery known for the unique taste of its beer. This taste is primarily the result of using sparkling spring water that flows from a particular stream made famous in the brewery's advertisements. The brewery is located on 20 acres at the foot of a large mountain. The famous stream flows down the mountain out of North Carolina and through the brewery's property in Georgia.

Your client paid a high price for these brewing operations—$1 million above the fair market value of the tangible assets acquired. The president of Smooth Brew has made it clear that the main reason he agreed to pay the price is to get access to the special water. Accordingly, he has requested that an account entitled "Water" be set up in the balance sheet and valued at $1 million.

As Smooth Brew's CPA, you know your firm will have to take a position on this issue. Should your firm allow the client to account for the $1 million the way he suggests? If not, what will be the position of your firm on how the transaction should be accounted for?

Write a memo to your boss, Claire Sanders, recommending what position your firm should take with this client and why. Chapter 10 discusses memos.

Exercise 8–7 [Auditing]

Prepare a research report on the impact of technology on auditing in areas such as (but not limited to) comprehensiveness, risk assessment, and data analytics. Assume your report will be distributed to all auditing staff in your firm. Chapter 11 discusses reports.

Exercise 8–8 [Managerial]

Prepare a research report on the use of GPK (Grenzplankostenrechnung) and ABC (Activity Based Costing) cost systems. Discuss some actual experiences of companies as well as some advantages and disadvantages of using each system. Assume your report will be made available to your manufacturing clients. Chapter 11 discusses reports.

Exercise 8–9 [Tax]

You are a member of the tax department of a sizable pharmaceutical company, Ansley Pharmaceuticals, which is considering a merger with a smaller company in Germany. The president of your company, George Matterhorn, wants to engineer the terms of the prospective merger to maximize its potential favorable effects on U.S. taxes. He has heard that by constructing the merger as a corporate inversion and establishing the merged company's tax address in Germany, he may be able to achieve his objective.

Mr. Matterhorn has asked you to prepare a technical memo discussing corporate inversions. Your memo should cover these topics:

- Definition and explanation of a corporate inversion
- Tax effects of corporate conversion: benefits and risks

Chapter 10 discusses technical memos.

NOTES

1. Prior to 2009, the FASB issued FASB Statements, FASB Interpretations, Emerging Issue Task Force (EITF) Abstracts, etc. The content of these documents has since been incorporated into the *FASB Accounting Standards Codification®*.

2. This information is taken from the "FASB Accounting Standards Codification®, Notice to Constituents (v 4.1), About the Codification."

3. See http://ria.thomsonreuters.com/IntegratedSolutions/ (25 January 2016).

4. Stephen Reid, *The Prentice Hall Guide for College Writers*, Brief Tenth Edition (Upper Saddle River, NJ: Pearson Education, Inc., 2014), 492.

5. There are many documentation styles in current use. The sample entries in this chapter and its appendices illustrate acceptable usage, but you may use another acceptable style as long as you're consistent within each paper. Note that some publishers will require a particular style of citation be used when quoting material they have published.

6. *The Chicago Manual of Style*, 16th ed. Chicago: The University of Chicago Press, 2010.

7. Kate L. Turabian, *A Manual for Writers of Term Papers, Theses, and Dissertations*, 8th ed. Chicago: The University of Chicago Press, 2013.

8. Janice R. Walker and Todd Taylor, *The Columbia Guide to Online Style, 2nd ed.* New York: Columbia University Press, 2006.

9. Lee Burton, "Take Heart, CPAs: Finally a Story That Doesn't Attack You as Boring," *The Wall Street Journal* (13 May 1987), 33.

10. David. A. Ziebart, et al, 2nd ed., *An Introduction to Applied Professional Research for Accountants* (Upper Saddle River, N.J.: Prentice Hall, 2001), 3.

Appendix 8 – A

*Sources of Accounting and Financial Information on the Internet**

Accounting and auditing and related
organizations

Academy of Accounting Historians	http://www.aahhq.org
Association of Chartered Certified Accountants (ACCA)	www.accaglobal.com/us/en.html
Association of Government Accountants	www.agacgfm.org/homepage.aspx
American Accounting Association (AAA)	http://aaahq.org/index.cfm
American Institute of CPAs (AICPA)	www.aicpa.org
Center for Audit Quality	http://www.thecaq.org
The Chartered Global Management Accountant (CGMA)	www.cgma.org
Chartered Institute of Management Accountants (CIMA)	www.cimaglobal.com/
Committee of Sponsoring Organizations (COSO)	www.coso.org/
CPA Consultants' Alliance (CPACA)	http://cpaconsultantsalliance.com/
Cybersecurity Resource Center (AICPA)	www.aicpa.org/InterestAreas/FRC/AssuranceAdvisory Services/Pages/cyber-security-resource-center.aspx
Financial Accounting Standards Board (FASB)	www.fasb.org
Financial Executives International	www.financialexecutives.org
Governmental Accounting Standards Board (GASB)	www.gasb.org
International Forum of Independent Audit Regulators (IFIAR)	www.ifiar.org/Home.aspx
Institute of Internal Auditors, The (IIA)	www.theiia.org
IMA (Formerly: Institute of Management Accountants)	www.imanet.org
ISACA (Formerly: Information Systems Audit and Control Association)	www.isaca.org/
National Association of Black Accountants, Inc. (NABA)	www.nabainc.org/
National Association of Professional Accountants (NAPA)	www.proaccountants.org
National Association of State Boards of Accountancy (NASBA)	www.nasba.org

---

*These Web addresses were accurate when this book went to press. However, Web addresses change frequently.

National Association of Tax Professionals (NATA)	www.natptax.com/Pages/default.aspx
National Society of Accountants (NSA)	www.nsacct.org/home
Public Company Accounting Oversight Board (PCAOB)	http://pcaobus.org/Pages/default.aspx
Sustainability Accounting Standards Board (SASB)	www.sasb.org/

Business and accounting news network services

Accounting Today	www.accountingtoday.com
Accounting WEB	www.accountingweb.com/
BNA (Bloomberg)	www.bna.com
CNN Money.com	http://money.cnn.com
MSN Money	http://money.msn.com

Business newspapers

Barrons Online	www.barrons.com/
Financial Times of London	www.ft.com/home/us
Investors.com (Investors Business Daily)	www.investors.com/
The Wall Street Journal	www.wsj.com/

Business magazines

Business 2.0	http://money.cnn.com/magazines/business2
Business Week	www.bloomberg.com/businessweek
CGMA Magazine	www.cgma.org/MAGAZINE/Pages/MagazineHome.aspx
CPA Journal	www.nysscpa.org/news/publications/the-cpa-journal/issue
Fortune Magazine	http://fortune.com/
Journal of Accountancy	www.journalofaccountancy.com/
Worth	www.worth.com

Data on the economy, industries, market indexes, and financial statistics—domestic and foreign

Bloomberg.com	www.bloomberg.com
Briefing.com	www.briefing.com
Dow Jones	www.dowjones.com
International Monetary Fund (IMF)	www.imf.org
New York Federal Reserve Bank	www.newyorkfed.org/index.html
The World Bank	www.worldbank.org

Information about stocks—company performance, corporate financial data, charts, company home pages, etc.

Hoover's Inc.	www.hoovers.com
Internetnews.com	www.Internetnews.com/bus-news/
INVEStools	www.investools.com
Morningstar.com	www.morningstar.com
NASDAQ	www.nasdaq.com
NYSE	https://nyse.nyx.com/
OTC Bulletin Board	www.finra.org/industry/otcbb/otc-bulletin-board-otcbb

StockMaster	www.stockmaster.com
Zacks Investment Research	www.zacks.com

Information about mutual funds
Morningstar.com	www.morningstar.com
Standard and Poor's Rating Service	www.standardandpoors.com/ en_US/web/guest/home
StockMaster	www.stockmaster.com

Securities exchanges
NASDAQ	www.nasdaq.com
New York Stock Exchange (NYSE)	https://nyse.nyx.com/

Government sites
Federal Accounting Standards Advisory Board	http://fasab.gov
Fed World (National Technical Information Service)	http://fedworld.ntis.gov/
Government Accountability Office (GAO)	www.gao.gov
Internal Revenue Service (IRS)	www.irs.gov/
Securities and Exchange Commission (SEC)	www.sec.gov
U.S. Congress	www.congress.gov
USA.gov (Index of Government Departments & Agencies	www.usa.gov
U.S. House of Representatives	www.house.gov
U.S. Senate	www.senate.gov

International accounting and finance organizations and sites
European Financial Reporting Advisory Group	www.efrag.org/Front/Home.aspx
IFRS (International Financial Reporting Standards) Foundation/International Accounting Standards Board (IASB)	www.ifrs.org/Pages/default.aspx
International Auditing and Assurance Standards Board (IAASB)	www.iaasb.org/about-iaasb
International Ethics Standards Board for Accountants (IESBA)	www.ethicsboard.org/
International Federation of Accountants (IFAC)	www.ifac.org
International Integrated Reporting Council (IIRC)	www.iasplus.com/en/resources/ sustainability/iirc
International Monetary Fund (IMF)	www.imf.org/external/index.htm
International Public Sector Accounting Standards Board (IPSASB)	www.ipsasb.org/
World Bank	www.worldbank.org

Links to other organizations, firms, journals, newspapers, etc.
CCH Daily [UK]	www.cchdaily.co.uk/
AccountantsWorld	www.accountantsworld.com/

Accounting Historians Journal	www.olemiss.edu/depts/general_library/dac/files/ahj.html
Accounting Review	http://aaajournals.org/loi/accr
Accounting Today	www.accountingtoday.com/
AccountingWEB	www.accountingweb.com/
AICPA (accounting publications)	www.cpa2biz.com/index.jsp
Analyst's Accounting Observer, The	http://accountingobserver.com/
Association of Certified Fraud Examiners	www.acfe.com
Big 4	www.big4.com/blog
Chartered Professional Accountants [CANADA]	www.cpacanada.ca/
CPA Magazine [CANADA]	www.cpacanada.ca/en/connecting-and-news/cpa-magazine
CPA Center of Excellence	www.cpacoe.com/
CPA Journal, The	www.nysscpa.org/news/publications/the-cpa-journal/issue
CPA Trendlines	http://cpatrendlines.com/
Financial Industry Regulatory Authority	www.finra.org/
Internal Auditor Magazine	https://na.theiia.org/periodicals/Pages/Internal-Auditor-Magazine.aspx
International Integrated Reporting Council (IIRC)	www.theiirc.org/
International Journal of Accounting Information Systems, The	www.sciencedirect.com/science/journal/14670895
Journal of Accountancy	www.journalofaccountancy.com/
Journal of Accounting Research	http://onlinelibrary.wiley.com/journal/10.1111/(ISSN)1475-679X/issues
Journal of International Accounting Research	http://aaajournals.org/loi/jiar
Management Accounting Quarterly	www.imanet.org/resources-publications/management-accounting-quarterly
New York Times, The (Accounting Accountants)	http://topics.nytimes.com/top/reference/timestopics/subjects/a/accounting_and_accountants/index.html?8qa
Rutgers Accounting Web	http://accounting.rutgers.edu/
Social Science Research Network	www.SSRN.com
Smart Brief	www.smartbrief.com/industry/finance/accounting

Appendix 8 – B

Online Database Services *

- *ABI/INFORM*® provides online indexing to business-related material occurring in thousands of publications from 1923 to the present. For additional information go to www.proquest.com/en-US/catalogs/databases/detail/abi_inform.shtml.
- *Accounting Research Manager*®, *by Commerce Clearing House (CCH*®), is available through Wolters Kluwer. It contains primary source data from all major standard setting bodies. For additional information go to www.cchgroup.com/roles/accounting-firms/accounting-and-audit/research/accounting-research-manager?gclid=CMm1vtG3xcoCFZQjgQodxlgF3A. This database requires a user name and password.
- *Accounting Standards Codification*® *Research System*, by the FASB, covers accounting literature issued by several standard setters. FASB publications included are Statements, Interpretations, Technical Bulletins, Staff Positions, Staff Implementation Guides, and Statement 138 Examples. Abstracts and Topic D of the Emerging Issues Task Force are included as are Derivatives Implementation Group Issues, Accounting Principles Board Opinions, Accounting Research Bulletins, and Accounting Interpretations. AICPA Statements of Position, Audit and Accounting Guides, Practice Bulletins, and Technical Inquiry Service issuances are also available here along with "relevant portions of authoritative content issued by the SEC and selected SEC staff interpretations and administrative guidance."[†] For additional information go to https://asc.fasb.org/.
- *Business Source*, by EBSCO Information Services, provides citations and abstracts to articles in about 600 business periodicals and newspapers. Full text is provided from selected periodicals, covering accounting, communications, economics, finance, management, marketing, and other business subjects. For additional information go to www2.ebsco.com.
- *Capital IQ Compustat*, by Standard and Poor's. Financial data on publicly held U.S. and some foreign corporations. For additional information go to www.compustat.com/?gclid=COL10NyyvaACFUFM5QodxDySUQ.
- *Checkpoint Catalyst*, by Thomson Reuters, is a good online research database for tax research. For additional information go to https://tax.thomsonreuters.com/checkpoint/catalyst/.
- *EconLit*, by the American Economic Association, covers the worldwide literature of economics. Subjects include microeconomics, macroeconomics, economic history, inflation, money, credit, finance, accounting theory, trade, natural resource economics, and regional economics. For additional information go to www.aeaweb.org/econlit/index.php.

---

*These Web addresses were accurate when this book went to press. However, Web addresses change frequently.

[†] Financial Accounting Foundation, "Notice to Constituents (v 4.1) – About the Codification." 2010. (Stamford, Conn.: Financial Accounting Foundation, 2010), 8.

- *FRED® Economic Data (Federal Reserve Economic Data)*, by the St. Louis Federal Reserve, contains 61,000 U.S. and international economic time series. For additional information go to https://fred.stlouisfed.org/.
- *Governmental Accounting Research System*™ (GARS), by the Governmental Accounting Standards Board (GASB), provides online access to accounting standards and related literature for state and local governments including GASB Codification, Original Pronouncements, and Implementation Guides. For additional information go to http://gars.gasb.org.
- *International Financial Statistics*, by the International Monetary Fund (IMF), provides statistical data on "all aspects of international and domestic finance." For additional information go to www.imf.org/external/data.htm.
- *IntelliConnect®*, by CCH, can be indispensable for tax research. It includes IRS Regulations, the Internal Revenue Manual, and various charts, interactive tools and calculators. For more information go to www.cchgroup.com/roles/accounting-firms/tax/research/cch-intelliconnect?gclid=CI-QlYXnx8oCFYcjgQodUEYExQ.
- Thompson ONE, hosted by the University of Chicago, is a database containing analyst reports from investment banks and advisors. For additional information go to http://guides.lib.uchicago.edu/thomson/analyst.
- *LexisNexis® Tax Center* contains a wide selection of tax content. For additional information go to www.lexisnexis.com/legalnewsroom/tax-law/b/research-toolbox/archive/2008/06/03/lexisnexis-tax-center.aspx?Redirected=true#sthash.NJIwM161.dpuf.
- *The Corporate Reports Collection at MIT Dewey Library* includes corporate annual reports, SEC filings, and other public company information over 150 years. For additional information go to http://libguides.mit.edu/c.php?g=176014. Many other useful sources of company information are listed at http://libguides.mit.edu/bizcat/companies.
- *ProQuest Banking Information Source*™ provides indexing, abstracting, full text, and images of more than 690 publications from 1971 to present, with weekly updates. Covers the financial services industry, including banks, savings institutions, investment houses, credit unions, insurance companies, and real estate organizations. Emphasis is on marketing and management. For additional information go to www.proquest.com/products-services/pq_accounting.html.
- *U.S. Basic Economics Database* presents more than 6,000 statistical series relating to business, industry, finance, and economics. Time period is 1947 to present, with daily updates. For additional information go to www.bsu.edu/mcobwin/econ/database/dri/index.html.
- *World Economic Outlook Database*, by the International Monetary Fund (IMF) contains "data series on national accounts, inflation, unemployment rates, balance of payments, fiscal indicators, . . . for countries and country groups . . . whose data are reported by the IMF." For additional information go to www.imf.org/external/pubs/ft/weo/2009/01/weodata/index.aspx.

Other Printed Sources of Accounting and Financial Information

Business news, articles, market data;
stock, bond, and mutual fund price quotes

Barron's	*Investor's Business Daily*
USA Today	*The Wall Street Journal*

Business news, articles

Business Week	*Fortune Magazine*
Forbes Magazine	*Money Magazine*

Data on the economy and industries;
financial and economic statistics

Business Conditions Digest	*Standard & Poor's Statistical Surveys*
Economic Report of the President	*Statistical Abstract of the*
Federal Reserve Bulletin	*United States*
Standard & Poor's Industry	*US Industrial Outlook*
Surveys	*World Almanac*

Summary data about industries, companies;
advice on industries, stocks; analyses and forecasts

Standard & Poor's Outlook	*Value-Line Investment Survey*

Stock information, company performance;
corporate financial data

Annual reports of companies	*Moody's OTC Manual*
Moody's Bank & Finance Manual	*Moody's Public Utility Manual*
Moody's Bond Record	*Moody's Transportation Manual*
Moody's Bond Survey	*Standard & Poor's Corporation*
Moody's Handbook of Common Stocks	*Records*
Moody's Industrial Manual	*Standard & Poor's Stock Reports*
Moody's International Manual	

Bond information

Moody's Bond Record	*Moody's Bond Survey*

Mutual fund information

Morningstar Mutual Funds

Internal Documentation Style

C = Citation within the text
R = Entry in reference list

Book—Single Author
C   (Pacter 1994, 12)
R   Pacter, P. 1994. *Reporting financial information by segment*. London, UK: International Accounting Standards Committee.

Book—Single Editor
C   (Frankel 1994, 64)
R   Frankel, J. A., ed. 1994. *The internationalization of equity markets*. Chicago: University of Chicago Press.

Book—Two Authors
C   (Romney and Steinbart 2014, 621)
R   Romney, Marshall B., and Paul John Steinbart. 2014. *Accounting Information Systems*, 13th ed. Upper Saddle River, N.J.: Prentice Hall.

Book—More than Two Authors
C   (Ahrens, Elder, and Beasley 2014, 84)
R   Ahrens, Alvin A., Randal J. Elder, and Mark S. Beasley. 2014. *Auditing and Assurance Services*, 15th ed. Upper Saddle River, N.J.: Pearson Education, Inc.

Book—Author Is an Association, Institution, or Organization
C   (AICPA 1993, 2)
R   American Institute of Certified Public Accountants (AICPA). 1993. *The information needs of investors and creditors: A report on the AICPA special committee's study of the information needs of today's users of financial reporting, November, 1993*. New York: AICPA.

Article in a Journal—Single Author
C   (Schwartz 1996, 20)
R   Schwartz, Donald. 1996. The future of financial accounting: Universal standards. *Journal of Accountancy* 181, no. 5 (May): 20–21.

Article in a Journal—Two Authors
C   (May and Schneider, 1988, 70)
R   May, G. S., and D. K. Schneider. 1988. Reporting accounting changes: Are stricter guidelines needed? *Accounting Horizons* 2, no. 3 (September): 68–74.

Article in a Journal—More Than Two Authors
C   (Barth, Landsman, and Rendleman, 1998, 75)
R   Barth, Mary E., Wayne R. Landsman, and Richard J. Rendleman, Jr. 1998. Option pricing-based bond value estimates and a fundamental components approach to account for corporate debt. *The Accounting Review* 73, no. 1 (January): 73–102.

Article in a Magazine
C   (Blinder 1988, 25)
R   Blinder, Alan S. 1988. Dithering on hill is crippling a key agency. *Business Week*, 26 September, 25.

Article in a Newspaper—Author Not Identified
C   (*The Wall Street Journal*, 16 July 1986)
R   *The Wall Street Journal*, 16 July 1986, Words count.

Article in a Newspaper—Author Identified
C   (May 1987)
R   May, Gordon S. 1987. No accounting for poor writers. *The Wall Street Journal*, 29 May.

Primary Source Reprinted in a Secondary Source
C   (FASB, *SFAC 1*, par. 3)
R   Financial Accounting Standards Board (FASB). 1978. *Objectives of financial reporting by business enterprises, statement of financial accounting concepts no. 1*. Stamford, Conn.: FASB. Reprinted in *Original Pronouncements, As Amended, 2005/2006 Edition: Accounting Standards as of June 1, 2006*, Vol. II. New York: John Wiley & Sons, 2006.

FASB Accounting Standards Codification[®][‡]
C   (FASB ASC par. 350-10-05-01)
R   Financial Accounting Standards Board (FASB), 2017. *Accounting Standards Codification*[®]. Stamford, Conn.: FASB.

Legal Citation
C   (*Aaron v. SEC*, 446 U.S. 680, 1980)
R   Aaron v. SEC, 446 U.S. 680 (1980).

Internal Revenue Code Section
C   (*Internal Revenue Code* Sec. 6111(a))
R   *Internal Revenue Code*. Sec. 6111(a).

Government Document
C   (SEC 1995, 3)
R   United States Securities and Exchange Commission (SEC). 1995. *Self-regulatory organizations; notice* of filing and order granting accelerated approval of proposed rule change by the National Association of Securities Dealers, Inc., relating to an interim extension of the OTC Bulletin Board (R) service through September 28, 1995. Securities Exchange Act Release No. 35918, 60 FR 35443. Washington, D.C. (July 7).

Federal Register
C   (61 Fed. Reg. 1996, 208:55264)
R   "Revision to NASA FAR supplement coverage on contractor financial management reporting." *Federal Register* 61, no. 208 (25 Oct. 1996): 55264.

[‡]The numbers shown in the in-text citation refer to the Codification Topic (350), Subtopic (10), Section (05), and Paragraph (01). The date in the accompanying reference list entry is the date of the edition of the ASC. Since the ASC is continuously updated, this will usually be the date you consulted it.

World Wide Web
C   (Cohn, 2016)
R   Cohn, Michael. "IMA Sees Record Growth in CMAs," Accounts Media
        Group. 2016. www.accountingtoday.com/news/firm-profession/ima-sees-
        record-growth-in-cmas-76966-1.html?utm_medium=email&ET=webcp
        a:e5937711:2482484a:&utm_source=newsletter&utm_campaign=daily-
        jan%2019%202016&st=email (25 January 2016).

Email
C   May, Gordon S. "The PCAOB." personal email (3 Aug. 2004).
R   Personal email messages are usually not included in reference lists.

More than One Work in Reference List by Same Author or Authors—Different
Years
C   (Lang and Lundholm, 1993)
R   Lang, M., and R. Lundholm. 1993. Cross-sectional determinants of analyst
        ratings of corporate disclosures. *Journal of Accounting Research* 31, no.
        2 (Autumn): 246–271.
        _____. 1996. Corporate disclosure policy and analyst behavior. *Account-
        ing Review* 71, no. 4 (October): 467–492.

More Than One Work in Reference List By Same Author or Authors—Same Year
C   (Frost and Pownall, 1994b, 61)
R   Frost, C. A., and G. Pownall. 1994a. Accounting disclosure practices in the
        United States and United Kingdom. *Journal of Accounting Research* 32,
        no. 1 (Spring): 75–102.
        _____. 1994b. A comparison of the stock price response to earnings
        measures in the United States and the United Kingdom. *Contemporary
        Accounting Research* 11, no. 1 (Summer): 59–83.

Endnotes or Footnotes and Bibliography Style

N = Endnote or footnote (Endnotes are numbered with full-sized or superscript Arabic numerals in a Notes section at the end of each chapter or at the end of the paper.)

B = Bibliographical entry

Book—Single Author
N   [1]P. Pacter, *Reporting Financial Information by Segment* (London, UK: International Accounting Standards Committee, 1994), 12.
B   Pacter, P. *Reporting Financial Information by Segment*. London, UK: International Accounting Standards Committee, 1994.

Book—Single Editor
N   [1]J. A. Frankel, ed., *The Internationalization of Equity Markets* (Chicago: University of Chicago Press, 1994), 64.
B   Frankel, J.A., ed. *The Internationalization of Equity Markets*. Chicago: University of Chicago Press, 1994.

Book—Two Authors
N   [1]Marshall B. Romney and Paul John Steinbart, *Accounting Information Systems*, 12th ed. (Upper Saddle River, N.J.: Pearson Prentice Hall, 2012), 622.
B   Romney, Marshall B., and Paul John Steinbart. *Accounting Information Systems*, 12th ed. Upper Saddle River, N.J.: Pearson Prentice Hall, 2012.

Book—More than Two Authors
N   [1]Alvin A. Ahrens, Randal J. Elder, and Mark S. Beasley, *Auditing and Assurance Services*, 15th ed. Upper Saddle River: Pearson Education, Inc., 2014.
B   Ahrens, Alvin A., Randal J. Elder, and Mark S. Beasley. *Auditing and Assurance Services*, 15th ed. Upper Saddle River: Pearson Education, Inc., 2014.

Book—Author Is an Association, Institution, or Organization
N   [1]American Institute of Certified Public Accountants (AICPA), *The Information Needs of Investors and Creditors: A Report on the AICPA Special Committee's Study of the Information Needs of Today's Users of Financial Reporting, November, 1993*. (New York: AICPA, 1993), 2.
B   American Institute of Certified Public Accountants (AICPA). *The Information Needs of Investors and Creditors: A Report on the AICPA Special Committee's Study of the Information Needs of Today's Users of Financial Reporting, November, 1993*. New York: AICPA, 1993.

Article in a Journal—Single Author
N [1]Donald Schwartz, "The Future of Financial Accounting: Universal Standards," *Journal of Accountancy* 181, no. 5 (May 1996): 20.
B Schwartz, Donald, "The Future of Accounting: Universal Standards." *Journal of Accountancy* 181, no. 5 (May 1996): 20–21.

Article in a Journal—Two Authors
N [1]G. S. May and D. K. Schneider, "Reporting Accounting Changes: Are Stricter Guidelines Needed?" *Accounting Horizons* 2, no. 3 (Sept. 1988): 70.
B May, G. S., and D. K. Schneider. "Reporting Accounting Changes: Are Stricter Guidelines Needed?" *Accounting Horizons* 2, no. 3 (Sept. 1988): 68–74.

Article in a Journal—More than Two Authors
N [1]Mary E. Barth, Wayne R. Landsman, and Richard J. Rendleman, Jr., "Option Pricing-Based Bond Value Estimates and a Fundamental Components Approach to Account for Corporate Debt," *Accounting Review* 73, no. 1 (January 1998): 75.
B Barth, Mary E., Wayne R. Landsman and Richard J. Rendleman, Jr. "Option Pricing-Based Bond Value Estimates and a Fundamental Components Approach to Account for Corporate Debt." *Accounting Review* 73, no. 1 (January 1998): 73–102.

Article in a Magazine
N [1]Alan S. Blinder, "Dithering on Hill is Crippling a Key Agency," *Business Week*, 26 September 1988, 25.
B Blinder, Alan S. "Dithering on Hill is Crippling a Key Agency." *Business Week*, 26 September 1988, 25.

Article in a Newspaper—Author Not Identified
N [1]*The Wall Street Journal*, 16 July 1986, "Words Count."
B *The Wall Street Journal*, 16 July 1986, "Words Count."

Article in a Newspaper—Author Identified
N [1]Gordon S. May, "No Accounting for Poor Writers," *Wall Street Journal*, 29 May 1986.
B May, Gordon S. "No Accounting for Poor Writers," *Wall Street Journal* 29, May 1986.

Primary Source Reprinted in a Secondary Source
N [1]Financial Accounting Standards Board (FASB). *Objectives of Financial Reporting by Business Enterprises, Statement of Financial Accounting Concepts No. 1*. (Stamford, Conn.: FASB, 1978), par. 3; reprinted in *Original Pronouncements, As Amended, 2005/2006 Edition: Accounting Standards as of June 1, 2005*, Vol. II. (New York: John Wiley & Sons, 2005), 1005–1020.
B Financial Accounting Standards Board (FASB). *Objectives of Financial Reporting by Business Enterprises, Statement of Financial Accounting Concepts No. 1*. Stamford, Conn.: FASB. Reprinted in *Original Pronouncements, As Amended, 2005/2006 Edition: Accounting Standards as of June 1, 2005*, Vol. II, 1005–1020. New York: John Wiley & Sons, 2005.

N   [1]Financial Accounting Standards Board (FASB). *Accounting for Income Taxes, Statement of Financial Accounting Standards No. 109.* (Stamford, Conn.: FASB, 1992), par. 17; available in *Financial Accounting Research System (FARS)*. Stamford: Financial Accounting Standards Board, 2010.

B   Financial Accounting Standards Board (FASB). *Accounting for Income Taxes, Statement of Financial Accounting Standards No. 109.* Stamford, Conn.: FASB. Available in *Financial Accounting Research System (FARS)*. Stamford: Financial Accounting Standards Board, 2010.

Legal Citation

N   [1]*Aaron v.* SEC. 446 U.S. 680 (1980).

B   *Aaron v.* SEC. 446 U.S. 680 (1980).

Internal Revenue Code Section

N   [1]*Internal Revenue Code* Sec. 6111(a).

B   *Internal Revenue Code.* Sec. 6111(a).

Government Document

N   [1]United States Securities and Exchange Commission (SEC), *Self-Regulatory Organizations; Notice of Filing and Order Granting Accelerated Approval of Proposed Rule Change by the National Association of Securities Dealers, Inc., Relating to an Interim Extension of the OTC Bulletin Board (R) Service Through September 28, 1995.* Securities Exchange Act Release No. 35918, 60 FR 35443 (7 July 1995): 3.

B   United States Securities and Exchange Commission (SEC). *Self-Regulatory Organizations; Notice of Filing and Order Granting Accelerated Approval of Proposed Rule Change by the National Association of Securities Dealers, Inc., Relating to an Interim Extension of the OTC Bulletin Board (R) Service Through September 28, 1995.* Securities Exchange Act Release No. 35918, 60 FR 35443 (7 July 1995).

Federal Register

N   [1]"Revision to NASA FAR Supplement Coverage on Contractor Financial Management Reporting." *Federal Register* 61, no. 208 (25 Oct. 1996): 55264.

B   "Revision to NASA FAR Supplement Coverage on Contractor Financial Management Reporting." *Federal Register* 61, no. 208 (25 Oct. 1996): 55264.

World Wide Web

N   [1]Michael Cohen, "IMA Sees Record Growth in CMAs," Accountants Media Group. 2016. http://www.accountingtoday.com/news/firm-profession/ima-sees-record-growth-in-cmas-76966-1.html?utm_medium=email&ET=webcpa:e5937711:2482484a:&utm_source=newsletter&utm_campaign=daily-jan%2019%202016&st=email (25 January 2016).

B   Cohen, Michael. "IMA Sees Record Growth in CMAs," Accountants Media Group. 2016. http://www.accountingtoday.com/news/firm-profession/ima-sees-record-growth-in-cmas-76966-1.html?utm_medium=email&ET=webcpa:e5937711:2482484a:&utm_source=newsletter&utm_campaign=daily-jan%2019%202016&st=email (25 January 2016).

Email
N   [1]Gordon S. May, "The PCAOB." personal email (3 Aug. 2009).
B   May, Gordon S., "The PCAOB." personal email (3 Aug. 2009).

More than One Work in Bibliography by Same Author or Authors
N   [1]M. Lang and R. Lundholm, "Cross-Sectional Determinants of Analyst
         Ratings of Corporate Disclosures," *Journal of Accounting Research* 31,
         no. 2 (Autumn 1993): 246–271.
B   Lang, M., and R. Lundholm, "Cross-Sectional Determinants of Analyst
         Ratings of Corporate Disclosures," *Journal of Accounting Research* 31,
         no. 2 (Autumn 1993): 246–271.
         _____. "Corporate Disclosure Policy and Analyst Behavior," *The
         Accounting Review* 71, no. 4 (October 1996): 467–492.

CHAPTER

Letters

9

Learning Objectives

After studying this chapter, you should be able to

9.1 Plan and organize a business letter.

9.2 Write letters in an appropriate style and tone.

9.3 Write attractive letters in a standard business format.

9.4 Respond effectively to correspondence you receive from others.

9.5 Write letters typical in the accounting profession, such as engagement letters, management advisory letters, and tax research letters.

All accountants, no matter what their specialty, write letters to a variety of people, including clients, government agencies, and fellow professionals. Auditors write engagement letters, letters regarding deficiencies in internal control, management letters, and other letters to clients. Tax accountants may write letters seeking data about a client's tax situation, or to clarify issues for a client. Accountants may also write letters to communicate the results of research into a technical accounting problem or for a wide variety of other reasons.

For any letter to get the best results, of course, it must be well written. This chapter begins with principles of good letter writing: organization, style, tone, and format. We then look at some typical letters that accountants write.

PLANNING AND ORGANIZING A LETTER

LO9.1 Plan and organize a business letter.

Effective letters have the characteristics of any good writing: They contain correct, complete information, and they are usually written with specific readers in mind. They are also written in an active, direct style. In other words, they are coherent, clear, and concise. The letters are also neat and attractive, with a professional appearance. To achieve these qualities of good letters, the first step is to plan the content carefully and then arrange your ideas into an effective organization.

Planning for Purpose and Audience

A letter can vary in length from one paragraph to several pages, although many business letters are no longer than a page. Whatever the length, think carefully about what the letter should cover before you begin.

As in other writing tasks, analyze the purpose of the letter before you write it. If you are answering another person's written correspondence, keep that document on hand and note any comments for which a reply is needed. Finally, jot down a brief outline to organize the material logically.

Think also about the reader or readers of your letter, especially when writing about a technical topic. Readers' knowledge and experience may vary greatly and should determine how much detail you use when explaining the technical material. Sometimes you must explain complex accounting procedures in words that a non-accountant can understand.

Organizing a Letter

Like other kinds of writing, a letter is organized into an introduction, a body, and a conclusion. Each section uses summary sentences to emphasize main ideas and help the reader follow the train of thought.

The *introduction* of a letter establishes rapport with the reader and identifies the subject of the letter or the reason it was written. You can mention previous communication on the subject, such as an earlier letter or phone call, or remind the reader of a recent meeting or shared interest. The introduction should also briefly summarize the main ideas discussed in the letter and may specify recommendations the letter will discuss. If the letter is longer than a page, you should identify in the introduction the main issues or topics the letter will cover.

The *body* of the letter is divided logically into discussions of each topic. Arrange the topics in descending order of importance *from the readers' point of view*. Start with the most important issue and work your way down to the least important. Begin the discussion of each issue with a summary sentence stating the main idea.

Paragraphs should be short, usually a maximum of four or five sentences, and each should begin with a topic sentence that summarizes the paragraph's main idea.

The letter's *conclusion* may be a conventional courteous closing:

Thank you very much for your help.

The conclusion is also a good place to tell your correspondent exactly what you want him or her to do, or what you will do to follow up on the subjects discussed in the letter:

May I have an appointment to discuss this matter with you? I'll be in Chicago next week, October 7–11. I'll call your administrative assistant to set up a time that is convenient for you.

The conclusion may also summarize your main ideas and recommendations, especially if the letter is longer than a page.

STYLE AND TONE

LO9.2   Write letters in an appropriate style and tone.

As you compose and revise your letter, be sure that you write in an effective style and tone. Conciseness and clarity, two qualities of all good writing, are particularly important in letters. You don't want to waste your readers' time, nor do you want them to miss important ideas. Come to the point quickly and say it in a way they will understand.

Many techniques already presented in this handbook are useful for writing short, clear letters. Your writing should be unified: paragraphs with a central idea that is easy to spot. The letter should also be as brief and simple as possible, while still conveying a precise meaning.

Yet another important characteristic of a well-written business letter is its tone, or the way it makes the reader feel. Chapter 4 discussed writing from your readers' point of view, emphasizing readers' interests and needs. Courtesy and respect are important qualities of business letters, as they are in all forms of communication.

In general, effective letters reflect a personal, conversational tone. However, the best tone to use for a given letter depends to some extent on the purpose and reader of that letter. Review the discussion of tone in Chapter 4 to see how the content of the letter and your relationship with the reader can affect the tone you choose for your correspondence.

FORMAT AND APPEARANCE

LO9.3   Write attractive letters in a standard business format.

One of the primary characteristics of an effective letter is a neat appearance and standard business format. Good stationery is important: 8½ × 11-inch paper of a high-quality bond, about 24-pound weight. Envelopes, 4 × 10 inches, should match the stationery. White or cream is usually the best color choice. Software programs will allow you to design and print your own letterhead stationery. If you design your own letterhead, be conservative when you select font styles and sizes.

Business letters should be printed on a good-quality printer. Envelopes should also be printed. Both the letter and the envelope should be free of errors. Neatness is essential!

A letter is usually single-spaced, with double-spacing between paragraphs, although letters can be double-spaced throughout (see the sample formats in Figures 9–1and 9–2). Margins should be at least 1 inch on all sides and as even as possible without justifying the right margin, although a shorter letter may allow you to set wider

FIGURE 9–1   Diagram of a Letter Format—Block Style

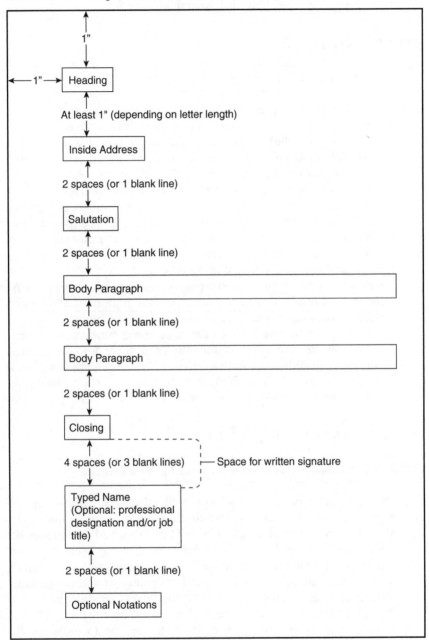

FIGURE 9–2   Diagram of a Letter Format — Modified Block Style

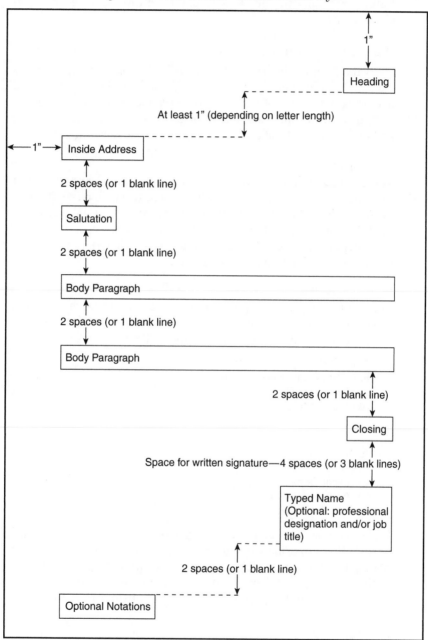

margins. One-page letters should be placed so that the body of the letter, excluding the heading, is centered on the page or slightly above center.

Parts of the Letter

Study the diagrams in Figures 9–1 and 9–2, which illustrate the parts of a letter and their proper placement for two formats, the block and the modified block styles. The following sections describe each part of the letter in more detail. Remember also that formatting techniques, such as headings and set-off lists, can make your letters attractive and easy to read.

Heading

The heading contains your address (not your name) and the date of the letter. If you use stationery without a letterhead, place the heading on the left margin (for block style) or next to the right margin (for modified block style). If you use letterhead stationery, omit the heading except for the date. Center the date below the letterhead or place it next to the left margin for block style.

Inside Address

The inside address is a reproduction of the address on the envelope. Place the title of the person to whom you are writing either on the same line as his or her name, or on the following line:

Anna O'Rourke, President
Excellent Consulting Services
2110 Winners Circle
Atlanta, GA 30378

or

Anna O'Rourke
President
Excellent Consulting Services
2110 Winners Circle
Atlanta, GA 30378

It's better to address a letter to a specific person rather than to an office or title. You can usually find the name of the person to whom you are writing by phoning the company or organization, or possibly by consulting its Web page. You should also verify the spelling of the name and the gender of the person, if gender isn't obvious from the name.

Salutation

If possible, address your correspondent by name:

Dear Ms. O'Rourke:

or

Dear Mr. Smith:

For a female correspondent, use Ms. unless she prefers another title.

If you know your correspondent well, you may use his or her first name in the salutation:

Dear Anna:

Be careful with the use of first names, however, especially when writing to someone you haven't met in person. A title and last name may be especially appropriate for an older person or one in a position of greater authority than yours. In many situations, a respectful, courteous tone requires using a title and last name.

If you don't know the name of the correspondent, use a salutation such as the following:

Dear Human Resource Division:
Dear Registrar:

Note that a colon (:) always follows the salutation in a business letter.

Closing

The letter's formal closing is placed at the left margin for a block-style letter and next to the right margin for the modified block style. Capitalize the first word of the closing and put a comma at the end. Either of the following closings is correct:

Sincerely yours,
Sincerely,

Signature

Your name should be printed four lines below the closing; your position or professional designation (or both) can be added as shown below:

Sincerely yours,

Anna O'Rourke

Anna O'Rourke, CPA
Managing Partner

The space between the closing and printed name is for your handwritten signature.

Optional Parts of a Letter

Sometimes you'll need additional notations, which are placed below the signature at the left margin. First, if someone else types your letter, a notation is made of your initials (all capital letters) and the typist's (all lowercase):

AO'R:lc

or

AO'R/lc

Second, if your letter will be mailed with enclosures, refer to the enclosures in the body of the letter and make a notation at the bottom of the letter:

Enclosure(s)

Finally, if you will distribute copies of the letter to other people, note the people who will receive a copy:

cc: John Jones

Second Page

Many business letters are only one page long. If you need additional pages, each should have a heading identifying the addressee, the date, and the page number. This information is printed at the left margin:

Mr. Richard Smith
November 18, 2018
Page 3

A second page (and any subsequent pages) should have at least three lines of text, in addition to the heading and closing.

RESPONDING TO CORRESPONDENCE

LO9.4 Respond effectively to correspondence you receive from others.

When you reply to a letter written by someone else, you should respond in a way that will build a good working relationship between you and the correspondent. Many of the techniques for effective letters already discussed apply to responses. Here is a summary of those techniques, as well as a few pointers that particularly apply when you are answering someone else's letter:

1. Respond promptly, by return mail if possible.
2. Reread carefully the letter you received, noting questions that need answers or ideas that need your comment.
3. For the opening paragraph:
   - Refer to the earlier correspondence, such as the date of the letter you received.
   - If your letter is good news, or at least neutral, state clearly and positively the letter's main idea.
   - If your letter contains bad news, such as the denial of a request, identify the subject of the letter in the opening paragraph. State the explicit refusal later in the body of the letter.
4. Answer all your correspondent's questions fully and cover all relevant topics in sufficient detail. However, the letter should be as concise as possible.
5. End with a courteous closing.

TYPICAL ACCOUNTING LETTERS

LO9.5   Write letters typical in the accounting profession, such as engagement letters, management advisory letters, and tax research letters.

Before we begin this section, we should note that many accounting firms and other organizations have standardized letters for some situations. The management of a firm may have decided on the organization and even the specific wording that it requires its staff to use for engagement letters, management advisory letters, and the like. If your employer uses standardized letters, simply adapt the basic letter to the specific case you are concerned with, adding dates, names, figures, and other relevant facts.

Sample letters for various situations are presented in the following pages, along with general comments on the content and organization of these letters.

Engagement Letters

Engagement letters put into writing the arrangements made between an accounting firm and a client. Engagement letters can confirm the arrangements for a variety of services: audit, review, compilation, management advisory services, or tax. The main advantage of an engagement letter is that it clarifies the mutual responsibilities of the accountant and client and thus prevents possible misunderstandings.

Engagement letters can vary a great deal in content, depending on the firm writing the letter, the type of services to be provided, and the facts of the case. However, most engagement letters will include the following:

- A description of the objectives and nature of the service the accountants will provide, including any non-audit services such as the preparation of tax returns or management consulting.
- A description of the responsibilities of both the client and the auditor.
- A description of any limitations, restrictions, or deadlines imposed on the work to be done.
- A description of any assistance to be provided by the client.
- A statement that an audit will possibly not uncover all acts of fraud.

In addition to these elements, an engagement letter may also include other information, such as information about the fee and a space for the client to indicate acceptance of the arrangements outlined in the engagement letter. Figure 9–3 is a sample audit engagement letter.

Management Advisory Letters

At the conclusion of an audit, an accountant often writes a letter to the client suggesting ways the client can improve the business. This type of

FIGURE 9–3 Audit Engagement Letter[1]

Collins & Yancey
Certified Public Accountants
356 Woodale Avenue
Austin, TX 78712

July 15, 2018

Robert Samson, President
Samson Manufacturing Company
167 Abbey Road
Austin, TX 78712

Dear Mr. Samson:

You have requested that we audit the financial statements of Samson Manufacturing Company, which comprise the balance sheet as of December 31, 2018, and the related statements of income; changes in stockholders' equity and cash flows for the year then ended; and the related notes to the financial statements. We are pleased to confirm our acceptance and our understanding of this audit engagement by means of this letter. Our audit will be conducted with the objective of our expressing an opinion on the financial statements.

Our Responsibilities

We will conduct our audit in accordance with generally accepted auditing standards (GAAS) in the United States. Those standards require that we plan and perform the audit to obtain reasonable assurance about whether the financial statements are free from material misstatement. An audit involves performing procedures to obtain audit evidence about the amounts and disclosures in the financial statements. The procedures selected depend on the auditor's judgment, including the assessment of the risks of material misstatement of the financial statements, whether due to fraud or error. An audit also includes evaluating the appropriateness of accounting policies used and the reasonableness of significant accounting estimates made by management, as well as evaluating the overall presentation of the financial statements.

Because of the inherent limitations of an audit, together with the inherent limitations of internal control, an unavoidable risk that some material misstatements may not be detected exists, even though the audit is properly planned and performed in accordance with GAAS.

In making our risk assessments, we consider internal control relevant to the entity's preparation and fair presentation of

FIGURE 9–3   (*Cont∂.*)

Robert Samson, President
July 15, 2018
Page 2

the financial statements in order to design audit procedures
that are appropriate in the circumstances, but not for the
purpose of expressing an opinion on the effectiveness of the
entity's internal control. However, we will communicate to
you in writing concerning any significant deficiencies or material weaknesses in internal control relevant to the audit of the
financial statements that we have identified during the audit.

Management Responsibilities

Our audit will be conducted on the basis that management
acknowledges and understands that they have responsibility
a. for the preparation and fair presentation of the
     financial statements in accordance with accounting
     principles generally accepted in the United States;
b. for the design, implementation, and maintenance of
     internal control relevant to the preparation and fair
     presentation of financial statements that are free of ma-
     terial misstatement, whether due to fraud or error; and
c. to provide us with
     i.   access to all information of which management is
          aware that is relevant to the preparation and fair
          presentation of the financial statements such as
          records, documentation, and other matters;
     ii. additional information that we may request from
          management for the purpose of the audit; and
     iii. unrestricted access to persons within the entity from
          whom we determine it necessary to obtain audit
          evidence.

As part of our audit process, we will request from management written confirmation concerning representations made
to us in connection with the audit.

Other Services

As part of our engagement for the year ending December
31, 2018, we will also prepare the federal and state income
tax returns for Samson Manufacturing Company.

Our fees will be billed as work progresses and are based on the
amount of time required at various levels of responsibility, plus
actual out-of-pocket expenses. Invoices are payable upon presentation. We will notify you immediately of any circumstances
we encounter that could significantly affect our initial estimate
of total fees of $150,000.

FIGURE 9–3   (*Contd.*)

Robert Samson, President
July 15, 2018
Page 3

We will issue a written report upon completion of our audit
of Samson Manufacturing Company's financial statements.
Our report will be addressed to management and the board
of directors of Samson Manufacturing. We cannot provide
assurance that an unmodified opinion will be expressed.
Circumstances may arise in which it is necessary for us to
modify our opinion, add an emphasis-of-matter or other-
matter paragraph(s), or withdraw from the engagement.

Please sign and return the attached copy of this letter to
indicate your acknowledgement of, and agreement with,
the arrangements for our audit of the financial statements
including our respective responsibilities.

Accepted: Yours very truly:

Robert Samson   *Mary Collins*
By: Robert Martinez   Mary Collins
Date: July 27, 2018   Partner

letter may contain suggestions on a variety of topics, such as internal
control, budgeting, or tax matters.

If the auditor includes many recommendations in the management
letter, the letter may be quite long. If you write a management letter
that is more than three pages long, consider organizing it into a report
with a transmittal letter. Address the transmittal letter to the president
or board of directors of the client company and summarize in the letter
the major recommendations made in the report. Chapter 11 provides
information on report writing.

In any case, whether the management letter is a single document
or a report with a transmittal letter, remember that documents are
more attractive and easier to read if they contain headings. These
headings divide the letter into logical sections.

Whatever the format of the management letter, write it in a way that
is helpful to the client and builds a good professional relationship between
the client and your firm. The techniques for effective writing discussed so
far in this book certainly apply to management letters: clear and logical
organization, readable style, and specific and concrete explanation.

An example of a short, but effective, management advisory letter
appears in Figure 9–4.

FIGURE 9–4   Management Advisory Letter

JADAU AND HERNANDEZ
Certified Public Accountants
1553 W. Ellis Street
Atlanta, GA 30316

March 15, 2018

Arthur Sanders, President
Art Products, Inc.
24 N. Broad Street
Atlanta, GA 30327

Dear Mr. Sanders:

Our examination of Art Products' financial statements
for the year ended December 31, 2017, revealed two areas
where we believe you could improve your business:

- Stronger budgeting system
- Review of credit policies

The following paragraphs explain these recommendations in
greater detail.

Budgets

Operating, selling, and general administrative expenses for 2017
as compared with 2016 increased from $1 million to $1,050,000,
a change of 5 percent. Although management has been able to
control expenditures, we believe efforts in this area would be
assisted by implementation of a strong system of budgeting.

Under such a system, responsibility for actual performance is
assigned to the employees most directly responsible for the
expenditures involved. (It is best that such employees have a
role in establishing the budgets.) Periodic reports reflecting
actual and budgeted amounts, together with explanations of
significant variances, should be provided to the management
personnel responsible for approving the budgets initially.
We cannot overemphasize the value of sound budgeting and
planning in all areas of the company's activities

Credit Policies

The history of write-offs of bad accounts over the past few
years indicates that the write-off percentage has declined.
Considering the low net earnings margin under which the
company operates (slightly less than 0.6 percent of net
sales), it is most important that this favorable record continue because a significant increase in bad debts could have
a substantial negative impact on net earnings.

FIGURE 9–4 (*Contd.*)

Arthur Sanders
March 15, 2018
Page 2

In view of the high cost of money for business in general,
management should consider reviewing its credit policies to
reasonably ensure that the risk inherent in continued sales to
customers of questionable credit standing is justified. This is
a delicate area of policy; it is not desirable to so restrict sales
representatives that profitable sales are lost because of overly
stringent credit policies. However, the credit and collection
department should exercise a reasonable amount of control
to ensure a minimum of bad accounts. For example, a limit
could be set on the amount sales representatives could extend
to customers whose accounts have reached a certain balance.

We will be glad to discuss these suggestions with you and
help you implement them.

Sincerely,

Juan Hernandez

Juan Hernandez
Jadau and Hernandez
Certified Public Accountants

Tax Research Letters

Accountants who provide tax services often write letters to their clients
communicating the results of the research into some tax question. These
letters can be for either tax planning or after-the-fact tax situations.

The content and organization of these letters can vary, but the
following basic outline is a good one:

- Introduction, giving background, and summarizing main ideas
- Facts on which the research was based with a caution that the
  advice is valid only for these facts
- Tax questions implicit in these facts, with analysis of the issues
- Conclusions, with the authoritative support for the conclusions
- Areas of controversy that the IRS might dispute (tax accountants
  do not all agree that the letter should identify the vulnerable areas
  in the client's situation.)
- Courteous closing

In addition to a logical organization, such as the one outlined
here, tax research letters should be understandable to the client.
You may need to explain technical terms. Figure 9–5 illustrates a

FIGURE 9–5   A Letter Reporting the Results of Tax Research[2]

Professional Accounting Associates
2701 First City Plaza
Suite 905
Dallas, TX 75019

December 12, 2018

Elizabeth Fegali, Chief Administrator
Mercy Hospital
22650 West Haven Drive
Arlington, TX 75527

Dear Ms. Fegali:

It was great to see you at last Thursday's football game. If not for that last minute fumble, the Longhorns might have taken the conference championship!

In our meeting of December 6, you asked us to research whether the value of the meal vouchers that Mercy provides to its medical employees is taxable to the employees. I regret to inform you that if the vouchers are redeemed at MacDougal's, their value is likely to be taxable to the employees. On the other hand, if the vouchers are redeemed in the hospital cafeteria, their value is likely to be excludible from the employee's income.

In reaching this conclusion, we consulted relevant provisions of the Internal Revenue Code (IRC), applicable Treasury Regulations under the IRC, and a pertinent Supreme Court case. In addition, we reviewed the documents on employee benefits that you submitted to us at our earlier meeting.

Facts

The facts as we understand them are as follows: Mercy provides meal vouchers to its medical employees to enable them to eat while on emergency call. The vouchers are redeemable either in the hospital cafeteria or at MacDougal's. MacDougal's is a privately-owned institution that rents business space from the hospital. Although Mercy's employees are not required to remain on or near the premises during their meal hours, they generally do.

Applicable Laws

Under the IRC, the value of meals is excludible from an employee's income if two conditions are met: first, the meals are furnished "for the convenience of the employer" and second, they are provided "on the business premises of the employer."

FIGURE 9–5   (*Contd.*)

Elizabeth Fegali
December 12, 2018
Page 2

Although the IRC does not explain what is meant by "for the convenience of the employer," "business premises of the employer," and "meals," other authorities do. Treasury Regulations define "business premises of the employer" to be the place of employment of the employees. The regulations state that providing meals during work hours to have an employee available for emergency calls is "for the convenience of the employer."

Moreover, under the IRC, if more than half the employees satisfy the "for the convenience of the employer" test, all employees will be regarded as satisfying the test. The Supreme Court has interpreted "meals" to mean food-in-kind and has held that cash allowances do not qualify as "meals."

Analysis

Clearly, the meals furnished by Mercy are "for the convenience of the employer." They are furnished during the employees' work hours to have the employees available for emergency calls. Although the meals provided in the hospital cafeteria appear to be furnished "on the business premises of the employer," the meals provided at MacDougal's do not appear to be. The hospital is the place of employment of the medical employees. MacDougal's is not. What is unclear is whether the meal vouchers are equivalent to food-in-kind. On the one hand, they are redeemable at more than one institution and thus resemble cash allowances. On the other hand, they are redeemable only in meals and thus resemble food-in-kind.

Recommendation

Because of this lack of clarity, we suggest that you modify your employee benefits plan to allow for the provision of meals-in-kind exclusively in the hospital cafeteria. In this way, you will dispel any doubt that Mercy is furnishing "meals," "for the convenience of the employer," "on the premises of the employer."

Please call me at (817) 475-2020 if you have any questions concerning this conclusion. I also suggest that we meet next week to discuss the possibility of revising your employee benefits plan.

Very truly yours,

Rosina Havacek

Rosina Havacek, Junior Associate
Professional Accounting Associates

letter written to a client to report the results of tax research. The letter deals with a technical tax question, but is clearly written with a friendly, courteous tone.

Standardized Letters: A Caution

As already mentioned, many organizations have standardized letters that they use for situations that occur often, such as engagement letters. These form letters save time, and they also convey the message precisely and reliably. If your employer expects you to use these standardized letters, then, of course, you should do so.

One word of caution: Remember that in many situations personalized letters are more appropriate than standardized letters. If you use standardized letters, be sure they are responsive to the readers' needs and concerns.

If you know your correspondent personally, a friendly reference to a topic of mutual interest can add warmth to your letter. The opening paragraph of the letter in Figure 9–5 provides a friendly, personalized opening to a client letter:

> It was great to see you at last Thursday's football game. If not for that last minute fumble, the Longhorns might have taken the conference championship!

Letters Sent by Email

Until a decade or two ago, business letters were always printed on paper and sent via the postal service. Today, much business correspondence is sent electronically, either as the body of an email or as an email attachment, as might be the case for a formal letter. The use of electronic correspondence is often convenient, but it must be done carefully, with attention to possible breaches of security. Chapter 12 provides detailed information on the use of electronic communication.

EXERCISES

Exercise 9–1 [General]

Suppose you received the letter shown in Figure 9–6. How would you react? What, specifically, is wrong with this letter? What about it is effective?

Revise this letter so that it would make a better impression on a reader.

Exercise 9–2 [General]

A friend of yours, Greg Mattis, has a daughter, Rachel, who wants to major in accounting. She believes that the only skills she needs for

FIGURE 9–6 Letter for Exercise 9–1

Smith, Barnum, and Bailey
Certified Public Accountants
301 MacDonald Place
Atlanta, GA 36095

Members
American Institute of   Telephone: (306) 782-5107
Certified Public Accountants

May 21, 2018

Mr. John W. Simmons
234 Myers Hall, UGA
Athens, GA 30609

Dear John:

After considerable debate about our needs, we have decided to offer the internship to someone else. Our offer was excepted, so the position is now filled. I enjoyed talking with you and felt you would of been a positive impact to our firm and would work well with our present staff. Upon graduation we would be most interested in talking with you regarding full-time employment. If I can be of assistance in the near future, please feel free to call.

Sincerely,

Jason A. Smith

Jason A. Smith
JASjr/mlk
Enclosures

success as an accountant are technical skills: knowledge of accounting principles, the ability to research accounting issues, and computer expertise. Your friend Greg suspects that success in accounting requires a wider range of skills than Rachel realizes. However, Rachel isn't receptive to suggestions from her father.

You are a successful CPA who has been in practice for over twenty years, and your family has been friends with the Mattis family for a long time. Greg asks you to write a letter to Rachel about the skills necessary to become a successful accountant. He is sure Rachel will take your advice seriously.

Write a letter to Rachel, a freshman at State University.

Exercise 9–3 [Managerial]

Your client, Janice Rush, is the owner/manager of a store that sells jewelry, fine china, sterling silver flatware, and other gifts. The store has 10 employees, mostly sales personnel who advise customers and handle the sales transactions. Ms. Rush is an astute business person, but she has little training in business and has asked for your help as she has noticed discrepancies in the amount of inventory she believes should be on hand and the amount of inventory actually on hand based on the physical inventory taken. After talking with Ms. Rush, you realize that she needs a better system of internal control over inventory.

Write a letter to Ms. Rush in which you explain the concept of internal control and outline a system of internal control over inventory that she can put in place.

Exercise 9–4 [Financial]

Lori Tripp wants to invest in an annuity for her grandchild Charles, who is 10 years old. She wants the annuity to pay exactly $10,000 a year for 5 years, beginning on Charles's 21st birthday (September 15, 2028). She wants to know how much money she will have to invest on March 15, 2018, when she expects to receive an inheritance check, in order to provide such an annuity. You have already determined that the annuity will earn three percent interest, compounded annually.

Write a letter to Ms. Tripp explaining annuities and the amount she would need to invest on March 15, 2018, to set up the plan she has in mind. Invent any facts you may need to complete the letter.

Exercise 9–5 [Auditing]

Assume that you are a partner of Black and White, CPAs. During the last year, you were part of the team that audited Parker and Smith, Inc., a small publicly held company. The audit went quite well, and the client had high praise for the work done by you and the other members of the audit team. One day six months after the completion of the audit, you receive this email from Jerome Parker, president of Parker and Smith:

Hi [your name],

We are still talking around here about the good job you and the other members of the audit team did on our audit. You all seemed to have a thorough understanding of our business, and we found working with you a pleasure. Based on the good experience we had with the audit, we would like to engage your firm to do additional work for us. Specifically, we'd like your help in designing a new financial information system for our company. We're also considering investing in stock being offered by one of our suppliers, and we'd like your input into that decision.

Hope you can help us here! Looking forward to hearing from you.

Regards,
Jerome

Write a letter to Mr. Parker in response to his email. Remember that you want to maintain a good working relationship with Parker and Smith. You also want to maintain proper professional and ethical standards particularly as they may regard conflicts of interest.

Exercise 9–6 [Tax]

Assume you are a CPA specializing in tax accounting for individuals in your community. One of your clients, Alicia Evans, has sent you the following email.

As you know, I have recently returned to work full time and need to hire someone to help me with house cleaning. I need to know what, if any, obligations I will have for withholding social security. Will I have any other tax or reporting obligations? I am considering the following possibilities:

1. Hiring an individual who has a business license and is self-employed as a contractor. This person would clean my house weekly. In return, I would pay this person $100 a week for 50 weeks of the year.
2. Using a cleaning service, who would send one of its employees to my home. I would use this service bi-weekly at $125 per visit, for a total of 26 visits per year.
3. Hiring my neighbor who does not have a business license. She would clean my house biweekly, and I would pay her $75 each visit, for a total of 26 visits each year.

(cont.)

I have one more question. Can I deduct any of the above expenses for house cleaning from my own income tax? After all, if I were not working I would not need to hire someone else to clean my house. It seems to me the house cleaning should be a legitimate business expense.

Please send the answer to the above questions to my home by registered mail. You have my address on file.

Write a letter to Ms. Evans in which you answer her questions. Invent any information you feel is necessary to make your letter complete.

Exercise 9–7 [Auditing/Ethics]

In the process of completing a tax return, your client, Sam Rhodes, refused to provide evidence to support some rather large deductions for business travel, saying, "Oh, I don't know about receipts. Just put it down and if and when the IRS questions me, I'll worry about receipts then."

Write a letter to Mr. Rhodes explaining why you cannot prepare a tax return showing these deductions unless he can provide the receipts. Remember the importance of tact and diplomacy in an awkward situation such as this. Use the proper format, effective organization, and appropriate style. Invent any information you feel is necessary to make your letter complete.

Exercise 9–8 [Auditing]

You are a partner in the firm of Shipley, Pyburn & Bynum, a local CPA firm. Your firm has received a letter from George Rayburn of Rayburn Industries, a potential audit client, that asks the following questions:

- What are the objectives of auditing your firm follows?
- How much responsibility does your firm take for the financial statements you produce as a result of an audit? Will your firm guarantee the accuracy of financial statements following your audit?
- What sort of guarantee does your firm provide that it will find any and all errors and fraud during the completion of an audit?

It is evident that Mr. Rayburn has sent a similar letter with the same questions to several CPA firms and plans to select a firm based upon the answers he receives.

Write a letter to Mr. Rayburn responding to his questions. Invent any information you feel is necessary to make your letter complete.

Exercise 9–9 [Auditing]

During your first audit of a new client, Capital Food Supplies, a small restaurant food supply company, you become aware of a major weakness in internal control: One employee keeps the accounts receivable and payable records, pays bills, and does the bank reconciliation each month. When you casually mention the problem to Scott Devin, the owner and general manager, he dismisses the issue. He says he trusts all his employees, has never had any problems, and can't afford to hire another employee just to deal with such a small internal control technicality.

Write a letter to your client tactfully explaining why you do not consider the problem to be "a small technicality." Explain the possible ramifications of not dealing with the issue, both in terms of the audit and in terms of asset protection. Use the proper format, effective organization, and appropriate style. Invent any information you feel is necessary to make your letter complete.

Exercise 9–10 [Financial/Theory]

Your boss, John Creedy, is a partner in the small local CPA firm for which you work. One morning a client, Jeff Altman, the owner of Altman Manufacturing, storms into Mr. Creedy's office and delivers a complaint. An edited version follows:

> This morning at my breakfast club I spoke with my competitor, Tony Dodd. He uses the LIFO inventory method just as I do. He boasted that his accountant had told him that by speeding up his purchases of raw materials at year-end he could significantly increase reported profits. If he can do that, why can't I? And why haven't you discussed this gimmick with me? I don't expect to rely on Dodd for financial advice; I pay you for that.

After Altman's departure, Mr. Creedy calls you, the accountant-in-charge of the Altman account, into his office to discuss Mr. Altman's complaint. You explain to your boss that your concern is your client's very large raw material inventory and slow turnover rate caused by years of over-buying. Mr. Creedy advises you that Altman needs new capital in his business and is trying to interest another local businessperson in becoming a limited partner. An increase in reported profits could be advantageous to Mr. Altman's plans and, therefore, left to his own devices, Mr. Altman would likely follow Mr. Dodd's accountant's advice.

Mr. Creedy asks you to draft a letter to Mr. Altman. The letter should discuss the problems of maintaining an overly large inventory as well as the disadvantage of a low turnover rate. Although you are not familiar with Mr. Dodd's company, you are reasonably certain his accountant would not have made the comment he did if Mr. Dodd's company had the same existing inventory problems as Altman Manufacturing. Use the proper format, effective organization, and appropriate style for your letter. Invent any information you feel is necessary to make your letter complete.

Exercise 9–11 [Financial]

Your audit client, Steven Dabbs, has written a letter to you. He is concerned because he has just received an offer to purchase his business for $1,000,000 more than the net carrying value of the assets as reported in the most recent financial statements that you had audited. He is not interested in selling the business, but he is now convinced that you have certified financial statements that do not properly reflect the value of his company.

Write a letter to your client explaining why the figures in the balance sheet should not be changed. You may assume your client is an astute businessman with no background in accounting. Use good format, effective organization, and appropriate style. Invent any information you feel is necessary to make your letter complete.

Exercise 9–12 [Systems]

James Gipper, one of your consulting clients, is the CEO of Glassplex, a rapidly growing plexiglass manufacturing company. Because his company is quickly developing its Internet presence, he is becoming increasingly concerned about Internet security. At his request, you are to write a letter to him outlining the basics of Internet security. Write the letter using good format, effective organization, and appropriate style. Invent any information you feel is necessary to make the letter complete.

Exercise 9–13 [Cost/Managerial]

One of your clients is Corporate Sentry, Inc., which manufactures alarms and other security devices. Due to competitive pressures, it plans to reduce costs so that it can more competitively price its products. In preparation for its internal deliberations, the CFO of the company, Charles Sargent, has asked your consulting firm to write a letter to him explaining the difference between engineered costs and discretionary costs and how such a distinction may be relevant to their downsizing plans. Write the letter using proper format, effective organization, and appropriate style. Invent any information you feel is necessary to make your letter complete.

Exercise 9–14 [Systems]

One of your clients, Jim Vaught, owns a very successful regional medical supply business. He has recently become interested in implementing an image processing system to improve cash collections. Mr. Vaught has asked you to write a letter to him describing the basics of a good image processing system. Write the letter using proper format, effective organization, and appropriate style. Invent any information you feel is necessary to make your letter complete.

Exercise 9–15 [Managerial/International/Current Professional Issues]

You are a successful management accountant employed by a large international corporation. The son of a good friend of yours is considering majoring in accounting in college. He is interested in accounting and international business and has recently learned that the AICPA and the Chartered Institute of Management Accountants jointly offer a Chartered Global Management Accountant (CGMA) designation, but knows nothing more about it. Your friend has asked you to write his son, Mitch Wilson, a letter explaining what a CGMA designation is, how to obtain it, and what benefit this credential might be to him if he is eventually employed in an international business environment. Write the letter using proper format, effective organization, and appropriate style. Invent any information you feel is necessary to make your letter complete.

Exercise 9–16 [Tax]

One of your tax clients, Stan Reid, has sent you various documents that you will use to construct his 2017 tax return. Included in this information is a cancelled check for $1,000 dated December 30, 2017, and payable to his church. The statement he received from the church listing his contributions during 2017 does not list this check. When asked about this discrepancy, Mr. Reid explained that he had made out the check on December 30, 2017, and intended to put it in the church's collection plate on Sunday, December 31. However, he forgot to do so and instead mailed it to the church the next day. According to Mr. Reid, the church then "wrongly counted it as a contribution for 2018 instead of 2017." He maintains that since the check was written in 2017 and the contribution was "clearly intended to be for 2017," it should properly be considered a deductible contribution for his 2017 taxes.

Write a letter to Mr. Reid responding to this issue and explaining how his contribution must be treated for tax purposes. Invent any information you feel is necessary to make your letter complete.

NOTES

1. Adapted with permission from Alvin A. Arens, Randel J. Elder, and Mark S. Beasley, *Auditing and Assurance Services: An Integrated Approach*, 15th ed. (Upper Saddle River, N.J.: Pearson Education, Inc., 2014), 212.

2. Adapted with permission from Rupert, Timothy J., Thomas R. Pope, and Kenneth E. Anderson, *Pearson's Federal Taxation 2017, Comprehensive* (Boston: Pearson Education, Inc., 2017), A-7.

CHAPTER 10

Memos and Briefing Documents

Learning Objectives

After studying this chapter, you should be able to

10.1 Summarize and apply the basic guidelines for writing memos.

10.2 Organize a coherent memo, with a focus on main ideas.

10.3 Write memos in an appropriate format.

10.4 Write memos in an effective style and tone.

10.5 Plan, organize, and write a technical memo.

10.6 Plan, organize, and write a briefing document.

10.7 Plan, organize, and write memos to clients' files.

Memos, sometimes called memoranda or memorandums, are often used for communication within an organization—between departments, for example, or between a supervisor and other members of the staff.[i] Memos may be of any length, from one sentence to several pages. They may be printed and distributed as hard copy, or they may be circulated electronically. (Chapter 12 covers special considerations for email and other forms of electronic communication.) They may inform decision makers in an organization about a current problem or issue, or record work done for a client in a document that will be stored in the client's file. While memos are often less formal than letters written to people outside the organization, some technical memos or briefing documents may be as formal as a report.

In spite of these differences in the types and styles of memos, well-written memos have the same qualities as good letters or any other business document: clarity, conciseness, coherence, and courtesy.

---

[i]In the past, some organizations, such as the FASB, used the term *Discussion Memorandum* to describe a formal document widely distributed to encourage discussion of a proposed standard or ruling. Such documents are now commonly referred to as *Discussion Papers*. They are issued by many accounting organizations currently, including the FASB, IASB, and IFRS. Discussion papers are covered in Chapter 11 of this book.

They are written with a clear purpose in mind, and they address the needs and expectations of readers.

In this chapter, we first discuss guidelines that apply to all effective memos. Then we look at several specialized memos that accountants often write: technical memos, briefing documents, and memos to client files.

We should note that the terminology used to identify the different kinds of memos can vary. For example, some organizations will not use the term *technical memo*, even when the subject of the memo is a highly technical topic. They may refer to these documents as *research memos*, or just simply *memos*. As another example of varied terminology, some people consider *briefing memos* to be identical to *briefing notes*, but for others *briefing notes* suggests a shorter document than a *briefing memo*. While inconsistent terminology can be confusing when you first encounter these terms, in actual practice you will know what kind of document you're expected to write for a given situation. If you're not sure, you can ask for clarification and look for examples written by others within your organization. As always, you will write the kind of document your readers expect.

MEMOS: BASIC GUIDELINES

LO10.1   Summarize and apply the basic guidelines for writing memos.

Often memos are quite short—from one sentence, perhaps, to several paragraphs. Figure 10–1 is an example of a short memo. Notice the heading of the memo: the person or persons addressed, the writer, the subject, and the date. For short memos, the writer's initials may replace a formal signature.

Sometimes memos are much longer than the one in Figure 10–1; in fact, technical memos may serve as short reports and have many pages. For longer memos, organization and structure are more complicated, so you need to think of writing the memo in terms of the writing process discussed in Chapter 2. Note also that for a memo longer than one page, later pages need a heading, such as this one:

> To: Mercy Hospital File
> From: Regina Havacek
> Date: December 10, 2018
> Page 2

Here is a summary of the steps you should take when writing a memo:

1. *Write with a specific purpose in mind.*
   - What are the main ideas of the memo?

FIGURE 10–1   Sample Memo

TO: Fourth-floor employees
FROM: Skip Waller *SW*
DATE: September 12, 2018
SUBJECT: Scheduled painting

Our painting contractors are scheduled to repaint the offices and public areas on our floor next week, September 24–28. The contractors understand that we will continue to work in the offices during this time and will try to disturb us as little as possible. But the work is bound to be disruptive, so let's all stay flexible and keep a sense of humor during this time that is bound to be somewhat inconvenient.

Thanks for your cooperation as we complete this much-needed maintenance.

- Should the memo summarize information, make a request, evaluate alternative courses of action, or recommend a solution to a problem?

2. *Write appropriately for your readers.*
   - Who will your readers be?
   - How familiar are your readers with the topic of the memo?
   - Are your readers familiar with technical terminology and accounting standards?

3. *Organize your memo into a coherent structure and appropriate format.*
   - Are you expected to present your ideas in a specialized memo format, such as a technical memo?
   - Do your readers expect an initial summary of your conclusions and recommendations?
   - How will you organize the subtopics in the memo's body, so that it meets the readers' needs?
   - Should you use formatting techniques, such as headings and bulleted lists, so that your memo is easier to read?

4. *Revise your memo so that it is polished and professional.*
   - Is your information complete and correct?
   - Have you explained the information clearly and concisely?
   - Did you proofread the final document carefully?

ORGANIZING FOR COHERENCE: PARTS OF A MEMO

LO10.2 Organize a coherent memo, with a focus on main ideas.

Like most kinds of writing, a memo is organized into an introduction, a body, and a conclusion. Summary sentences are used throughout the memo to make it more coherent. Even very short memos have this structure. The memo shown in Figure 10–1, which contains only two paragraphs, begins by summarizing the main idea of the memo. The remainder of the first paragraph provides additional information, and the final paragraph, which is only one sentence, concludes by thanking the readers for their cooperation.

Introduction

The introduction of a memo may vary from one sentence to several paragraphs. The introduction should identify what the memo is about and why it was written. If the memo will discuss more than one topic or be divided into several subtopics, the introduction should identify all important issues to be covered. The introduction might contain a sentence such as the following to indicate the memo's contents:

> This memo explains how to account for patents, copyrights, and trademarks.

An introduction should also identify the main ideas of the memo and may summarize your conclusions and any recommendations. Sometimes the main ideas, conclusions, and recommendations can be summarized in a few sentences, but at other times, you might need an entire paragraph or more. Longer summaries are better placed in a separate section following the introduction.

Summary or Recommendations

If the summary of your main ideas, conclusions, and recommendations is longer than a paragraph, it's better to put them in a separate section immediately following the introduction. This section should have a heading such as *Summary* or *Recommendations*. Note that in some memos, however, such as the one shown in Figure 10–3 on pages 192–194, the conclusions and recommendations may be presented in the final section of the memo, following the analysis of the issues. Yet another variation in structure is to summarize the main findings in both places, briefly near the beginning of the memo and in more detail in the final section. Later sections of this chapter will discuss these various formats more fully.

Body

The body of the memo can be divided into sections, as illustrated in Figures 10–2 and 10–3 on pages 191–194, each with a heading that describes the contents of that section. Remember to begin by summarizing the main idea of the section.

FIGURE 10–2   A Memo

MEMORANDUM   Date: August 16, 2018
TO: David Sanders
FROM: Jeff Ward _jw_
SUBJECT: Valuing Avalon Manufacturing

This memo is in response to your questions concerning the nature of goodwill and the role it plays in the valuation of a company such as Avalon Manufacturing. The memo explains what goodwill is and discusses how to determine its value.

What Is Goodwill?

The value of any business that is a going concern is greater than the sum of the values of its separately identified assets acquired, less liabilities. Goodwill is an intangible asset made up of items that may contribute to the earning power of a company, but that are not otherwise listed on the company's balance sheet. Sometimes this is called "going concern value." For example, some items that may contribute to goodwill for Avalon Manufacturing that are not on its balance sheet may be:

1. Highly capable engineering staff
2. Highly skilled labor
3. Strong reputation for quality work
4. Highly effective management
5. A widely recognized and respected brand name
6. A large loyal customer base

These items are not separately identified on Avalon's balance sheet. However, they obviously contribute to the earning power of the company and should be included in the purchase price of the business.

How to Value Goodwill

Generally, the value of goodwill is established by comparing the present value of future cash earnings of a company (the overall purchase price) with the total value assigned to the separately identified assets acquired and shown on its balance sheet, less liabilities. The difference between the two is the value of goodwill.

The key to determining the value of goodwill is, of course, the determination of the overall purchase price (estimating the present value of future cash earnings). We can do this by completing a cash-flow analysis similar to the ones we perform in our capital budgeting process.

Let me know if you have any further questions about goodwill or the valuing of Avalon Manufacturing.

FIGURE 10–3   A Memo to a Client's File[1]

Memorandum to the Mercy Hospital File

FROM: Regina Havacek RH

DATE: December 10, 2018

RE: The taxability of meal vouchers furnished by
            Mercy Hospital to its medical staff.

Facts

Our client, Mercy Hospital ("Mercy"), provides meal vouchers
to its medical employees to enable them to remain on emergency call. The vouchers are redeemable at Mercy's onsite cafeteria and at MacDougal's, a privately owned sandwich shop.
MacDougal's rents business space from the hospital. Although
Mercy does not require its employees to remain on or near its
premises during their meal hours, the employees generally do.
Elizabeth Fegali, Mercy's Chief Administrator, has asked us to
research whether the value of the meal vouchers is taxable to
the employees.

Issues

The taxability of the meal vouchers depends on three issues:

- Whether the meals are furnished "for the convenience of
  the employer."
- Whether they are furnished "on the business premises of
  the employer."
- Whether the vouchers are equivalent to cash.

Applicable Law

Section 119 provides that the value of meals is excludible
from an employee's income if the meals are furnished for
the convenience of, and on the business premises of, the
employer. Under Reg. Sec. 1.119-1, a meal is furnished "for
the convenience of the employer" if it is furnished for a
"substantial noncompensatory business reason." A "substantial noncompensatory reason" includes the need to have
the employee available for emergency calls during his or
her meal period. Under Sec. 119(b)(4), if more than half the
employees satisfy the "for the convenience of the employee"
test, all employees will be regarded as satisfying the test.
Regulation Sec. 1.119-1 defines "business premises of the
employer" as the place of employment of the employee.

A Supreme Court case, *Kowalski v. CIR*, 434 U.S. 77, 77-2 USTC
9748, discusses what constitutes "meals" for purposes of Sec.
119. In *Kowalski*, the State of New Jersey furnished cash meal

FIGURE 10–3   (*Contd.*)

TO: Mercy Hospital File
FROM: Regina Havacek
DATE: December 10, 2018
Page 2

allowances to its state troopers to enable them to eat while on duty. It did not require the troopers to use the allowances exclusively for meals. Nor did it require them to consume their meals on its business premises. One trooper, R.J. Kowalski, excluded the value of his allowances from his income. The IRS disputed this treatment, and Kowalski took the IRS to court. In court, Kowalski argued that the allowances were excludible because they were furnished "for the convenience of the employer." The IRS contended that the allowances were taxable because they amounted to compensation. The U.S. Supreme Court took up the case and decided for the IRS. The Court held that the Sec. 119 income exclusion does not apply to payments in cash.

Analysis

Issue 1: The meals provided by Mercy seem to be furnished "for the convenience of the employer." They are furnished to have employees available for emergency calls during their meal breaks. This is a "substantial noncompensatory reason" within the meaning of Reg. Sec. 1.119-1.

Issue 2: Although the hospital cafeteria appears to be the "business premises of the employer," MacDougal's does not appear to be. The hospital is the place of employment of the medical employees. MacDougal's is not.

Issue 3: Based on the foregoing authorities, it is unclear whether the vouchers are equivalent to cash. On the one hand, they are redeemable only in meals. Thus, they resemble meals-in-kind. On the other hand, they are redeemable at more than one institution. Thus, they resemble cash. Nor is it clear whether a court deciding this case would reach the same conclusion as the Supreme Court did in *Kowalski*. In the latter case, the State of New Jersey provided its meal allowances in the form of cash. It did not require its employees to use the allowances exclusively for meals. Nor did it require them to consume their meals on its business premises. In our case, Mercy provides its meal allowances in the form of vouchers. Thus, it indirectly requires its employees to use the allowances exclusively for meals. On the other hand, it does not require them to consume their meals on its business premises.

FIGURE 10–3   (*Contd.*)

TO: Mercy Hospital File
FROM: Regina Havacek
DATE: December 10, 2018
Page 3

Conclusion

Although it appears that the meals acquired by voucher in
the hospital cafeteria are furnished "for the convenience
of the employer" and "on the business premises of the
employer," it is unclear whether the vouchers are equivalent to cash. If they *are* equivalent to cash, *or* if they are
redeemed at MacDougal's, their value is likely to be taxable
to the employees. On the other hand, if they are not equivalent to cash, *and* they are redeemed only in the hospital cafeteria, their value is likely to be excludible.

Conclusion

Memos often end with a conclusion, which can be very brief. Consider
this example:

Let me know if you have any further questions about these procedures.

A conclusion such as this one brings the memo to a close and ends
in a courteous, helpful tone. A word of caution, however, about conclusions like the one just given: Be careful not to end all your memos with
the same sentence (or some slightly altered variation). The conclusion
should be a meaningful addition to the memo, not just an empty string
of words added out of habit. Also, be sure your conclusion (like the
rest of the memo) is appropriate to your reader. Consider why the
conclusions in Figures 10–1 and 10–2 might be unsuitable for a memo
you're sending to your boss. The sample memos in this chapter show
several different conclusions; all are appropriate to the content of the
memo and the readers.

One misconception some people have about conclusions is that
they should always repeat the memo's main ideas. For short memos,
this repetition is usually not necessary, although for longer memos,
such an ending summary is helpful and in some cases, such as a technical memo, may be essential.

Whatever the length of the memo, the conclusion is a good
place to tell your readers what you want them to do, or what you

will do, to follow-up on the ideas discussed in the memo. The memo shown earlier in Figure 10–1 has such a conclusion. It implies tactfully that readers should cooperate with the painting project, without complaining.

FORMATS

LO10.3   Write memos in an appropriate format.

Memos can be written in a variety of formats, as the examples in this chapter show. The memo in Figure 10–2 is typical of the format used in many organizations. Notice especially how the headings and set-off list make this memo attractive and easy to read.

Some organizations may prefer another format that has become customary within the organization. As always, you should prepare your memos according to your employer's expectations. The examples in Figures 10–2 and 10–3 illustrate formats some accounting firms may prefer when the memos are to be part of a client's file.

If you are free to design the format of your memos, be conservative; avoid oversized fonts and a great deal of inked space.

CONCISE, CLEAR, READABLE MEMOS: STYLE AND TONE

LO10.4   Write memos in an effective style and tone.

Memos should be as concise as possible: no unnecessary repetitions, digressions, or wordiness. They should be written in a clear, direct style, so that readers find them interesting and informative. Finally, memos should have flawless grammar and mechanics.

Memos can vary considerably in tone, depending on what they are about and how they will be circulated. Some memos, such as the one shown previously in Figure 10–1, are informal. For these memos, a conversational, personal tone is appropriate.

Other memos are more formal and might serve as short reports. Technical memos are usually longer, more formal memos. These memos, such as the one shown in Figure 10–3, may report the results of research or work performed, and may thus become part of the permanent records in a client's file. These memos are usually written with a more impersonal, formal tone. Whether formal or informal, however, all memos should be clear and concise.

As an example of the guidelines we've discussed, consider again the example memo in Figure 10–2. This memo was written in response to the hypothetical situation described here:

Situation:

David Sanders is the proprietor of the firm for which you work. Mr. Sanders wants to acquire a manufacturing business. The business he wants to acquire, Avalon Manufacturing, is insisting that he pay not only for the identifiable net assets of the business, but also for "goodwill." Mr. Sanders asks you: "What is goodwill? Should I pay for it? If I should pay for it, how much should I pay?"

Study the memo shown in Figure 10–2 to see how it illustrates the principles of memo writing already discussed. Do you think Mr. Sanders will be pleased with the memo?

TECHNICAL MEMOS

LO10.5   Plan, organize, and write a technical memo.

As a practicing accountant, you may be asked to prepare a technical memo in response to an unusual transaction or a complicated problem encountered by a client or the organization for which you work. You will conduct careful research in preparation for writing the memo, using your higher order thinking skills to analyze the problem and evaluate alternative solutions. Your conclusions will be based on a complete, documented set of facts and thorough research into the relevant literature and authoritative standards.

A technical memo, as its name suggests, describes the research done on a technical topic. It is usually specific to a particular, real-world situation, as opposed to being theoretical or hypothetical. While well grounded in careful research and authoritative standards, the emphasis on a technical memo is conclusions, rather than details of the methodology you used to reach those conclusions.

Figure 10–3 on pages 192–194 shows an example of a technical memo, in this case one that will be part of a client's files.

Purpose and Audience

As with all the writing you will do as part of your professional responsibilities, you must ensure that you understand the purpose and intended readers of the technical memos you write. In general, technical memos summarize the results of research into a technical topic. However, these memos can differ in an important way: some technical memos are an even-handed investigation into alternative solutions to a problem, leaving the final choice of alternative to the decision makers in an organization. Other technical memos will recommend the best alternative. In this case, you will present all alternatives you have considered, giving the pros and cons of each, and supporting your recommendation with evidence, analysis, and authoritative support. Technical memos such as this may thus include both arguments and counterarguments. (See Chapter 7 for a further discussion of these terms.)

The readers of a technical memo might be other accountants, managers, or occasionally clients. You should write the memo so that it will be appropriate for these different readers, both current readers and those who might consult your memo in the future. Pay particular attention to the needs and expectations of current readers, anticipating their questions and providing them with enough information to make decisions.

Technical memos are often stored for future reference, such as in client files. Future readers will need to have enough background information that they understand the facts of the situation and the research on which you based your conclusions.

Structure

A technical memo is usually several pages long, perhaps two to five pages, and sometimes even longer. The format of a technical memo can vary, but the one shown below is typical.

Heading

Your memo may begin with a heading such as this one:

To:	Identify the person(s) who requested the memo, and any other recipients, and add their titles. You may also indicate that the memo is intended for the client file, as in Figure 10-3.
From:	Your name and title.
Date:	The date the memo is written.
Subject:	Be specific in identifying the subject of your memo. This part of the heading should be one or two lines of type.

Introduction

Begin your technical memo with an introduction that defines the purpose of the memo and identifies the topics it will cover. You may also identify who authorized or requested the research, or stress the importance of the topic. The introduction may also provide background information on the situation you're discussing, unless this information appears within the body of the memo. Especially in longer memos, the final portion of the introduction may also identify the main topics the memo will cover, either in a sentence or a bulleted list.

Notice that the introduction in Figure 10–3 is labeled *Facts*. In addition to summarizing key facts of the situation, the paragraph identifies the memo's purpose and authorization.

Initial Summary

You will often summarize your conclusions and/or recommendations near the beginning of the memo, either as part of the introduction or in a separate section with a heading such as *Summary*. However, some organizations prefer that the conclusions and recommendations appear only at the end of the memo; in such situations, you will of course omit an initial summary. If you have both an initial summary and concluding sections in the memo, the summary will be a briefer version of the conclusions you explain in greater detail at the end of the memo. In Figure 10–3, the conclusions appear only in the final section of the memo.

Body or Discussion

This section of the memo may begin with background information of the situation or a summary of the facts, unless this information has appeared in the introduction. Divide the body into the different issues, or different alternatives or types of information you have considered to solve a problem.

Conclusion

The conclusion of a technical memo may be as short as a sentence or as long as several paragraphs. For a short memo in which you have provided an initial summary, the conclusion can be a conventional courteous closing:

> Please let me know if I can provide any further information about how to account for this transaction.

For many technical memos, however, you will discuss your conclusions and recommendations in some detail in the final section of the memo, as based on the analysis and research discussed in the body of the memo. In deciding on what kind of conclusion to write, consider the expectations of your readers and the custom of the organization in which you work.

BRIEFING DOCUMENTS

LO10.6   Plan, organize, and write a briefing document.

Briefing documents, which may be referred to as *briefing notes* or *briefing memos*, are short documents that inform the reader or readers about an issue. Such documents may distill information about an issue for senior decision makers or those about to participate in discussions or presentations who may not have the time to research the issue themselves. These briefing documents are short, usually from one to three pages; they cover the key points of an issue without going into great detail. As mentioned earlier in the chapter, some people use the terms *briefing notes* and *briefing memos* interchangeably. Other writers consider briefing notes to be shorter than briefing memos.

Purpose and Audience

Whatever the terminology used, the purposes of briefing documents can be divided into three broad possibilities: (1) they may recommend a solution to a problem, including pros and cons for this recommendation, (2) they may present an even-handed, objective discussion of all alternatives for readers to evaluate before making a final decision, or (3) they may provide background information for a speech or other presentation to an audience. As always when you write, clarify your purpose before you begin your analysis and research, and write the document so that it meets your readers' expectations.

Structure

The organization of briefing documents, whether memos or notes, may vary, but they will generally have the following structure:

Heading

Your memo will begin with a heading such as this one:

To: Identify the person(s) who requested the memo, and any other recipients, and add their titles.

From: Your name and title.

Date: The date you write the document.

Subject: Be specific in identifying the subject of your memo. This part of the heading should be one or two lines of type.

Statement of the Problem or Issue Addressed in the Document

This section will state the purpose of the document and identify the major topics it will consider. Where a recommendation has been requested, this section will specify action you recommend.

Summary of the Facts and Issues

This section, which may be divided into subsections with headings, may stress the topic's importance, summarize relevant background information, or report the current status of work already performed on the issue. The summary will identify key considerations and will summarize relevant facts, analyses, options, and arguments.

Conclusion

This section will summarize your conclusions and, where requested, your recommendations. Your conclusions should be supported by the facts and analysis you discussed in the Summary.

MEMOS TO CLIENTS' FILES

LO10.7   Plan, organize, and write memos to clients' files.

Accountants often record information about a client's situation in a memo that is placed in the client's file for later reference. Other members of the staff may refer to the information recorded in these memos months or even years later, so the information must be recorded clearly, accurately, and correctly.

For example, a client might write or call an accounting firm about a tax question. The person receiving the letter or handling the call might then write a memo to record the pertinent facts of the client's situation. Later, another member of the staff may research the question. The researcher needs adequate information to identify the issues and solve the client's problem.

A sample memo written for a client's file appears in Figure 10–3. This memo, which has the structure of a technical memo, summarizes research into a tax question. Memos to clients' files may be technical memos, such as the one in Figure 10–3, or they may be organized in some other format.

EXERCISES

Exercise 10–1 [General]

Two years ago you were hired as an accountant in the tax department of a small regional accounting firm. This year you have been asked to help mentor an intern from the local university. This intern, Jeff Golightly, has been following your progress as you've researched a client's tax problem. Your conclusions, which are complex and technical, have been approved by your supervisors.

Jeff sent you an email to suggest that you and he meet with the client over lunch and present the results of your research orally. That way, he argues, you can avoid the work and aggravation of putting your findings into a written client letter.

Write a memo to Jeff in which you explain why his idea is not a good one. Invent any information you feel is necessary to make your memo complete.

Exercise 10–2 [General]

You are a manager in a local CPA firm, Barry, Peters, & Travis. While attending the symphony in your city you noticed in the program that a couple of other CPA firms in the area were listed among the donors; one had given $100,000 and another had given $40,000. As a fan of the symphony, you would like to see your firm also make a donation. However, beyond wanting to support the symphony, you want to encourage such a donation because you think it would enhance the image of your firm and be a good marketing move. You note that several of your firm's clients have also made donations.

Write a memo to the partner-in-charge of your firm, John Hoffman, persuading him to support such a donation.

Exercise 10–3 [General]

You have just graduated from college and been hired as an entry-level accountant in a local CPA firm, Olde, Aged, and Outofit, CPAs. When you arrived on the job, you were shocked to learn that the firm's partners, Elmer Olde, Thaddeus Aged, and Ethel Outofit, know almost nothing about social media, especially as it is now being used in business. They boast that they do business "the old-fashioned way" and regard social media as the trendy hobby of inexperienced young people.

At a recent meeting with one of the firm's main clients, however, Mr. Olde heard some disturbing news. This client, Rodney Current, believes that all businesses, if they are to remain competitive and effective, must understand and in some cases incorporate social media into their business practices. Mr. Olde was horrified to hear Mr. Current's views, but he and his partners have begun to suspect that their own views might be just a little behind the times.

Mr. Olde called you into the office because he knows you are fully up-to-date on the use of electronic communication and social media. He has asked you to research the use of social media in professional accounting practices. He has not asked you to recommend whether the firm should embrace these media, but he does want to be fully informed about the topic, so that he and the other partners can evaluate whether their firm will need to update their attitudes, and possibly their practices.

Research the topic and write a memo to Mr. Olde, as he has requested. Invent any information you feel is necessary to make your memo complete.

Exercise 10–4 [Managerial]

You are a staff accountant for Mitchell Manufacturing, Inc., a large electronics manufacturing company. Mitchell has four sales divisions, three manufacturing plants, and a home office in Dearborn, Michigan, which houses all the administrative offices. Management is considering using the cloud in accounting and auditing for the first time. Jeff Smart, Chief Operating Officer of Mitchell, has asked you to answer the following questions in a memo:

- What is the cloud?
- How might Mitchell Manufacturing use the cloud in accounting and auditing?
- What advantages might there be to Mitchell Manufacturing's use of the cloud?

Write a memo to Mr. Smart responding to these questions. Invent any information you feel is necessary to make your memo complete.

Exercise 10–5 [Financial]

You are newly hired as an accountant for Hill Business Technologies, Inc., a small service business that has no formal capital budgeting system. The president of your company, Janice Hill, has requested that you write a memo to her explaining what the internal rate of return method of investment evaluation is, how it differs from the net present value and payback period methods, and why Hill Business Technologies should use the internal rate of return method for capital budgeting purposes instead of either of the other methods. Write the memo. Invent any information you feel is necessary to make your memo complete.

Exercise 10–6 [Auditing]

In recent years, assessment of organizational culture has become an important issue in internal auditing. As an accountant employed in your company's financial division, you have been asked by the comptroller, Janice Graham, to write a briefing memo for her that she can use in several meetings she has set up with company managers to discuss this issue. Write the briefing memo for Ms. Graham. Invent any information you feel is necessary to make your memo complete.

Exercise 10–7 [Managerial]

You are a managerial accountant at Gourmet Restaurant Supplies, which supplies fresh produce, meat, seafood, and food staples to the area's finest restaurants. You have been asked by the controller to write a memo to the company's regional managers that will explain cost-volume-profit (CVP) analysis. In particular, the controller hopes that managers will understand how CVP analysis can help them perform their responsibilities.

Write the memo to Gourmet's three regional managers: Lupe Garcia, Sybil Alexander, and Paul Chan. You can make up hypothetical examples if needed to illustrate your memo.

Exercise 10–8 [Tax]

You are a CGMA working for a large multinational manufacturing firm that has operations in 37 countries, mostly in Europe, North and South America, and Southeast Asia. Some of your company's competitors in the United States have recently been subjected to transfer pricing audits by the IRS. Your controller, James Wheat, has asked you to prepare a briefing memo concerning transfer pricing audits.

The memo should cover the issues of why the IRS is motivated to conduct them, and what your company can do to either avoid such audits or mitigate the burden should one be conducted. Write the memo inventing any information you feel is necessary to make your briefing memo complete.

Exercise 10–9 [Financial]

Daniel Gordon, the president of the Skinner Company, is considering a bond issue to raise $1,000,000 for the company. Mr. Gordon notes that long-term treasury bonds yield 3%, which he thinks is a good loan rate. Before proceeding with the bond issue, however, Mr. Gordon wants to know more about it. Specifically, he wonders what the annual interest payments would be on the bonds.

You are a financial analyst at Skinner Company. Write a memo to Mr. Gordon explaining what the interest payments on a $1,000,000, 20-year bond issue would be if the bonds were issued at a 3% yield. Also explain in your memo why the Skinner Company would probably not be able to issue the bonds at 3%.

Exercise 10–10 [Systems]

You are a new employee at Southwest Parts Distributors, Inc. As a specialist in accounting information systems, one of your responsibilities is to recommend adequate controls to ensure the safety of Southwest's data, including the data it keeps on suppliers and customers. You recently recommended that the company adopt a new set of control procedures. However, Southwest's regional manager, Bill Tomlinson, has expressed impatience with your recommendations. He views the new procedures as "unnecessary red tape."

Write a memo to Mr. Tomlinson that explains the advantages of strong controls to protect the company's data.

Exercise 10–11 [Auditing]

Assume you are a staff accountant working for Kim & Kirkpatrick, Inc. (K&K), a small publicly traded company that will soon have its financial statements audited by a local CPA firm, Young, Mitchell, and Gregory. Eleanor Lee, a rising manager at K&K, expects to work closely with the auditors. Ms. Lee has a general business background and several years experience working for K&K, but her knowledge of auditing is limited. She sees you in the hall one day and during the conversation, she tells you she is confused about a term she's heard of that will somehow affect the upcoming audit. The term she refers to is *materiality*. You talk with her briefly about materiality, but as she walks away she still seems to be a little confused. Later she asks you to write her a memo explaining the concept of materiality and possible ways it might affect the audit of K&K.

Write the memo, inventing any details you need to make your discussion clear and readable.

Exercise 10–12 [Auditing/Current Professional Issues]

You are an audit partner in a medium-size CPA firm, Kilmer, Kissenger, and Kennedy. Several of your larger audit clients have read in the news about the possibility that audit firm rotation might at some time be required and have asked whether they should be prepared to comply with such a requirement in the near future. You have been asked by your partners to prepare a memo for distribution to your firm's clients that discusses the pros and cons of such a requirement and your evaluation of the likelihood of its occurrence in the near future.

Write the memo, inventing any details you need to make your discussion clear and readable.

NOTES

1. Adapted with permission from Rupert, Timothy J., Thomas R. Pope, and Kenneth E. Anderson, *Pearson's Federal Taxation 2017, Comprehensive* (Boston: Pearson Education, Inc., 2017), A-6.

CHAPTER 11

Reports and Discussion Papers

11

Learning Objectives

After studying this chapter, you should be able to

11.1 Plan and organize a formal report using a standard report format.

11.2 Plan and organize a discussion paper.

Most of the documents accountants write in practice are relatively short—from a one-sentence email perhaps, to a memo or letter of one or two pages. For some situations a longer document is appropriate. These documents, which may take the form of a formal report or discussion paper, are helpful to summarize research into a complicated topic, to present arguments (pro and con) for alternative solutions to a complex problem, or to delve into issues on a theoretical topic being considered by the accounting profession. In addition to these longer documents, some situations, such as the reports issued at the end of an audit, require a shorter formal report.

This chapter will first discuss and illustrate formal reports, including auditors' reports and longer documents that report the research into a complex problem. The final section of the chapter will cover discussion papers.

REPORTS

LO11.1 Plan and organize a formal report using a standard report format.

Sometimes accountants prepare formal reports, such as a report for a client that a CPA in public practice might prepare. Managerial accountants might prepare reports for other departments in their firm or perhaps for a group of managers with a particular need. Auditors prepare reports to summarize their findings for auditing engagements. Figure 11–1 shows an example of an auditor's report,

FIGURE 11–1   A Standard Auditor's Unqualified Report on Comparative Financial Statements

Coffey & Nelson, P.C.
Certified Public Accountants
2300 Peachtree St., Suite 100
Atlanta, GA 30000

Independent Auditor's Report

To the Stockholders
DVD Enterprises, Inc.

We have audited the accompanying balance sheets of DVD Enterprises, Inc., as of December 31, 2017, and 2016, and the related statements of income, changes in stockholders' equity, and cash flows for the years then ended and the related notes to the financial statements.

Management's Responsibility for the Financial Statements
Management is responsible for the preparation and fair presentation of the financial statements in accordance with the accounting principles generally accepted in the United States of America; this includes the design, implementation, and maintenance of internal control relevant to the preparation and fair presentation of financial statements that are free from material misstatement, whether due to fraud or error.

Auditor's Responsibility
Our responsibility is to express an opinion on these financial statements based on our audits. We conducted our audits in accordance with auditing standards generally accepted in the United States of America. Those standards require that we plan and perform the audit to obtain reasonable assurance about whether the financial statements are free of material misstatement.

An audit involves performing procedures to obtain audit evidence about the amounts and disclosures in the financial statements. The procedures selected depend on the auditor's judgment, including the assessment of the risks of material misstatement of the financial statements, whether due to fraud or error. In making those risk assessments, the auditor considers internal control relevant to the entity's preparation and fair presentation of the financial statements in order to design audit procedures that are appropriate in the circumstances, but not for the purpose of expressing an opinion on the effectiveness of the entity's internal control. Accordingly, we express no such opinion. An audit also includes evaluating

FIGURE 11–1 (*Contd.*)

the appropriateness of accounting policies used and the reasonableness of significant accounting estimates made by management, as well as evaluating the overall presentation of the financial statements.

We believe that the audit evidence we have obtained is sufficient and appropriate to provide a basis for our audit opinion.

Opinion
In our opinion, the financial statements referred to above present fairly, in all material respects, the financial position of DVD Enterprises, Inc., as of December 31, 2017, and 2016, and the results of their operations and cash flows for the years then ended in accordance with accounting principles generally accepted in the United States of America.

COFFEY & NELSON, P.C., CPAs
Atlanta, GA

February 23, 2018

---

in this case, a standard unqualified report on comparative financial statements. This report uses standard wording required by AICPA auditing standards.

Other reports may involve analyzing an accounting problem and applying accounting principles, or applying provisions of the tax code to a particular situation. A report may also require researching professional literature or other material, so the research techniques discussed in Chapter 8 are often part of report preparation.

Reports may vary in length, but all reports should meet certain basic criteria. The technical content should be accurate and complete, the organization should be coherent, the report should be presented attractively, and the writing style should be clear and concise. Like all forms of writing, a report should be designed and written with the readers' needs and expectations in mind.

Planning a Report

If you are preparing a report on the job, your company may have an established format for you to follow for all reports. Find out your organization's expectations and policies before you begin work on your report. If you are free to design your own report format, the format presented in this chapter can serve as a generic model that is typical of those used in business and industry.

When planning the report, consider the purpose of the report and who its readers will be. Analyzing the purpose and audience for a report may be more difficult than it is for some letters and memos because a report can have many groups of readers, and each group may have different interests and needs.

For example, a report recommending that a firm invest in a new information system might be circulated to the management information systems (MIS) department, the accounting department, the departments that would actually use the system, and senior management. The accounting department would be interested in the accounting information aspects of the acquisition as well as how the system could be used for various accounting tasks. The MIS department would be interested in the technical features of the system and how it would affect MIS personnel. Other departments would want to know how the system would make their work easier or more difficult, whether it would affect their budgets, and what additional training, if any, their personnel would need to use the system. Senior management would be interested in the bigger picture, such as how the system would affect the firm's efficiency, competitiveness, and cash flow.

To write this report, you would need to identify clearly who the readers are and what information they want the report to include. You would obviously be writing to readers with different degrees of knowledge about the technical features of the new system and with different interests and concerns as well. The way to handle this complicated situation is to write different parts of the report for different groups of readers.

Fortunately, reports are not usually as difficult to plan and write as this one, but this example shows how important it is to analyze carefully the needs and expectations of different groups of readers.

Most reports require a great deal of research. They may report the results of empirical studies or pilot projects, or report research involving generally accepted accounting principles or other technical literature. Review the organization principles discussed in Chapter 3, and then organize your research and discussion into an outline that will give your report a coherent structure.

1. Is the subject covered adequately?
   - Background information when necessary
   - Adequate explanations, supporting data, and examples
   - Citations from GAAP and other authoritative sources, as needed
   - Application to the specific needs and interests of the readers
2. Is the report too long?
   - Digressions—off the subject
   - Too much explanation or detail
   - Repetitions or wordiness

3. Is the report logically organized?
- In order from most to least important—from the readers' point of view
- Summary sentences where helpful
- Transitions to link ideas
- Short, well-organized paragraphs with topic sentences

The format of a report—how its various parts are put together—also determines how coherent the report is.

The Parts of a Report

Reports can be presented in a variety of formats that are all designed to make the report easy to read. The format presented here shows a typical structure.

A report may include these sections:

Transmittal document

Title page

Table of contents

List of illustrations

Summary section

Introduction

Body of the report

Conclusion

Appendices

Notes

Bibliography

Graphic illustrations

Transmittal Document

The transmittal document can be either a cover letter or a memo. It presents the report to the people for whom it was written and adds any other information that will be helpful.

The transmittal document will not be long, but it should include essential information, such as the report's title, topic, and purpose; you might also identify who requested or authorized the report. Summarize the report's main idea or recommendation if you can do so in a few sentences. You may want to add other comments about the report that will be helpful to the readers. Always end with a courteous closing. Whereas the style of the actual report is usually formal and impersonal, the transmittal document can usually be more conversational, including the use of personal pronouns.

Title Page

The title page might look something like this:

Title of Report
Prepared for . . .
Prepared by . . .
Date

Table of Contents

The table of contents appears on a separate page with a heading. The contents listed are the major parts of the report, excluding the transmittal document, with the appropriate page numbers.

List of Illustrations

The list of illustrations, if applicable, includes titles and page numbers of graphs, charts, and other illustrations.

Summary Section

Most formal reports have a section near the beginning of the report that summarizes the main ideas and recommendations. This section can vary in length from one paragraph to several pages, and can come either immediately before or immediately after the introduction. The summary section may be called an executive summary, abstract, synopsis, summary, or some other term.

An executive summary is especially helpful for long reports. This section gives the readers an overview of the report's contents without the technical detail. The executive summary identifies the purpose and scope of the report and possibly the methods used for research. It includes the major findings of the research, the conclusions of the researcher, and the recommendations, if any. The length of an executive summary varies with the length of the report, but it's generally about one to three pages long. The summary begins on a separate page following the table of contents or list of illustrations, and is entitled *Executive Summary*. The sample report at the end of this chapter uses this kind of summary.

For shorter reports, a section right after the introduction can provide a summary of the report's main ideas and recommendations. This section is labeled *Summary*; it's usually one or two paragraphs long.

Introduction

The introduction of a formal report is longer than that of a letter or memo—perhaps two or three short paragraphs, and for long reports, even longer than a page. The introduction identifies the subject of the report and states why it was written—who requested or authorized it, or for whom it was prepared. The introduction states the purpose of the report in specific terms:

The purpose of this report is to discuss the feasibility of offering a stock bonus plan to employees of Gulf Coast Industries.

Not:

The purpose of this report is to discuss stock bonus plans.

Sometimes an introduction includes additional information to help the reader, perhaps a brief background of the report's topic. However, if it's necessary to include a great deal of background information, this material should be presented in a separate section in the body of the report.

Finally, the introduction of a report should end with a plan of development that gives the reader an overview or forecast of the topics the report covers and the order in which they are presented. A simple plan of development can be in sentence form:

This report describes the proposed pension plan and then discusses its costs and benefits.

Sometimes a set-off list makes the plan of development easier to read:

This report discusses the following topics related to the proposed pension plan:

- Major provisions
- Benefits to employees
- Benefits to the corporation
- Cost
- Accounting for the plan

Body of the Report

The body of the report should be divided into sections, and possibly subsections, each with an appropriate heading. Remember to begin each section with a statement that summarizes the main idea to be covered in that section.

The body of the report can also contain graphic illustrations, as discussed below.

Conclusion

In addition to the summary section at the beginning, a report should have a conclusion to remind the reader of the report's main ideas and recommendations. This section may be from one paragraph to several pages.

Appendices (Optional)

Depending on the report's audience and purpose, you may want to place technical information and statistics in appendices at the end of the report. If you use an appendix, give it a title and refer to it in the body of the report.

Notes and Bibliography

What to put at the end of the report depends in part on the style of documentation you use. If you use endnotes, they should usually begin on a separate page and be labeled *Notes*.

Almost all reports have some sort of bibliography or reference list. This list identifies the sources you cited in your paper, and it may also include additional references the reader might want to consult. This section should begin on a separate page following the notes (if any), and should have a title such as *Bibliography* or *References*.

Appendix 8–E in Chapter 8 demonstrates the proper form for endnotes or footnotes and bibliographical entries.

Graphic Illustrations

Sometimes graphic illustrations, such as graphs or tables, make a report easier to read and more interesting, especially if you are presenting statistical or numerical data or if the subject of the report concerns a process. You can place graphic illustrations either in an appendix or in the body of your report, just after the place in the text where they are discussed.

Graphic illustrations are discussed more fully in Chapter 6.

Appearance

Presenting your report as attractively as possible is important. Reports can be single-spaced or double-spaced, depending on the situation. Students' reports are usually double-spaced to provide space for annotations when they are graded. In all reports, the transmittal document and any set-off material are single-spaced. Pages should be numbered, using lowercase Roman numerals for front matter (table of contents, list of illustrations, executive summary) and Arabic numerals for the remainder of the report, from the introduction through the end matter.

Style and Tone

The tone of a formal report is usually just what its name implies: formal, and therefore impersonal. You probably won't use personal pronouns or contractions in a formal report, for example. However, a formal style should still be readable and interesting, so you should use the effective style techniques discussed in Chapter 4. Even a formal document can be written simply, clearly, and concretely.

The report in Figure 11–2 illustrates many effective report writing techniques.

FIGURE 11–2   A Report

B&H Financial Consultants
125 Easy Street
Athens, GA 36150
August 8, 2018

Mr. Sam Hamilton
Hamilton Manufacturing
1890 Meerly Avenue
Atlanta, GA 30306

Dear Mr. Hamilton:

Enclosed is the report about convertible bonds that you requested in your letter of July 21. The report, titled *Convertible
Bonds: Financial and Accounting Considerations*, examines the
nature of convertible debt, the pros and cons of such an issue,
and the accounting treatment of the securities.

The report shows that convertible bonds may represent a relatively less expensive method of raising capital than noncon-
vertible bonds. Another advantage is that should the convertible bonds be converted, the existing shares of common stock
will not be diluted as severely as they would if common stock
had been issued. However, as the report makes clear, these
effects are by no means certain.

I believe the report will provide you with the information you
need. If you have any further questions, however, don't hesitate
to give me a call.

Sincerely yours,

Joyce Samuels

Joyce Samuels
jhw

FIGURE 11–2   *(Contd.)*

CONVERTIBLE BONDS:
FINANCIAL AND ACCOUNTING CONSIDERATIONS

Prepared for Hamilton Manufacturing

by

JOYCE SAMUELS

AUGUST 8, 2018

FIGURE 11–2   (*Contd.*)

CONTENTS

i

FIGURE 11–2 *(Contd.)*

EXECUTIVE SUMMARY

This report provides information about convertible bonds for the managers of Hamilton Manufacturing. Included is information about the nature of convertible bonds, financial advantages and disadvantages of issuing such bonds, and their accounting treatment.

A convertible bond is a debt security that carries the option of exchange for an equity security, usually common stock. The bond indenture specifies when the bonds may be converted and a conversion ratio.

Convertible bonds would offer Hamilton several advantages:

- The company could issue the bonds at a premium or at a low stated interest rate, which investors would accept because of the conversion privilege.
- The company could avoid another stock issue now, when the price of Hamilton's stock is low.
- The company may avoid a decrease in share price caused by issuing a large number of new shares on the market at one time.
- Total stock issuance costs may be less.
- Management would avoid possible conflict with its major stockholders.

There are also potential disadvantages management should consider before issuing the convertible bonds:

- Before conversion, the uncertain conditions of the economy make a future increase in the market price of the company's stock uncertain. If conversion does not occur, Hamilton may have difficulty meeting the debt requirements.
- Bond conversion will reduce basic earnings per share. Conversion will also increase Hamilton's income tax liability because of the loss of interest expense.
- The required accounting treatment of convertible bonds may have an unfavorable effect on the company's financial statements: a high level of debt may be presented alongside a lowered diluted earnings per share (DEPS).

ii

FIGURE 11–2   (*Contd.*)

CONVERTIBLE BONDS:
FINANCIAL AND ACCOUNTING CONSIDERATIONS

Introduction

The purpose of this report is to provide information for the management of Hamilton Manufacturing about convertible debt as a means of financing. Convertible debt is an issue of debt securities (bonds) with the option to exchange those debt securities for equity securities (usually common stock).

This report covers three major topics:

* The nature of convertible bonds.
* Financial advantages and disadvantages Hamilton can expect if it issues the bonds.
* Accounting treatment for the bonds.

Nature of Convertible Bonds

When convertible bonds are issued, the bond indenture defines a time period after issuance during which the bonds may be converted. The indenture also gives a conversion ratio, which is the number of shares of stock for which each bond may be exchanged. The effective price of stock to the bondholder is determined by dividing the par value of the bond by the number of shares exchangeable for one bond.

The indenture usually includes a call provision so that the issuing entity can force bondholders to convert (usually at a premium over par). Thus, entities that issue convertible debt often do so as a means of raising equity capital. The following sections discuss why Hamilton might choose to issue convertible debt.

1

FIGURE 11–2 (*Contd.*)

Financial Advantages and Disadvantages

<u>Advantages</u>

Use of convertible debt would offer Hamilton advantages over straight debt or stock issues.

Investors in bonds that are convertible into stock are usually willing to accept a lower stated interest rate on such bonds, to pay a premium and accept a lower yield, or to accept less restrictive covenants. Thus, by issuing convertible debt, Hamilton will probably be able to obtain funds at a lower cost than if it issued debt that is not convertible.

Depending upon economic conditions, there may also be a timing advantage to issuing convertible debt. If current conditions make it unfavorable to sell stock because of depressed value, issuing convertible debt will allow Hamilton to raise capital debt now that may later be converted into stock when the stock price has recovered.

In addition, by issuing convertible debt, Hamilton may avoid a decrease in stock price caused by a large new issue of stock being made available on the market all at once.

Another advantage to Hamilton of issuing convertible bonds is that the company might avoid creating a conflict with major stockholders, who want to maintain their percentage interests. The stockholders might vote against a large issue of stock. However, the bond issue could be convertible into a number of shares small enough not to significantly injure the stockholders' interests.

<u>Disadvantages</u>

Most disadvantages of issuing convertible bonds are related to the uncertainty of conversion. If Hamilton's stock price does not rise, conversion may not occur without call, the company may not obtain the equity financing it desires, and Hamilton might then be saddled with long-term debt obligations.

Another disadvantage is the impact on either diluted earnings per share (DEPS) before conversion, or basic earnings per share (BEPS) after conversion. In either case the earnings per share figure will be reduced. After conversion, income tax expense will increase because of the reduction in interest expense.

2

FIGURE 11–2 (*Contd.*)

Accounting Treatment

According to Generally Accepted Accounting Principles (GAAP), if convertible bonds are "sold at a price or have a value at issuance not significantly in excess of the face amount . . . [n]o portion of the proceeds from the issuance . . . shall be accounted for as attributable to the conversion feature" (ASC pars. 470-20-25-10b and 470-20-25-12). In other words, the expectation that some or all of the bonds will be converted into stock is not recognized in the accounts.

Because convertible bonds are normally sold at a premium, the amount of the cash proceeds from the issue is usually greater than the face value of the bonds. The premium is amortized over the life of the bonds. The effect of the amortization is that the interest expense recorded by Hamilton each period would not equal the amount of the interest *payment*, but would reflect the effective yield to the bondholders.

When the bonds are converted, Hamilton will remove from the accounts the balance associated with those bonds. The value assigned to the stock equals the book value of the bonds, and no gain or loss is recognized or recorded.

If Hamilton decides to retire its convertible bonds for cash before their maturity date, the transaction will be recorded in the same way as the early bonds, and the cash paid to retire them will be a gain or a loss on the income statement.

Although convertibles are accounted for solely as debt, Hamilton must also consider the equity characteristics of such issues in computing diluted earnings per share (DEPS). GAAP require that corporations having issued securities that are potentially dilutive of EPS, such as convertible bonds, must present both basic earnings per share (BEPS) and diluted earnings per share (DEPS) for income from continuing operations and for net income in the income statement "with equal prominence" (ASC par. 260-10-45-2).

The DEPS figure represents EPS *as if* the bonds had been converted into stock. If they had been converted, the removal of the bonds would have caused a reduction of interest expense, which would have increased earnings. However, the positive effect of the earnings adjustment may not offset the negative effect of the shares adjustment. Thus, convertibles reduce reported DEPS.

3

FIGURE 11–2 (*Contd.*)

Conclusion

In deciding whether to finance with convertible debt, Hamilton must consider whether it would benefit from using convertibles rather than straight debt or stock issues and whether it can meet the debt requirements, should conversion not occur as expected. In addition, management should analyze carefully the effect of the issue on readers of the financial statements, because until the bonds are converted, a possibly high level of debt will exist alongside a lowered presentation of DEPS.

WORKS CITED

Financial Accounting Standards Board (FASB), 2016.
Accounting Standards Codification®. Stamford, Conn.: FASB.

4

DISCUSSION PAPERS

LO11.2 Plan and organize a discussion paper.

A discussion paper is a long document that covers a topic thoroughly. Typically, discussion papers treat a theoretical or hypothetical issue, rather than a real world application of accounting standards to a concrete situation, or the solution of an actual problem, such as might be covered in a formal report or other document. Chapter 3 introduced basic principles you can use to organize a discussion paper. We look here at these documents in a little more detail.

Discussion papers are written only after extensive research and careful analysis. They cover all important issues related to the topic, and they present the issues from all possible informed perspectives. Discussion papers often discuss both pros and cons of possible positions, thus containing both arguments and counterarguments. They may conclude with a recommended point of view, or they may summarize all the alternatives, leaving the final decision to others, perhaps senior management or an authoritative accounting organization, such as the FASB.[i] You should of course clarify the purpose and audience for your discussion paper before you begin working on it.

You will recognize from the above description of discussion papers that they require a mastery of all the research, thinking, and writing skills covered in this book. If you are asked to compose a discussion paper, it will be particularly helpful for you to review these chapters:

Chapter 2—the sections on analyzing purpose and audience.

Chapter 3—organizing for coherence. This chapter discusses how to organize a discussion paper.

Chapter 6—formatting techniques, such as headings and graphics.

Chapter 7—higher order thinking skills.

Chapter 8—accounting research.

Structure and Format

Like most of the business documents you write, a discussion paper will be divided into an introduction, body, and conclusion. The body of the document will likely be divided into topics and possibly subtopics, each with an appropriate heading.

The introduction, which will be one or more paragraphs, will state the purpose of the discussion paper and indicate the major topics it will cover, perhaps with a bulleted list. Each bulleted item will indicate

---

[i] A special instance of discussion papers is the documents issued by organizations such as the FASB. While you may never participate in the writing of these official documents, you may find it helpful to examine a typical discussion paper, such as those issued by the FASB. You can find an example of an FASB discussion paper at http://www.fasb.org/DP_Revenue_Recognition.pdf.

a major division of the body. The introduction may summarize your major conclusions and any recommendations, or this information may appear in a separate section, either an initial summary, an abstract, or an executive summary.

The body of the discussion paper will develop the major topics you indicated in the introduction. Here you will discuss fully the important findings from your research, possibly including the background of the topic, its current status, and a summary of options for future treatment, including pros and cons of each. You may also summarize financial data or other statistical information, which you may include within the text as figures, or in an appendix at the end of the paper. You may also cite authoritative support for the options you've presented, documenting your sources either within the text or as endnotes, with a reference list. You should give each topic and subtopic a heading, and begin each section of the body with a summary sentence that identifies the main idea of the section; paragraphs should begin with topic sentences.

The concluding section of the discussion paper should summarize your findings, including any recommendations you've been asked to make. Your conclusions and recommendations should be thoroughly supported by the facts, analyses, and citations of authoritative literature you discussed in the body of your paper. The conclusion should also provide readers of the discussion paper with closure, a sense that the paper has come to an appropriate end.

Typically, especially for longer documents, a discussion paper may have the structure of a formal report, including some or all of the front matter discussed on page 210 of this chapter. It may also be presented in the format of a technical memo, as discussed in Chapter 10. As always, you will follow the custom or the organization for which you are preparing the discussion paper.

EXERCISES

Exercise 11–1 [General]

As a staff member of Swobe, Deal, and Grace, CPAs, you have been asked to prepare a report on the *FASB Accounting Standards Codification*™ that will be circulated to all staff as part of the firm's continuing education program. It has been suggested that the report should cover why and how the Codification has come about and how and when to use it. You may also include other aspects of the topic you believe to be important.

Write the report as requested.

Exercise 11–2 [Financial]

Assume you are a recently hired accountant working for Growing Bigger, Inc., a national business consulting firm with ambitions to expand into an international market. The President of Growing, Elizabeth Golightly, calls you into her office with a request. She has been asked to participate in a seminar on international accounting standards and wants to update her knowledge of the topic. She asks you to research the topic, with emphasis on the position taken recently by U.S. agencies and other authorities. She would like to know what the arguments are in favor of international accounting standards, as well as the disadvantages, especially to businesses based in the United States. She is not asking you to take a position on whether the United States should endorse international accounting standards, but she does want a balanced report on the topic.

Ms. Golightly has asked you to research the topic and prepare a report for her, which she will use to help her prepare for her seminar participation. Respond to her request.

Exercise 11–3 [Auditing]

You are a member of the auditing staff of a medium-size CPA firm, Reid, Daniels, & Luke. One of the audit partners, Alan Daniels, has asked you to prepare a report addressing the topic of the use of data analytics technology both in external financial statement auditing and in internal auditing. He has heard that the use of such technology is revolutionizing how larger CPA firms conduct audits and does not want RD&L to fall behind. He is particularly interested in more fully understanding exactly what data analytics technology is and how RD&L can use it to provide better service to its clients. Mr. Daniels plans to circulate your report to all partners and managers in the firm.

Write a report for Mr. Daniels addressing his concerns.

Exercise 11–4 [Financial]

A client, Manuel Rodriguez, has just inherited some money and has decided to invest it in stock. He is not interested in mutual funds because he prefers to have personal control over his stock investments. He currently has a diversified portfolio of stock to which this new investment will be added. Your client wants to invest about $500,000, but in keeping with his conservative investing strategy, he wishes to keep his risk as low as possible.

Mr. Rodriguez has asked you to evaluate the most recent annual reports of several corporations as possible investment options. Choose three corporations whose stock is listed on the NYSE or the NASDAQ and whose annual reports you can study. Compare the information found in these reports and then write a report for Mr. Rodriguez that explains which of the companies is likely to be his best investment. Explain your conclusions thoroughly, quoting from the annual reports as necessary.

Exercise 11–5 [Auditing][1]

Saylor & Company is a brokerage firm registered under the Securities Exchange Act of 1934, which requires Saylor to file audited financial statements with the SEC annually. Your firm, O'Brien and Sherrill, Saylor's CPAs, performed the annual audit for the year ended December 31, 2017, and rendered an unqualified opinion, which was filed with the SEC along with Saylor's financial statements. During 2017, a Saylor employee engaged in a massive embezzlement scheme that eventually bankrupted the company and resulted in substantial losses suffered by its customers and shareholders, including some shareholders who had purchased shares of Saylor & Company after reviewing the company's 2017 audit report. O'Brien and Sherrill's audit was deficient; if it had fully complied with auditing standards, the embezzlement would have been discovered. However, the CPA firm had no knowledge of the embezzlement, and their conduct cannot be characterized as reckless.

Hugh O'Brien, partner-in-charge of O'Brien and Sherrill, has asked you to write a report discussing the different theories of liability available to the customers and stockholders of Saylor & Company under common law and what liability your firm may have under the Securities Exchange Act of 1934.

Write the report requested by Mr. O'Brien.

Exercise 11–6 [Systems]

Your employer, Nalley, Nellie, & Nicholson, CPAs, is considering the use of cloud-based systems to grow its business and better serve its clients. As one with some knowledge of information technology, you have been asked to prepare a report for the managing partners of your firm evaluating the pros and cons of cloud-based systems. Your managing partners have asked that you give specific attention to the ability of cloud-based solutions to cut costs, build client and employee relationships, improve the exchange of information with clients, and build sales capabilities and sales management. You have also been asked to address the issue of security of sensitive information that may be placed in the cloud.

Prepare the report for Peter Nalley, the managing partner of your firm.

Exercise 11–7 [Auditing]

As a staff member of Norton, Price, and Cummings, CPAs, you have been asked to prepare a report on "Materiality" that will be circulated to all staff as part of the firm's continuing education program. It has been suggested that the report should cover the definition of materiality, why the concept is important to auditing, and how to measure it. You should also discuss any other aspects of materiality you find important. Write the report as requested.

Exercise 11–8 [Tax]

You are on the financial staff of Governor James Cash, who is governor of a large state. He has been a prominent supporter of the flat tax idea for many years. Now, as governor, he is considering pushing for the adoption of a flat tax to replace the current progressive state income tax. He has asked you to prepare a report for him covering the pros and cons of a flat tax and how, if he decides to pursue the idea, he should respond to critics.

Write the report for Governor Cash.

Exercise 11–9 [Financial/Current Professional Issues]

You are a partner in a regional CPA firm, Swearingen & Gray, with 14 offices covering the Eastern United States. Your firm routinely publishes and distributes reports to its clients that cover current accounting and financial reporting topics. You have been asked by James Swearingen, the managing partner of your firm, to prepare such a report on the use of non-GAAP measurements in annual reports, an issue about which the SEC has recently voiced serious concern. In your report, Mr. Swearingen has asked you to cover these topics and others you consider important.

- What are some of the more commonly used non-GAAP measurements?
- Why is the SEC concerned about the use of such measurements?

Do the necessary research for this project and write the report for Mr. Swearingen.

NOTES

1. Adapted with permission from Arens, Alvin A., Rendal J. Elder, and Mark S. Beasley, *Auditing and Assurance Services: An Integrated Approach*, 15th ed. (Upper Saddle River, N.J.: Pearson Education, Inc., 2014), 139.

CHAPTER

E-Communication and Social Media

12

Learning Objectives

After studying this chapter, you should be able to

12.1 Communicate via email in a professional, effective manner.

12.2 Use electronic media for job searches and applications.

12.3 Explain the opportunities and risks of social media use within the accounting profession.

12.4 Compose effective blogs for accounting and business sites.

12.5 Use instant messaging and texts effectively.

12.6 Use telephone calls in an effective, courteous manner.

12.7 Explain situations when face-to-face communication is needed.

In earlier chapters, we discussed ways you can use technology to help you research accounting literature and then compose and revise business documents. This chapter focuses on how to use electronic media to communicate with others, both within the organization where you work and to those outside your firm or business, such as clients, other professionals, and agencies. The chapter also discusses how you can use electronic media in your search for employment.

Electronic communication, especially email, is now used almost universally for both personal and business use. In recent years, we've seen the advent and development of other media, such as social networks, instant messaging, text messaging, blogging, podcasting, and online video. Many of these media were originally developed primarily for personal communication, but they are now becoming more common in many business settings, including the profession of accounting.

This chapter discusses the effective use of email in business, with a look at social media and its role in the life of a professional accountant, including the search for employment. We will see that the principles of effective writing stressed throughout this text for traditional forms of communication apply to messages sent via electronic media as well.

You should plan what you write to achieve your intended purpose in a way that is appropriate to your audience; write in a style that is clear and concise, with main ideas that are easy to spot; and review what you've written to ensure that it is both correct and professional.

The chapter concludes with a section on telephone etiquette.

EMAIL

LO12.1   Communicate via email in a professional, effective manner.

In most businesses, emails have replaced paper memos for much of the written communication that takes place within the organization. Like hard-copy memos, emails may be brief or lengthy, formal or informal. An email may announce a meeting or arrange a lunch, request help on a project or provide detailed information about a business's activities. Emails may also be used to communicate with clients or other people outside the organization, as substitutes or supplements to hard-copy letters. You should give the emails you write to business associates the same care and attention you use whenever you write.

Composing the Email

When you write an email, follow the guidelines for effective writing discussed throughout this text. Think carefully about the purpose of the email: Do you want to respond to a request, make your own request, or provide information? Who will your readers be, and what will they expect from your email? Write the email in a concise, clear writing style and structure so that main ideas are easy to spot. Emails also call for a number of special considerations. Keep the following guidelines in mind as you compose the email.

Address Messages Carefully

We've all heard stories of messages being sent to unintended recipients. This often occurs when a memo is sent using a distribution list or some general address, rather than to an individual. The results are sometimes humorous, as when an employee invites the entire corporation to lunch; or they can be disastrous, as might occur when the plans for a new product are sent by mistake to the firm's competitors. The lesson is to "think twice and click once" when addressing an email.

When replying to an email that was sent using a distribution list, remember that if you click on the "reply to all" button instead of the "reply" button, your reply will be sent to the entire distribution list. Is that necessary or what you intend?

Finally, when you reply to an email, consider whether you need to include previous email exchanges or attachments with your current email message — a series of replies to replies. The default mode for many email programs reproduces and thus continues old email exchanges including attachments, which can go on for pages. If you don't have a good reason to include previous exchanges or attachments in your reply, reply to your correspondent with a fresh original email.

Write a Strong Subject Line

Write a short, powerful subject line with key words near the beginning, since your recipients' software may truncate the subject line when the message appears in their inbox. You want to catch readers' attention to ensure that they open and read your message. Compare the following subject lines:

Subject: Meeting

vs.

Subject: Required staff meeting May 19, 3 PM

Which subject line is more likely to ensure attendance at the meeting?

Begin with a Salutation

Most of your emails should begin with a salutation, especially if you're writing to only one person. While email salutations are usually informal, some situations, such as an email that serves as a cover letter for a résumé, call for a more formal salutation. The email shown in Figure 12–1, which is an informal message between colleagues, uses an informal salutation:

Hi Bob,

For a more formal situation, such as email connected with a job search, address your reader with the same formality you would use if you were talking with this person face-to-face:

FIGURE 12–1   Example of an Informal Email

From:	Jack Wilson <jwilson@whateversite.com>
To:	Robert Gonzalez <rgonzalez@whateversite.com>
Subject:	Lunch today?
Date:	Jan. 15, 2018

Hi Bob,

Do you have time for lunch today? This would give us a chance to discuss the Fairweather audit. I should be free by 12:30, and we could try the new brew pub down the street. Let me know if this works for you.

Jack

Dear Ms. Allison,

Note that a comma follows the salutation for both formal and informal emails.

As these examples show, the choice between a formal and informal salutation depends on the purpose of the email and your relationship with the recipient. The degree of informality within a firm or office may also reflect the culture of the organization, so you should look for models of customary usage in the emails you receive from others with whom you work.

Put Important Ideas First

The first line of your email should catch the readers' attention so that they will want to read the rest of your message. Begin with the most important information, from the readers' point of view, and progress to ideas of less importance. Remember that people often read email hurriedly, scanning for what is important and closing the email before they read it completely. Short paragraphs with clear topic sentences are especially important for longer emails, because they enable readers to spot important ideas quickly.

If you're replying to an email, your opening paragraph may refer to the email you received. If you're responding to a request, for example, you should mention that request specifically in your opening sentence.

Use Conventional Grammar and Mechanics

Follow conventional usage for grammar and mechanics, including standard spelling, punctuation, and capitalization. Avoid the codes often used for text messages sent via cell phone, such as all lower-case letters or abbreviations for frequently used words and phrases.

Use an Email Signature

Your email system will enable you to create a file with an automatic signature that you can use at the end of your emails. This signature will include such information as your name, position, firm or business, and contact information. For example,

Susan Reid
Audit Manager
Clifford, Sims & Rogers, CPAs
1822 Market Square
Pittsburgh, PA 15212
Phone: 412-867-7820

Use Attachments Carefully

Sometimes you may attach another document to an email, especially if you're conveying a great deal of information, or if you're transmitting a more formal or technical document, such as a report. When you use attachments, the cover email should be brief: Tell the recipient what is attached, and why it's important.

Attachments require some caution. First, be sure that the file you attach is the file you intend to send. Open the attached file from the email you've composed before you send the email to check that it is the correct file. Also, review the name of the file: Will it clearly identify the attachment's contents, and be suitable for your reader? Another safeguard is to follow up with your recipient to ensure that the attachment was actually received with your cover email.

Uses for Email: Informal or Formal?

Accountants use email for such a wide variety of purposes, and in so many situations, that the distinction between formal and informal is more a question of degree than a clear-cut difference. Email used for business will likely be more formal than purely social email, however, so you should write in Standard English, as clearly and concisely as possible, in a friendly, respectful tone that is appropriate to your reader.

As an example of an informal email that might be common within a business or firm, consider the email in Figure 12–1. This is being sent to one person only, but emails may be sent to several people or even an entire distribution list, if the information is relevant to a group. Figure 12–2 shows

---

FIGURE 12–2   Example of A More Formal Email Sent to a Distribution List

From:	Mary Ellen Parker <meparker@othersite.com>
To:	Staff <distribution list>
Subject:	Vacation Requests for Fiscal Year 2019
Date:	May 15, 2018
Attachment:	Vacation Request Form

In order that we may plan our staffing schedules for the upcoming fiscal year, we need to have everyone's vacation requests as soon as possible. Please complete the attached request form and return it to me no later than May 25.

Thank you very much for your help.

Mary Ellen Parker

Director of Human Resources
Big and Little, CPAs
111-222-3333
meparker@othersite.com

an example of a more formal email that might be sent to several departments, or even an entire organization via a distribution list.

You will notice that this email seems more formal than the lunch invitation in Figure 12–1, in keeping with the purpose of the second email and its wide distribution. The second email also contains an email signature at the close of the email.

Email Within an Organization

You probably recognize that standard email headings resemble the format of a memo: sender's name, recipient's name, subject line, and date. In fact, email has largely replaced paper memos for inter-office communication in most business settings. However, the guidelines for effective memos discussed in Chapter 10 apply as much to email used within an organization as they do to paper memos.

External Email

In the past, business correspondence addressed to recipients outside an office was always sent via the U. S. mail or some other delivery service. Today some external business correspondence, both letters and memos, is sent electronically. A major advantage of sending these documents electronically is of course the speed with which they are transmitted. The recipient can also reply quickly.

Business correspondence sent electronically carries risks, however. Security can be an issue. In addition, emails used in business, especially to people outside the writer's organization, are not always carefully written. As we've already seen, grammatical and mechanical conventions, such as correct spelling and punctuation, are as important for email as they are for documents sent in an envelope.

Email: A Few More Cautions

The use of email, while certainly convenient, requires caution. Be careful to do the following:

Compose Your Message as if It Will Be Read by Everyone
Remember that an email message may be read by people you do not intend to read it. Email messages are not private, and there are no "off-the-record" emails. Emails are sent over networks, where they can be easily intercepted.

All email messages are saved somewhere and can be used as proof that the communication took place. Usually, you are sending the email to record some information for the record, but occasionally people fall into the trap of treating email like a phone call. For example, they may say in an email something like "Steve thinks he's going to exercise

his options for $4,000, but it'll never happen as long as I'm the CFO."
Imagine how this CFO will feel if Steve turns up with a copy of the
email message. Again, the best advice is to assume that every email
message you write will be read by everyone else.

One more word of caution: Emails can be subpoenaed as evidence
in legal proceedings. Remember that nothing you post electronically,
whether an email, a text message, or a posting on any social media site, is
ever confidential. You must assume that your postings are permanently
available to whoever may have the time and resources to retrieve them.
You cannot delete them with assurance that there is no backup somewhere or that what you delete cannot be retrieved with software designed
to recover erased or deleted files. Never use emails to circulate gossip or
derogatory comments about another person or entity, nor to express anger
or frustration. Think carefully about anything you commit to cyberspace.

Review Before Sending

After you have composed your email, read it again slowly and carefully
to ensure that it is clear and correct. Check that the revisions you made
while composing actually show up on the screen as you intended them.
Depending on the word processing program you use, you may find that
the program's autocorrect function has introduced the wrong words
into your email, or changed the formatting. A few minutes' review can
prevent you from sending an email that is erroneous and unprofessional.

Avoid Sending Junk Email

Email resulting from forwarding jokes, humor, and other "items of
interest" that have little if any relevance to the work environment is a
form of junk email. You may find those photographs of baby animals
absolutely adorable, but they don't belong on the job. Save humor
and other nonbusiness items for people with whom you correspond
socially. Even if you are tempted to forward serious news items about
some topic related to your work, consider very seriously whether the
intended recipient will find them useful, or have the time to read them.

Email used for social correspondence, such as the email you
exchange with family or friends, can cause problems if you write or
receive it on the job. The computer on your desk, along with its supporting hardware and software, is the property of your employer, and
you should use it only for communication related to your professional
responsibilities. You should not, therefore, write or respond to personal email using the business's equipment. Recall also that all emails,
even those you delete, are saved somewhere in your employer's system. You don't want records of your personal life available for business
associates to access, even accidentally.

Many businesses have formal policies for the uses of email by their
employees. If your business has such a policy, you should of course
follow the rules carefully.

ELECTRONIC MEDIA AND EMPLOYMENT

LO12.2   Use electronic media for job searches and applications.

Electronic media have become an important tool for those seeking employment. In fact, some prospective employers require electronic submission of résumés, making paper résumés almost obsolete in some cases. You may also use the Internet, including business networking sites, to locate jobs for which you will apply. These sites may ask you to submit your résumé electronically, or they may require you to complete a profile that will be used to match your credentials and job objectives with prospective employers. Electronic media can help you find a good job, if you use it with care.

Use of Social Media for Job Searches

Electronic media enable you to access information about many jobs available in almost any location, and you can easily and quickly apply for the positions that interest you. In addition, electronic placement agencies and networking sites may enable prospective employers to identify you as someone they wish to interview. Many companies use social media and networking sites, such as LinkedIn, to find qualified candidates for employment. However, electronic media also carry serious risks for people seeking employment.

Employers have the same access to the Internet that you do. That means that they have access to what you've posted on the Web in other contexts, such as your postings to blogs, Twitter, YouTube, and Facebook. Many employers surf the Web to find out more about prospective employees than the information written on the résumé. Remember that for professional employment purposes you need to project a professional image. Also, remember that it is difficult, if not impossible, to separate your social image from your professional image on social media. This means that you should never post anything on social media that could conflict with your image as a professional.

Electronic Submission of Résumés

A prospective employer may ask you to submit your résumé via email. If you encounter this request, send the résumé as an attachment, using the cover email as a short letter of application. The cover email should identify specifically the position for which you're applying, summarize briefly your credentials, and refer to the complete résumé that you've attached. This cover email should be carefully composed, using a courteous, professional tone; it should also be written in Standard English using the guidelines discussed earlier in this book. Proofread the cover email carefully to make sure it's free of errors. Remember that this cover email may be your first opportunity to impress the prospective employer with your communication skills.

Since you will have prepared your résumé carefully, you will have a computer file that you can use for email submissions. You can also tailor your résumé to match the position for which you're applying.

Some employers, placement agencies, or networking sites may scan the résumés they receive into computer searchable databases, which they then search using industry-specific and job-specific key words in order to match applicants to specific positions. Include as many of those words as possible. Examples of key words you may wish to include when submitting a résumé for an accounting position include CMA, CPA, CGMA, auditing, tax, systems, cost, managerial, and locations you may be interested in, such as Atlanta, Chicago, Los Angeles, and New York. Also, include strong action words such as *achieved*, *improved*, *managed*, and *created*.

Chapter 14 provides additional information on the creation of an effective résumé and letter of application.

LinkedIn Profiles

One of the most widely used networking sites for business, including job searches and recruiting, is LinkedIn, and its use by companies seeking to hire accountants is on the rise. Creating a LinkedIn profile that will attract the notice of potential employers may be part of your search for employment.

The LinkedIn website specifies the information required for a profile. You will find much of the required information on your résumé, such as education, work experience, and skills. You will also be asked to supply a profile photograph. As you might imagine, the photograph should project a professional image.

It's important to follow the instructions for creating your profile. It should be as complete as possible, and you should update it often. Complete, current profiles are much more likely to result in job offers. You should also proofread your profile carefully to ensure that it is written in Standard English and is free of errors.

SOCIAL MEDIA USED IN THE ACCOUNTING PROFESSION

LO12.3 **Explain the opportunities and risks of social media use within the accounting profession.**

Social media, which many people use daily for personal communication, have become increasingly important in many business settings. Even networking sites that were originally designed for strictly social interaction, such as Facebook, have been adapted for some business purposes, such as recruiting, training, and market research.

If you are employed by a firm that embraces the use of social media, use it carefully. Compose written messages posted on social media with the same attention to detail you use for all business writing, including the use of Standard English.

Many companies have policies about their employees' use of social media. These policies specify the information and opinions that employees may, and may not, share via the Internet. Some of the prohibited material is obvious, such as classified or proprietary information about the business or its clients or associates. Some businesses also caution employees about saying anything negative about the business itself or the people who work there. This means that if you're upset about something that has happened on the job, or angry with your boss, you should not vent through email, Facebook, Twitter, or any other form of social media. Violation of a business's social media policy can result in termination, so you should become aware of its policy and use discretion about what you say on the Internet.

Once you are working in an accounting position, you may need to adjust your use of social media to be even more careful of potential misuse. Some companies may require their employees to maintain separate accounts for their personal and professional communication. They may also caution their employees to be especially discreet in making social connections so that they will maintain a professional public image.

ACCOUNTING BLOGS

LO12.4   Compose effective blogs for accounting and business sites.

In recent years, blogs (a shortened word for *weblogs*) have become more common within the profession of accounting. Blogs, which may be hosted by an organization or by an individual, enable users to communicate in a timely way on topics of common interest. They can be updated frequently, and many blogs allow readers to respond to the information and opinions posted, thus generating a conversation.Examples of blogs dealing with accounting topics are included among the online accounting publications shown in Figure 15–2 on pages 274–275.

Writing for a blog may be a good way for you to network with other accountants and business professionals who share your interests. If you decide to write a blog posting or join in a blog conversation, remember to review your employer's policy on social media, as we've already discussed. In addition to following your employer's policies, take care that what you say, and how you say it, projects a professional image. Remember that once something is posted to a blog, it is available to everyone and will last forever.

Tips for Writing Blogs

Once you've decided to write for a blog, keep these general guidelines in mind:

Review What Has Already Been Written on the Topic

Read what other people have already written on your topic so that what you write for the blog will be timely and responsive to what others have said. You may also want to review recent publications on the topic that have appeared in other news outlets, both print and electronic publications. Remember to document any sources you use to give credit for ideas and information that are not your own.

Plan What You Want to Say

As with other forms of professional writing, you should first consider the purpose of your writing and the main ideas you want to convey. An outline will help you organize your ideas.

Consider Your Audience

Analyze the readers of the blog so that you write about topics that they will find interesting and relevant. Write in a style that is appropriate for your readers, at a technical level they will understand. As a general rule, blog postings are written in an informal, conversational style.

Organize Your Thoughts

When you write a blog posting, begin with a brief introduction to introduce your main idea(s). Short paragraphs with strong topic sentences and transitions, as needed, will ensure that readers find your posting easy to read and understand.

Write Clear, Descriptive Headlines

You want to catch your readers' attention so that they read your blog posting.

Keep It Short

Blog postings are meant to be brief. Consult previous postings at the site you're using to get an idea about the preferred length for that site.

Edit Your Blog Posting Before You Post

Be sure that you've written in a clear, readable style. Like all professional writing, blog postings should be written in Standard English and proofread carefully before posting.

INSTANT MESSAGING AND TEXTING

LO12.5 Use instant messaging and texts effectively.

Like blogging, instant messaging and texting are becoming more common within the accounting profession. The extent to which you use them for professional communication will depend on your situation and your firm's policy.

Instant messaging, in which brief messages appear automatically on users' computer screens, may be used for both internal and external communication. It may be a stand-alone program or embedded into social networks, office software, or other platforms.

When you write a message that will be posted as an instant message, use the same principles of effective communication you use for all your writing. Many business people expect instant messages to be written in Standard English, rather than with abbreviations, acronyms, and other jargon more typically found in the messages exchanged in personal communication.

Instant messages are not the place for exchanging confidential information, unless you're using a secure server. Nor should you use them for personal communication as long as you're working in a business setting.

Texting, which uses a cell phone network to transmit brief written messages, is widely used socially and may be acceptable for some business uses. However, some people regard texting as too informal for professional use, and the language often used to text, with its many abbreviations, acronyms, and emoticons, may detract from a professional image.

As with all forms of electronic communication and social media, you should evaluate your particular work environment to see if texting is consistent with its culture. Recall the tip stressed throughout this book: Write with your audience in mind. If your audience expects you to text, then that's what you should do. But take care in composing even the briefest text to ensure that it's courteous and clear and maintains a professional image. Recall too that some professionals, including accountants, may expect texts to be written in Standard English. Here again you should write according to your reader's expectations.

It's also worth noting that as in the case of email, text messages do not disappear when deleted. So many of the same cautions relating to the use of email also apply to text messaging.

TELEPHONE ETIQUETTE

LO12.6 Use telephone calls in an effective, courteous manner.

Telephone conversations are an essential component of business, including the business of an accountant. Well-conducted telephone conversations can ensure smooth working relationships with clients, fellow professionals, and others within the business community. At the same time, careless, discourteous phone calls can ruin professional relationships. Here are some tips for using the telephone effectively.

Making a Call

Before you make call, know what you need to say. For some conversations, it may be a good idea to outline the questions you want to ask or the information you're looking for. If necessary, you can write notes in your outline as you're talking so that you remember what's important.

When you've reached the person with whom you wish to speak, introduce yourself, using your first and last name, and identify the company or firm for whom you work. Speak with courtesy and respect, in a pleasant tone of voice. If you're not sure you've understood something completely or correctly, paraphrase what you've heard so that the person can repeat or modify the information, if necessary.

Always thank the other person for taking the time to talk with you.

Receiving a Call

When you receive a call, give your caller your complete attention, and listen carefully. Don't try to accomplish some other task, such as working on your computer, during the call. Take notes so that you'll remember important points. Speak in a courteous, respectful manner with a pleasant, professional tone of voice.

Conference Calls

Always identify yourself by name before you speak during a conference call, every time you speak. Find a quiet place removed from background noise from which to speak, and when you're not speaking, mute your phone so that other callers won't hear background noise from your location. Listen carefully as others speak, taking notes as necessary. Treat the conference call as you would a meeting and always be respectful.

Cell Phones

Cell phones are a great convenience, but they too, like most social media, can cause problems in a business environment, most of which result from their use at inappropriate times. As a general rule, you should turn the phone off if you're having a conversation with a client, coworker, or other professional. In most cases, this means turning the phone completely off, not just setting it on "vibrate."

When you're talking with others, they deserve your undivided attention. Even the vibration of a silent phone can distract you, so that you don't listen carefully to what the other person is saying. Turning your cell phone completely off may also be desirable to avoid embarrassing interruption by alert tones from incoming emails, text messages, and so on.

The advice to leave your cell phone turned off will have exceptions. If you're expecting an urgent call on a business matter, you may need to leave the phone in its vibrating mode. The polite way to handle a situation where you may have to take a call is to alert the person with whom you're meeting that the call may come, and apologize if you have to interrupt the conversation. In truth, there are very few situations that justify letting a phone call interrupt a face-to-face conversation.

A FINAL WORD: SOMETIMES FACE-TO-FACE IS BETTER

LO12.7   Explain situations when face-to-face communication is needed.

In spite of the advantages and widespread use of electronic communication, it may be better to convey some messages in person. This may be particularly true if the communication involves a disagreement or is in some other way sensitive or difficult. If you communicate in person, you will be able to read the person's body language. Facial expressions or other body movements that aren't detectible over the phone or through a text message or email can alert you to how the other person is reacting to what you've said, as well as whether you've been understood. This may give you the chance to adjust your message or tone and avoid unintended complications, such as offending a client or damaging a working relationship with an employee or colleague.

EXERCISES

Exercise 12–1 [General]

You are the managing partner in the local firm of Mueller, Britt, & Little, CPAs. It has come to your attention that several employees, both professional and support staff, have recently begun wearing political buttons, displaying political posters in the office, and texting political jokes and quips.

Your firm uses an in-house instant messaging system. Write a draft for an instant message to be circulated to all personnel in your firm explaining that such political activity should cease and explaining why it is inappropriate.

Exercise 12–2 [General]

You are a partner in the CPA firm of Gregory & Rush. Recently you have noticed that your inbox on the local area network in your company accumulates ten to fifteen messages a day that are jokes and humorous stories downloaded from the Internet. These messages all take time to delete, and sometimes in the process of deleting them, you delete important messages by mistake. Clearly the situation has gotten out of hand. Write an email to the staff about the problem and ask that the practice of distributing humorous email messages be discontinued. Be sure to explain your reasoning so you won't come across as dictatorial.

Exercise 12–3 [Systems]

Assume you are a newly hired staff accountant in a local accounting firm, Johnson, Park, and Gonzalez (JPG). One of JPG's partners, Francis Park, stopped you in the hall with a question. He said he has read something about "cloud accounting," and he wants to learn more about what this term means. He's heard a rumor that some accounting firms are using this technology in their practices, and he wonders whether JPG should get on board—what the advantages would be, if any, as well as the risks.

Mr. Park asks you to research his concern about "cloud accounting" and send him your findings by email. Depending on the amount of information you find in your research, you may decide to summarize your findings in a report and send it as an attachment, with an appropriate cover email.

Exercise 12–4 [Financial]

You are newly hired as an accountant for the Regal Condominium Association, a condominium owners association with approximately 200 condo units. The Association is currently using the cash basis of accounting. The president, Brenda Galina, has asked that you explain what the accrual basis of accounting is, how it differs from the cash basis, and whether the Regal Condominium Association should switch from the cash basis to the accrual basis.

Write an email to Ms. Galina that answers her questions. You will need to identify the facts and issues the association should consider before making the decision. Invent any facts necessary to do this. If you find that your explanation will be lengthy, consider writing it as an attachment, with a cover email.

Exercise 12–5 [Auditing]

You are the managing partner of a medium-size CPA firm with several publicly traded clients. One of your partners, John DeFries, has served as lead partner for the audit engagement of Rousch Industries, a publicly traded client, for the last five years. He has just gotten the word that he will be replaced in that capacity by another partner beginning with next year's audit and is quite upset over this situation. He has emailed you arguing that he has invested years getting to know Rousch's business operations and is therefore the best qualified partner to lead the audit. He feels he is being penalized for some reason he does not understand.

Write an email to Mr. DeFries explaining the requirements of the Sarbanes-Oxley Act and the SEC regarding audit partner rotation and assuring him that he is not being penalized for anything.

Exercise 12–6 [Auditing/Ethics]

You are an audit partner of a small CPA firm. One of the audit managers who works for you, Alan Robinson, has emailed you about a prospective audit client, Stanley Thornton, with whom he has been talking. Mr. Robinson is concerned because the prospective client has made it clear that if he hires your firm he will expect your firm to be his advocate and always act in his best interests. In other words, Mr. Thornton expects your firm to be in a relationship with him similar to the relationship he has with his attorney. Alan Robinson is a little uncomfortable with that expectation, but does not know how to respond. He is seeking your advice. Reply to Mr. Robinson's email advising him to discuss the necessity for independence in the audit, the broader responsibilities of a CPA firm, and how CPA firms differ from other professionals in that regard. Elaborate upon these issues, giving Mr. Robinson some ideas of how to explain them to Mr. Thornton.

Exercise 12–7 [Managerial/Ethics]

As the newly appointed CFO of Celebrity Manufacturing, Inc., a medium-size publicly traded company doing business in North America and Europe, you have decided to further the development of a code of ethical conduct for accounting and finance employees in the company. Write an email to members of upper management encouraging them to attend a meeting on September 12th to organize a task force that will write the code. Explain why you think the development of such a code is desirable.

Exercise 12–8 [Managerial/Systems]

You are a managerial accountant in a large manufacturing company with over fifty branches around the world. The controller of your company, John Hipps, has recently heard about a kind of database called "blockchain" and how it might be much more secure than the kind of database technology the company currently uses. He has asked you to briefly tell him what "blockchain" is and why it might be more secure. Write an email to Mr. Hipps responding to his inquiry. Invent any information you may think is necessary to complete your email.

CHAPTER 13

Writing for Exams: Professional Certification and Academic Exams

---

Learning Objectives

After studying this chapter, you should be able to

13.1 Summarize the writing components contained in professional certification exams: CPA, CMA, and CGMA.

13.2 Write successful responses for professional certification exams: time management and content organization.

13.3 Write successful responses on academic exams that contain a writing component.

13.4 Explain the importance of both technical mastery and writing skills on certification and academic exams.

The importance of writing skills to the successful practice of accounting has been clearly documented, as we saw in Chapter 1. This chapter discusses the importance of writing skills on both professional certification and academic exams and suggests ways you can succeed on exams that require written responses.

PROFESSIONAL CERTIFICATION EXAMS

LO13.1   Summarize the writing components contained in professional certification exams: CPA, CMA, and CGMA.

Because writing skills are essential for success in an accounting career, accounting professional certification exams evaluate writing skills as well as technical competencies. The American Institute of Certified Public Accountants (AICPA) has tested writing skills on the Uniform

CPA Examination since 1994. Since 2013, written communication tasks have comprised 15 percent of the total score for the Business Environment and Concept (BEC) section of the CPA exam. Since 2012, the IMA (formerly the Institute of Management Accountants) has tested writing skills on the Certified Management Accountant (CMA) exam. And in 2014 the AICPA, in cooperation with the Chartered Institute of Management Accountants (CIMA), announced that it would require written answers as part of the Chartered Global Management Accountant (CGMA) designation. These answers are written in the form of emails, reports, memos, briefing notes, or discussion papers.[1] Thus, as the requirements for certification exams make clear, your professional future as an accountant depends on your ability to write well.

This chapter will look at these professional exams, including the criteria used to test candidates' mastery of effective writing. We'll discuss how to write responses to exam questions that show your mastery of the technical content as well as your writing skills. The advice given for the certification exams will work equally well for academic courses, when exams in those courses call for a written response. You will see that the criteria of effective writing tested on professional and academic exams are the same qualities stressed throughout this text: coherent organization, with main ideas that are easy to identify; adequate development of main ideas; a clear, concise writing style; precise vocabulary and Standard English.

Writing for the CPA Exam[2]

The BEC section of the CPA exam includes questions that require what the AICPA calls "constructed responses." These questions specify the format the constructed response should take, usually that of a typical business document such as a memo or letter. You will write your constructed responses using a word processor with a spell checker. The spell checker will help you identify and correct some misspelled words, but not all of them; for example, a spell checker will not discriminate between homonyms like *their* and *there*. The word processor will also make your editing and revision easier.

The specific writing skills tested on the CPA exam include these:[3]

- *Organization:* Structure, order of ideas, and connecting ideas, including using an overview or thesis statement, unified paragraphs, and transitions and connectives.
- *Development:* The use of supporting evidence and information to clarify thoughts, including using details, definitions, examples, and rephrasing.
- *Expression:* The use of Standard English including grammar, punctuation, word usage, capitalization, and spelling.

The AICPA has also specified that the written response should be accurate, clear, complete, and professional. Candidates are expected to respond directly to the topic identified in the question and will not receive credit for answers that are either off-topic or clearly illegal.

You should recognize from the above description of the exam that a successful response to a writing task requires skills that go beyond the ability to write well or understand the relevant accounting concepts. Specifically, you will need to read the question carefully and follow directions. In addition, you will need to use your higher order thinking skills, including analysis and evaluation. In fact, your ability to read carefully, follow directions, and think critically will affect your ability to succeed on the CPA exam in questions and tasks that don't explicitly evaluate writing skills.

The AICPA has identified judgment and problem-solving skills, among others, as important for success on the CPA exam.[4] Candidates should be able to:

- Develop and understand goals, objectives, and strategies for dealing with potential issues, obstacles, or opportunities.
- Analyze patterns of information and contextual factors to identify potential problems and their implications.
- Devise and implement a plan of action appropriate for a given problem.
- Apply professional skepticism, which is an attitude that includes a questioning mind and a critical assessment of information or evidence obtained.
- Adapt strategies or planned actions in response to changing circumstances.
- Identify and solve unstructured problems.
- Develop reasonable hypotheses to answer a question or resolve a problem.
- Formulate and examine alternative solutions in terms of their relative strengths and weaknesses, level of risk, and appropriateness for a given situation.
- Develop creative ways of thinking about situations, problems, and opportunities to create insightful and sound solutions.
- Develop logical conclusions through the use of inductive and deductive reasoning.
- Apply knowledge of professional standards and laws, as well as legal, ethical, and regulatory issues.
- Assess the need for consultations with other professionals when gray areas, or areas requiring specialized knowledge, are encountered.

The ability to analyze problems, think critically, and make sound judgments will thus be essential to your success on all parts of the CPA exam, not just the sections requiring written responses. These skills are stressed throughout this text, especially in Chapter 7, "Thinking on the Job: Higher Order Thinking Skills," and Chapter 8, "Accounting Research."

Figure 13–1 shows a sample question provided by the AICPA, typical of those that might appear on the CPA exam. This question requires a constructed response. Several features of this question, and the accompanying instructions, are worthy of note. The question appears in the form of a hypothetical business case scenario. The answer must be written in the form of a typical business document to a specific reader, in this case a memo addressed to the president of a company. The answer must be helpful to that reader and specifically address the issues raised in the question. The answer must also illustrate writing skills the AICPA has identified as important, that is, development, organization, and the appropriate expression of ideas in professional correspondence.

But note this restriction: The instructions state that you should not use a table or bulleted list to present the information in the memo. While bulleted lists and tables are often effective in business writing, the AICPA does not want them on the CPA exam. Therefore, you should follow the AICPA's instructions precisely.

By way of contrast, however, bulleted lists may be appropriate on the CMA exam, as we will see in the following section.

FIGURE 13–1   Sample CPA Exam Question Requiring a Constructed Response[5]

SkyView Inc., a small startup company, has hired you as a consultant to assess its financial systems and related processes. During your review, you learn that the company's accountant is responsible for providing general ledger access to others in the company, processing all financial transactions in the general ledger, and printing checks. The president of the company must authorize write-offs in the system, but the accountant has access to the president's username and password.

Prepare a memo to SkyView's president assessing these responsibilities in the context of segregation of duties. Also address the possibility of the accountant committing fraud.

Type your communication in the response area below the horizontal line using the word processor provided.

REMINDER: Your response will be graded for both technical content and writing skills. Technical content will be evaluated for information that is helpful to the intended reader and clearly relevant to the issue. Writing skills will be evaluated for development, organization, and the appropriate expression of ideas in professional correspondence. Use a standard business memorandum or letter format with a clear beginning, middle, and end. Do not convey information in the form of a table, bullet point list, or other abbreviated presentation.

Writing for the CMA Exam

Writing skills and critical thinking skills are also essential for success on the CMA exam. According to the IMA, the CMA exam tests for a candidate's ability "to analyze, evaluate, and communicate,"[6] as well as a candidate's mastery of accounting concepts and technical skills. As you will surely recognize, analysis and evaluation are components of higher order thinking skills, so the IMA is stressing both thinking skills and writing as essential to the successful practice of management accounting.

Candidates for the CMA designation answer four questions requiring written responses on the exam. The IMA has stressed that each answer must be relevant to the question asked. Thus, your ability to read carefully and follow directions will be essential to receiving credit for your answer. In addition, the IMA will evaluate these specific writing skills:[7]

- *Use of Standard English:* proper grammar, punctuation, and spelling
- *Organization:* logical and coherent arrangement of ideas
- *Clarity:* clear communication of analysis and recommendation(s), if any, with well-constructed sentences and appropriate vocabulary

Figure 13–2 shows a sample question from a CMA exam, with two possible answers that would receive full credit. Study these examples to see how they fulfill the requirements of the exam:

- Both answers are relevant to the question asked.
- Both answers are arranged logically and coherently, and main ideas are easy to identify. Each answer begins with a thesis statement that summarizes the answer and directly answers the question. Additional paragraphs form the body of the answer; each paragraph begins with a topic sentence and explains one part of the answer.
- Sentences are clearly and correctly constructed, with appropriate word choices. They have been edited and proofread so that they are free of misspelled words and other errors.
- Sample Answer 2 also uses a technique of document design—set-off lists. Notice that these lists are constructed with parallel grammatical structure; that is, all items in the lists are noun phrases.

Written responses to CMA exam questions should take 5 to 10 minutes to complete. Some questions can be answered in one or two well-constructed sentences. Other questions may require candidates to write brief essays, such as the answers shown in Figure 13–2. Candidates will type these written responses into a text box on a computer screen. Note that bulleted lists are permitted in answers to the CMA exam, unlike answers to the CPA exam or CGMA exam.

FIGURE 13–2   Sample CMA Exam Question Requiring a Written Response[8]

Sample Question

Identify and describe the two fundamental types of internal audits, and give two examples of each.

Sample Answer 1

The two types of internal audits are operational audits and compliance audits.

An operational audit is a review of the functions within an enterprise to evaluate the efficiency of operations and the effectiveness with which those functions achieve their objective. An example would be an audit to assess productivity. Another example would be an evaluation of processes to reduce rework.

A compliance audit is the review of both financial and operation controls to confirm that they conform to established laws, standards, and proce-dures. An environmental audit would be an example of a compliance audit. An examination of the company's investment portfolio to assess whether the credit ratings of issuers conform to investment policies would be another example of a compliance audit.

Sample Answer 2

There are two types of internal audits: operational and compliance audits.

Operational audits are reviews of operations to ensure efficiency and effectiveness. Examples include:

- Process efficiency review.
- Productivity review.

Compliance audits review controls to ensure compliance with regulatory guidelines, policies, and procedures. Examples include:

- Review of legal contracts to ensure compliance with contractual obligations.
- Review of bond covenant agreements to make sure the company is meet-ing requirements.

Writing for the CGMA Exam[9]

The CGMA designation and exam are offered by the Association of International Certified Professional Accountants, a joint venture of the AICPA in the United States and CIMA in Great Britain. The CGMA exam is designed to test competency in skills required to be an effec-tive financial and business strategist. These skills, as outlined in the CGMA Competency Framework,[10] include technical skills, business skills, leadership skills, and people skills. Successful CGMA candidates must demonstrate in their exam answers proficiency in all four types of skills; that is, demonstration of proficiency in any one skill category, such as in technical skills, will not be enough.

The CGMA exam is a case study exam requiring written answers to questions using various stipulated formats including reports, emails, briefing notes, memos, and discussion papers. The exam will require completion of three to six tasks related to a single business case. Although you will be given guidance about how to allot your time for these tasks, time management will be important. Each task will require a written response in one of the formats listed above and will test for several specific communication skills, including these:

- Identification of appropriate audience and purpose.
- Preparing and presenting verbal information that is accurate, clear, and concise using language and tone that are appropriate to the intended audience. Earlier chapters of this book discuss the formats that you may be required to use for written responses on the CGMA exam.

TAKING A PROFESSIONAL CERTIFICATION EXAM

LO13.2   Write successful responses on professional certification exams: time management and content organization.

Preparing for professional certification examinations is much more involved than studying for an exam in an academic course. You will study many long hours, perhaps with the help of an exam review text or course. The types of questions you are asked on the written portions of those exams may resemble those in your course exams, perhaps to explain a concept, describe a process, analyze a situation, or solve the problem of a hypothetical client. Exam questions may also resemble the writing assignments you completed as part of your course work, or possibly some of the more technical writing assignments included in this text.

Taking a certification exam may cause you anxiety, and the written responses asked for may seem especially daunting. We offer tips below to help you succeed in the examination, including ways to reduce the stress through time management. We also discuss strategies for reading the questions and planning your response, writing your answer, and editing for correct language. You can learn how to write an answer so that you receive full credit for what you know.

Manage Your Time

The pressure caused by the time constraints in a professional examination pose a challenge. You can meet this challenge, and reduce stress, if you manage the time you have to complete the required response. The key is to budget your time so that you can plan, write, and revise your answer.

First, take a few minutes to read the question carefully to be sure you know what is being asked. Underline key phrases in the question so that your answer won't overlook something important. Then jot down the main ideas you want to include in the answer. Put numbers by these ideas or draw arrows to arrange them in the most effective order. You might budget 1 to 5 minutes to plan your answer, depending on the total time you have for your response.

The next step, writing your answer, should take most of the remaining time. In this stage, you will write in well-organized paragraphs with main ideas that are easy to spot. You need an overview or thesis statement for the entire response, which should come at or near the beginning of your response. Then develop supporting paragraphs with relevant details—pertinent facts from the question, definitions, examples, and rephrasing, as the exam specifies. Paragraphs should be unified, devoted to the development of one idea. The main idea of a paragraph will appear at the beginning of the paragraph as the topic sentence, with appropriate transitions that achieve a coherent flow of thought.

As you compose your response, write as well as you can, but don't get stuck looking for the perfect word or phrase if it doesn't come quickly. The most important objective is to get the ideas down on paper to get credit for what you know. Write as well as you can, and keep going.

Finally, allow time to edit your answer. When you edit, check that all words are correctly spelled and that sentences are grammatically correct and clearly constructed.

Time is a big factor in answering the written components of professional exams, so use it wisely. Budget your time so that you can plan, write, and then revise.

Use the Exam Question to Organize the Response

We saw above that you should write in short paragraphs with strong topic sentences, enabling exam graders to identify your main ideas. The question itself can suggest the wording of the topic sentences or subheadings. The sample question and answers from the CMA exam in Figure 13–2 illustrate this approach to organizing your response. CGMA practice exams and answers which also illustrate this approach are available at www.cgma.org/becomeacgma/program-overview.html#?tab-1=3.

WRITING RESPONSES FOR ACADEMIC EXAMS

LO13.3 **Write successful responses on academic exams that contain a writing component.**

Some of the academic courses you will take in preparation for your career may also require you to write responses as part of a course exam. Sometimes these exams are called essay exams, or discussion questions. The writing you do for these exams will help prepare you for the certification exams you will take later.

Preparation

Although much of your studying for an objective examination will also help prepare you for questions requiring a written response, such as an essay or discussion question, you need to do a different kind of studying as well. Remember that these questions will require that you show a mastery of ideas. You may be asked to explain a concept, compare or contrast two methods of doing something, evaluate alternative treatments for a given situation, or justify a recommendation. Therefore, when you are studying for an exam, you should note concepts and explanations that would lend themselves to this type of question.

When you prepare for an exam, outline topics that may be subject to questions that call for a written response. When your outlines are ready, review them and try to guess questions that might appear on the exam. Then outline the information you would include in your answers to those questions.

Taking the Exam

Composing a written response is easier if you have a strategy for using your time and composing your answer. For some exams you may hand write your answers, or you may answer the exam question on a computer. This strategy works for either situation.

Budget Your Time

Managing your time well is a crucial part of your strategy. Budget the time you have to accomplish the three steps of the writing process: planning, writing, and revising. For example, if you have 30 minutes, allow 5 minutes to read the question carefully and plan your response, 20 to write, and the final 5 minutes to revise.

Organize Your Answer

The goal for organizing your answer is to help the grader read it easily so that you will receive full credit for what you know. Thus, you should apply one of the primary recommendations emphasized throughout this book: Use summary sentences so that your main ideas stand out. The key is to begin the answer with a thesis statement and to use topic sentences at the beginning of each paragraph.

The thesis statement should echo the question and summarize the main ideas of your answer. Suppose you find this question on an exam:

Explain the matching concept in accounting.

Your answer to this question might begin this way:

> The matching concept is used to determine what expense amounts should appear in the income statement for a particular period.

For short discussion questions, your answer might be only one paragraph long. In this case, the thesis statement for the answer would also function as the topic sentence for the paragraph. For more extensive questions, organize your answer into several paragraphs, each discussing one aspect of your answer. Each paragraph will have a topic sentence that provides a transition from the last paragraph, where needed, and that summarizes the main idea to be discussed in the new paragraph. Suppose you're asked this question on an exam:

> Discuss how the definition of an asset changed after the Accounting Principles Board was replaced by the Financial Accounting Standards Board.

Your answer might be organized like this:

> **Thesis (first paragraph of your answer):**
>
> When the Financial Accounting Standards Board replaced the Accounting Principles Board, it switched the focus of income determination from the Expense/Revenue View to the Asset/Liability View.
>
> **Topic sentence for paragraph 2:**
>
> Under the Expense/Revenue View previously taken by the Accounting Principles Board, assets were merely debit balances left over after deciding the proper amount of expenses to match with revenues in the income statement.
>
> **Topic sentence for paragraph 3:**
>
> Under the Asset/Liability View favored by the Financial Accounting Standards Board, net income is determined by directly measuring changes in the value of net assets adjusted for changes resulting from owners' equity transactions.

One final reminder about organization: When deciding how many paragraphs to use for your answer, remember that readers usually find shorter paragraphs easier to read, as long as you provide adequate transitions so that they can follow your train of thought.

Use Document Design

Sometimes the best way to include several points in your answer in a minimum amount of time is to use the document design principles explained in Chapter 6, especially set-off lists and headings. One of the sample answers to a CMA exam question shown in Figure 13–1 uses set-off lists. (Remember, however, not to use a set-off list on the CPA exam!) For a longer written response especially, headings may be a good way to divide your answer into its main components. If you are required to produce a memo or letter, be sure to follow the design principles discussed in Chapters 9 and 10.

Qualities of a Good Written Response

The discussion so far has already suggested several qualities of an effective answer to a question requiring a written response. Here is a summary of those qualities, plus a few additional pointers:

- If you hand write an answer, your handwriting should be legible and your pages neat and easy to read. Corrections, additions, and deletions should be made as neatly as possible.
- Main ideas should be easy to identify; the flow of thought should be easy for the grader to follow.
- Answer the question directly and completely. Supply adequate details and examples to support your assertions.
- Sentences should be concise, clear, and readable. Grammatical and mechanical errors should not distract the reader.

EFFECTIVE WRITING AND TECHNICAL MASTERY: BOTH IMPORTANT

LO13.4 Explain the importance of both technical mastery and writing skills on certification and academic exams.

To succeed in an exam that asks for a written response requires that you master technical accounting content, of course. Success also depends on your mastery of the effective writing and higher order thinking skills stressed throughout this text.

Like business document readers, exam graders want written responses to be coherent (main ideas easy to identify, flow of thought easy to follow), concise (no wasted words), and clear (no guesswork about meaning, no distractions caused by grammatical and mechanical errors). Thus, the writing skills emphasized in this book apply to professional certification and academic exams as well as to more common forms of business writing.

EXERCISES

Exercise 13–1 [Managerial]

Write an essay comparing and contrasting traditional and activity-based costing (ABC) systems. How do ABC systems provide value to a business's management?

Exercise 13–2 [Auditing]

There is often misunderstanding about the responsibilities of independent auditors when they audit a client's financial statements. Write an essay discussing those responsibilities and the degree of confidence users should have that audited financial statements are free of material misstatements and fraud. Include a discussion of the responsibility of management for the same financial statements.

Exercise 13–3 [Auditing]

The International Auditing and Assurance Standards Board (IAASB) has been actively involved in recasting old standards and casting new standards in a form that is intended to be clearer and easier to read and understand. Write an essay discussing the relationship between the IAASB and the Auditing Standards Board (ASB) in the U.S. and how this effort of the IAASB may affect the output of the ASB. Your essay should be long enough to cover the important issues involved.

Exercise 13–4 [Tax]

Write an essay discussing the important tax and legal advantages and disadvantages in organizing a business as either a partnership, an S Corporation, or a Limited Liability Company.

Exercise 13–5 [Financial]

Write an essay discussing the various valuation bases used in GAAP, for example, historical cost, fair market value, liquidation value, replacement value, depreciated or amortized cost, and so on. For each basis in your discussion, cover its definition, describe in general terms when it is proper to use it, and critique the advantages and disadvantages of its use. Address the issue of why we should (or should not) use so many different valuation bases in GAAP. Is it accurate to claim that GAAP is still based on historical cost?

Exercise 13–6 [Financial/International]

Write an essay discussing the advantages and disadvantages of adopting International Financial Reporting Standards (IFRS) in the United States. Assuming IFRS are adopted, include in your essay a discussion of the pros and cons of using a convergence approach versus a "condorsement" approach to adoption.

NOTES

1. See "The CGMA Exam Handbook," www.cgma.org/BecomeACGMA/CGMAexam/DownloadableDocuments/CGMA-exam-handbook.pdf. (4 Mar. 2017).

2. Much of the information in this section is from American Institute of Certified Public Accountants, "Written Communication." www.aicpa.org/BecomeACPA/CPAExam/ForCandidates/HowToPrepare/Pages/Written-Communication.aspx (4 Mar. 2017).

3. For a complete guide to the overall content of the exam, see American Institute of Certified Public Accountants, "Content and Skill Specifications for The Uniform CPA Examination" Approved May 15 2009; Update Approved May 28, 2015; Effective January 1, 2017. www.aicpa.org/becomeacpa/cpaexam/examinationcontent/contentandskills/downloadabledocuments/csos-ssos-effective-jan-2017.pdf (4 Mar. 2017).

4. American Institute of Certified Public Accountants, "Content and Skill Specifications for the Uniform CPA Examination" Approved May 15 2009; Update Approved May 28, 2015; Effective January 1, 2017. www.aicpa.org/becomeacpa/cpaexam/examinationcontent/contentandskills/downloadabledocuments/csos-ssos-effective-jan-2017.pdf (4 Mar. 2017), 37-38. The bulleted list of skills that follows is a direct quotation from this document.

5. American Institute of Certified Public Accountants, "The Uniform CPA Examination Sample Tests" https://sampletests.aicpa.org:8443/Citrix/STWeb/clients/HTML5Client/src/SessionWindow.html?launchid=1488652908795 (4 Mar. 2017).

6. William Cordes, Director of Exam Administration for the IMA, personal email (15 May 2013).

7. William Cordes, Director of Exam Administration for the IMA, personal email (15 May 2013).

8. William Cordes, Director of Exam Administration for the IMA, personal email (15 May 2013).

9. For a complete guide to overall content of the exam, see "The CGMA Exam Handbook," www.cgma.org/BecomeACGMA/CGMAexam/DownloadableDocuments/CGMA-exam-handbook.pdf. (4 Mar. 2017).

10. See www.cgma.org/Resources/Tools/DownloadableDocuments/competency-framework-complete.pdf (4 Mar. 2017).

Writing for Employment: Résumés and Letters of Application

Learning Objectives

After studying this chapter, you should be able to

14.1 Begin your job search by researching potential employers.

14.2 Prepare effective materials you will use in your job search: résumé, letter of application, thank-you letter.

Finding a job after graduation is a concern for most accounting students and some accountants who already have their degrees. Your communication skills can be a tremendous asset in finding that job. In fact, an applicant's communication skills may be the *single most important factor* in employers' hiring decisions. This chapter focuses on several important skills you need to get a good job: researching a targeted company, preparing a résumé and letter of application, and writing a thank-you letter to follow an interview.

STARTING THE JOB SEARCH: RESEARCHING EMPLOYERS

LO14.1 Begin your job search by researching potential employers.

The way you begin your job search depends to some extent on where you are when you start. If you are still a student in a large university, you will probably work with your school's job placement office, its faculty, and the recruiters who visit your campus. If you are a student in a small school, opportunities for on-campus interviews may be more limited, and you may find it helpful to work with the accounting faculty to identify potential employers. If you have already graduated, then you may be on your own in locating potential jobs and establishing initial contacts with employers, although the placement office of the school from which you graduated may still work with you.

Whether you're a student or already a practicing professional, you may also look for positions on networking sites, such as LinkedIn®. Chapter 12 discusses the use of electronic media to locate and apply for employment, including the email submission of résumés and the creation of profiles that some networking sites, such as LinkedIn®, require.

Regardless of how you begin your job search, you will need to write certain documents to secure the job, including a letter of application, a résumé, and a thank-you letter after you have had an interview. For all these documents, knowledge of the prospective employer is important so that you can tailor what you write to that employer's needs. You will also want to show the people who read these documents that you are familiar with the company and that you did the preparation necessary to make a good impression. You should be very familiar at least with the content of the company's Web site, but additional research into the company is desirable. At an interview, you may be asked whether you have questions about the company; it can be very embarrassing to ask a question if the answer is readily available on the company's Web site or some other material to which you've had access.

Thus, you may begin your research by studying the organization's Web page. It may also be that the company publishes a blog or some other online publication; you should become thoroughly familiar with the information you obtain from these sources. You can also search the Internet for articles and news items in the financial press, and you can talk with business faculty about the organization. Your school's job placement office may also have an information file on the company. Perhaps you will also be fortunate enough to meet recruiters from the organization on campus at accounting club meetings or at job fairs. If you have this opportunity, listen carefully to what the recruiters say about their organization and ask appropriate questions. Show with polite, attentive listening that you are interested in what the recruiters have to say, and remember the names of the people you meet!

You should also find as much information as possible about the job for which you are applying. If there is a specific job opening, you will probably have general information about the position in a job announcement. Read the announcement carefully so that you learn as much as possible about the position's requirements and the credentials the employer is looking for. This information can guide you when you prepare your résumé and application letter.

PREPARING YOUR MATERIALS

LO14.2   Prepare effective materials you will use in your job search: résumé, letter of application, thank-you letter.

All the information you gathered in your research will be important as you prepare the materials you will use for your job application. These materials may include a résumé, letter of application, thank-you letter, and possibly other materials as well.

Follow Instructions

Before you begin the actual process of applying for a job, study any instructions the employer has provided for the application process, including written materials the employer requests. Some employers specify the electronic submission of the résumé, for example. If you submit a hard copy rather than an electronic version, your résumé will likely be ignored. Similarly, the employer may specify that you include particular information in your application, such as your experience or training in a specific area. You should provide requested information exactly as requested. Failure to follow directions exactly will likely disqualify your application.

Prepare Your Résumé

Preparing a résumé may be one of the most important steps you take in finding a good job. If your résumé doesn't project a professional, competent image, your application won't be considered seriously.

Figure 14–1 illustrates an effective résumé. This example is not the only way to prepare a good résumé, however, and you may find other models in business communication texts or in materials supplied by your school's job placement office. We will consider the résumé in Figure 14–1 as a generic model that you can adapt to your own situation.

Format

First, look at the document design of the résumé in Figure 14–1. Notice the placement of text on the page and the pleasing use of white space, headings, fonts, and bullets. The résumé is arranged so that it has an attractive, professional appearance; it is also easy to read because it's not crowded, and important information is easy to find. You'll see how these design techniques can be used with the various parts of a résumé.

Name and Address

Center your name in bold print at the top of the page. On the next line, put your address at the left margin and your phone number (including your area code) at the right margin, as shown in Figure 14–1. Place your

FIGURE 14–1   Sample Résumé

Shane W. Brown

1324 Horsetooth Road	Phone: (970) 435-1234
Fort Collins, CO 80125	email: sbrown@csu.edu

CAREER OBJECTIVE	An accounting position that will allow me to build on my academic and employment background and provide opportunities for professional growth and development. Willing to travel.
SUMMARY OF QUALIFICATIONS	Degree in accounting; honor student; experience with corporate staff; experienced in customer service.
EDUCATION	Bachelor of Business Administration, University of Georgia Expected Graduation Date: June 2018 Major: Accounting GPA (cumulative): 3.55/4.0

WORK EXPERIENCE

June 2017–September 2017	**Jaymart, Inc.; Executive Offices,** Norcross, Ga. *Accounting Internship* • Assisted in the preparation of year-end audit work papers. • Worked on depreciation schedules; updated property, plant, and equipment accounts. • Participated in the preparation of the 2015 corporate tax return work papers, and set up schedules for the 2016 corporate return. • Prepared 2016 income tax projections for individual corporate officers.
March 2016–June 2017	**University of Georgia Language Laboratories,** Athens, Ga. *Laboratory Assistant* • Supervised foreign language students using the laboratory. Worked an average of 15 hours per week.
June 2015–September 2015	**AT&T Information Systems,** Atlanta, Ga. *Support Services* • Assisted AT&T employees with their mailroom needs.
June 2014–September 2014	**Food Giant,** Atlanta, Ga. *Courtesy Clerk, Produce Department* • Promoted to Produce Department Manager in July 2014. Assisted customers.
HONORS AND ACTIVITIES	Association of Students of Accounting; Beta Alpha Psi Initiate (Accounting Fraternity); University Honors Program, Recipient of Junior Division Honors; Beta Gamma Sigma (Business Honor Society); Dean's List (seven of eleven quarters); Tau Epsilon Phi (Social Fraternity); Finance Club; College Republicans; Intramural Softball, Volleyball.
INTERESTS	Racquetball, current events, travel, music.

email address below your phone number. Place a horizontal line under this portion to separate your identifying data from your qualifications.

Career Objective

Be as specific as possible about the kind of job you're looking for so the employer can easily determine whether your goals match any available openings. You might indicate an accounting specialty such as tax, auditing, or systems, for example. At the same time, you don't want to close any doors you will later wish you had left open, so consider describing your objective in a way that will allow for all reasonable possibilities of employment for which you're qualified. Even better, you can edit your résumé so that your objective fits specific openings for which you're applying.

Summary of Qualifications

Employers often receive many résumés and do not have time to study the detailed information the résumés contain. Therefore, you should provide a "snapshot" of your qualifications that will immediately catch the employer's eye.

Notice Shane Brown's Summary of Qualifications section in Figure 14–1. In one quick phrase he sums up why the employer should pick him for the job.

Education

Beginning with your most recent degree or school, provide information in reverse chronological order about your education to show your qualifications for employment. Include the following information:

- Degree(s) you have completed or are working on.
- Complete name of the school granting this degree.
- Date of the degree, or expected graduation date.
- Your major and, if applicable to the job, your minor.
- Grade point average, if it is above 3.0 on a 4.0 scale. (Figure your GPA several ways to try to reach at least a 3.0—for example, cumulative GPA, GPA in your major coursework, GPA in upper level courses, and so on—labeling it accordingly.)
- Approximate percentage of your college expenses you financed yourself, if this amount is significant.

If you have attended several colleges or universities, include information about all of them, especially if you received a degree. If you attended schools without completing a degree, give the dates of your attendance.

You shouldn't include information about your high school education, unless that information is relevant to a potential employer. If you're applying for summer employment, but still have some time before you graduate from college, then you might list your high school and date of graduation.

Work Experience

Again, in reverse chronological order, provide information about the jobs you have held, both full time and part time. You can also list volunteer work if it's relevant to the job for which you're applying. For each job that you list, provide the following information:

- Dates of employment. You may decide to put the dates in the left margin, as in the sample résumé.
- Name and location of the organization for which you worked.
- Your position.
- A description of your responsibilities, with emphasis on the ones that show you are qualified for the job you are now seeking. Note any promotions or honors you received. Whenever possible, describe your responsibilities using active voice verbs such as *assisted, completed, prepared,* and *supervised.* Quantify your accomplishments, if possible. In the example résumé in Figure 14–1, Shane Brown notes that he worked in the language lab an average of 15 hours per week.

Honors and Activities

List the organizations you have belonged to, the honors you have received, and any other activities that show you to be a well-rounded, active person. List these activities from most important to least important, *from the potential employer's point of view.* If you held an office in an organization or had significant responsibilities, add this information as well. Finally, if an organization or honor is not self-explanatory, explain it briefly, as illustrated in Figure 14–1.

Interests

Information about your hobbies and interests is optional on a résumé. The advantage of including this information is that it can show that you are a well-rounded person with interests that might help you relate to other people, such as your coworkers and clients.

References

If you provide the names, addresses, and phone numbers of your references on your résumé, the employer can contact them easily. However, you run the risk that an employer will call your reference at an inconvenient time, or that the reference will not immediately recall detailed information about you. As a general rule, do not include a list of references or letters of reference with your résumé unless they are specifically requested. However, you should prepare a list of references in advance of any interview you may have and give the list to your interviewer.

In addition, it is not necessary to include a statement on your résumé that "references are available upon request," as this is generally considered obvious. However, if you are enrolled or have recently graduated from a college or university, you may be able to place reference letters on file with your school's job placement office. Then your résumé or reference list can include a line such as this one:

References available upon request from:

Placement Office
University of Manhattan
Manhattan, GA 30678

Although placing reference letters on file with school's placement office may be useful, most employers will prefer to contact your references directly.

One final word about references: Never list people as references without first asking their permission. Ask people to be references who are likely to remember you well and have favorable things to say about you. Former instructors and employers are good candidates.

What *Not* to Put on a Résumé

Remember that there are laws against hiring discrimination on the basis of age, sex, race, religion, marital status, or national origin, so do not put information of this nature on a résumé. Also, when preparing your résumé avoid phrases such as these:

- gets along well with coworkers
- pleasant disposition
- always eager to please

These phrases make you sound as if you were applying to be a pet rather than an employee! "Fluff" phrases like these are guaranteed to send your résumé straight to the bottom of the pile.

Generally, employers hiring for accounting positions are interested in two things: what you know and what you can do. Therefore, your résumé should specifically state what you know and what you can do.

Write a Letter of Application

Usually you will send your résumé to a potential employer with a formal letter of application, or you will write to follow up some earlier communication. Like the résumé, the letter must be professional and well researched.

Your letter should follow the general advice for letters discussed in Chapter 9, including these guidelines:

- Address the reader by name. Get the appropriate name over the telephone or by other means, if possible.
- Give your letter an attractive, professional appearance. Use good stationery and a high-quality printer. The letter and résumé should be printed on matching paper and both should match the envelope.

- Write in short, concise paragraphs and clear sentences. A courteous, conversational tone is best.
- The spelling, grammar, and mechanics of your letter should be perfect.

The content of your letter will depend on your situation. The letter will typically have three paragraphs. The first paragraph will identify the specific position for which you're applying. It will also provide a context for your application, such as how you learned about the position. If you have already discussed the job or possible employment with an employee of the company, you should refer to this person by name and say exactly why you're sending the résumé. You might write a sentence such as this one:

> Sara Evans suggested that I write you about a possible opening in your auditing department. I had the pleasure of talking with Ms. Evans at a meeting of our Accounting Club here at the University of Central California.
>
> As you will see in my enclosed résumé, . . .

After the introduction to your letter, use your second paragraph to show the reader two things: that you are familiar with the organization doing the hiring and that you have the credentials the organization is looking for. Thus, you can briefly refer to what you've learned about the company from your research and highlight the information on your résumé that shows you to be especially interested in, and qualified for, the position. In other words, you use the letter of application to sell yourself as the best person for the job. The following paragraphs show examples from two different letters:

> As you will see on my enclosed résumé, I will graduate from the University of Northern Idaho in June with a Masters of Accounting degree and a specialty in tax, so my training should qualify me for an entry-level position in your tax department. In addition, I have worked as a tax assistant with the Smith Company during the past two summers.
>
> * * *
>
> While at the University of Tempe, I have worked an average of twenty hours a week to pay approximately half my college and living expenses. At the same time I have maintained a cumulative GPA of 3.3 and have been active in a number of campus organizations. I believe this record shows that I am a conscientious worker with an ability to organize my time and achieve goals in a deadline-intensive environment.

The final paragraph should include a courteous closing and suggest a response from the reader or follow-up action you will take. You might suggest that you will call in a week to see if the employer needs additional information. At the least, express enthusiasm for the position and a hope that you will hear from the employer soon:

I hope that you will find my education and experience suitable for this position and that we can set up an interview soon to discuss the position further. I look forward to hearing from you.

Figure 14–2 shows a letter of application.

FIGURE 14–2   Letter of Application

2134 Roxboro Road
Atlanta, GA 30378
January 15, 2018

Ann Bradbury, Partner
Bradbury, Ellis, and Gomez, CPAs
33 Hightower Building
Atlanta, GA 30391

Dear Ms. Bradbury:

It was a pleasure meeting you and George Ellis last week at the Accounting Club meeting here at Fulton University. As you suggested, I am sending you my résumé because you anticipate having an opening soon for which I would be qualified.

As my résumé shows, I will graduate from Fulton in May with an MACC degree and a specialty in auditing. As an intern with Brown and Hill, CPAs, I participated in several audits in the north Georgia area. I hope you will find that my education and experience make me a good candidate for an auditing position with Bradbury, Ellis, and Gomez.

I would very much appreciate the opportunity to talk with you further about possible future employment. I will call your office next week to see whether we might set up a time for an interview.

Sincerely,

Carla Brown

Carla Brown
Enclosure

Mail your letter of application and résumé in a flat business envelope so that you won't have to fold your documents. Alternatively, some employers may ask for applications and résumés to be submitted by email, as we discussed in Chapter 12.

Write a Thank-You Letter

With an impressive résumé and application letter, good credentials to support them, and a little luck, you will probably have one or more interviews for jobs. After the interviews, you need to write letters to the people who met with you to thank them for their hospitality and to show enthusiasm for what you learned about the organization and the position for which you're applying.

A thank-you letter need not be long; a letter of two or three short paragraphs is usually long enough. Again, you need to address your readers by name and refer specifically to your meeting and to one or two of the topics you discussed. If you met any of the firm's other employees, you should express pleasure at having had that opportunity. End your letter with a courteous closing and express the hope that you will hear from your reader soon.

This letter, like the application letter, should follow the guidelines for letters covered in Chapter 9. A sample thank-you letter is shown in Figure 14–3.

FIGURE 14–3 Thank-You Letter

> 2134 Roxboro Road
> Atlanta, GA 30378
> April 23, 2017
>
> Ann Bradbury, Partner
> Bradbury, Ellis, and Gomez, CPAs
> 33 Hightower Building
> Atlanta, GA 30391
>
> Dear Ms. Bradbury:
>
> Thank you very much for meeting with me last
> week to discuss the possibility of my working for
> Bradbury, Ellis, and Gomez after my graduation
> next month. I enjoyed the opportunity to visit
> your office and meet the other members of your

FIGURE 14–3   (*Contd.*)

auditing staff. The lunch with June Oliver and Richard Wang was particularly pleasant and informative because they were able to share their experiences as first-year auditors.

I would very much welcome the opportunity to work as an auditor with your firm, so I hope that you will decide my qualifications meet your needs. Please let me know if I can provide any additional information.

Thank you once again for your hospitality. I look forward to hearing from you.

Sincerely,

Carla Brown

Carla Brown

Electronic Submissions

For some jobs, you will submit your résumé and application letter electronically. Some job announcements request an electronic submission, or you may find it an advantage to submit your materials quickly. In situations such as these, you can attach your résumé to an email. The email itself will be your formal letter of application, with your résumé as an attachment. Select the rich text option for your email, or send it in PDF format, in order to preserve the formatting of your application letter.

Chapter 12 provides more information on the use of electronic media for job applications, including the email submission of your résumé.

EXERCISES

Exercise 14–1 [General]

Imagine that you are an employer who received the résumé shown in Figure 14–4. How would you react to the résumé? Would you be likely to give the applicant an interview? Why or why not?

Examine the résumé closely, noting the applicant's accomplishments and experience. Does this person have credentials that might make him a good employee?

Rewrite this résumé so that the applicant's credentials show to good advantage. You may have to make up some details so that the résumé is complete.

Exercise 14–2 [General]

Exchange résumés with one or more of your classmates. Critique the résumés, checking for effective organization, wording, and page design. Proofread each other's résumés to be sure there are no mechanical or typographical errors. After you receive suggestions from your classmates, revise your résumé accordingly.

Exercise 14–3 [General]

Imagine that you find the following job announcement at your school's placement office. Prepare your résumé and application letter for this position.

ACCOUNTANT Entry-level staff accountant for a mid-size manufacturing firm. Accounting degree required. Send résumé to William Willson, Director of Human Resources, Southern Cardboard Industries, Durham, NC 60314. An equal opportunity/affirmative action employer.

Exercise 14–4 [General]

The application letter you prepared for Exercise 14–3 was so effective and your résumé looked so impressive that you had an office interview with Southern Cardboard Industries. At the interview, you met the company'spresident, Stanley McDonald, and several staff accountants. You had lunch after the interview with Mary Vian, a senior accountant in the firm, as well as the controller, Robert Cron. You learned that the company has been in business for sixteen years, and that it is now expanding into a larger national market.

Write a thank-you letter to follow up on your interview.

FIGURE 14–4   Résumé to Accompany Exercise 14–1

William H. Bonney

PRESENT ADDRESS	PERMANENT ADDRESS
745 Main St.	1634 Scaffold Lane
Athens, GA 30600	Highnoon, GA 31200

EDUCATION	DEGREE	CUM GRAD. DATE	MAJ. GPA	GPA
University of Georgia		6/17	3.4	3.5
Oconee Springs High School		6/13		3.9

FIGURE 14–4   (*Contd.*)

William H. Bonney

MAJOR COURSES

Principles of Accounting I and II; Financial Accounting
I, II, III; Systems I.

WORK EXPERIENCE

	TITLE	FROM	TO
Auto Stores, Inc. Clark-stown, Ga.	Cashier	7/16	9/16
Hamilton's Coldwater, Ga.	Cashier	5/16	9/16
Tulips Discount Stores Roosevelt, Ga.	Clerk	6/15	9/15
Sam's Market Athens, Ga.	Salesperson	11/14	1/15
Esops, Inc. Athens, Ga.	Office/ Customer svc.	6/14	10/14
Telemarketing, Inc. Ath-ens, Ga.	Telemarketer	7/16	Present

HONORS AND ACTIVITIES

Honors Program
Dean's List
Golden Key
Outstanding College Students of America
Phi Chi Theta Business Fraternity
Association of Students in Accounting
James E. Cassidy Scholarship

PERSONAL

Date of Birth—October 20, 1998; excellent health; prefer to
work in the north Atlanta area.

Exercise 14–5 [Financial/Auditing]

The job listing for Johnson & Peters, CPAs, shown in Figure 14–5, is a
typical listing of an entry-level job opening in a small to medium-size
CPA firm. Assume you have all the qualifications for this job. Write
your résumé and a letter of application to respond to this listing. Invent
any facts you may need to complete this assignment. Address your
letter to James Sorbon, Director of Personnel.

FIGURE 14-5   Typical Entry-Level Job Listing for a Medium-Size CPA Firm

Johnson & Peters, CPAs
1231 Main St.
Houston, TX 77001

Opening for Audit Associate

Johnson & Peters provides an excellent opportunity for advancement and development of a life-long career. The firm is committed to the development of our future leaders. Associates may report to and receive instruction from staff, managers, principals, and partners with all levels of experience.

Audit Associate Specific Duties
- Become familiar with accounting and auditing procedures and perform them in accordance with Johnson & Peters' standards in an accurate, thorough, and timely manner.
- Work on preparation of financial statements, lease testing, payroll testing, cash disbursement testing, auditing accounts payable, searching for unrecorded liabilities, maintaining confirmation logs, and preparing audit files.
- Understand clients' accounting systems.
- Resolve audit issues by obtaining evidence and making inquiries of clients.
- Apply concepts of materiality and audit risk.
- Prepare audit file content that is informative, indexed, cross-referenced, and easily understood.
- Manage daily client workflow and multiple client projects.

Personal and Professional Development
- Pursue and pass the CPA Exam.
- Earn confidence, trust, and respect from clients and colleagues.
- Continually develop technical skills and industry knowledge.
- Demonstrate initiative, resourcefulness, creativity, independent thinking, and sound business judgment.
- Represent Johnson & Peters in a positive and professional manner.
- Develop an ability to motivate and train staff.
- Actively participate in Johnson & Peters' internal development programs, including staff training courses.

Requirements
- Bachelors degree in accounting.
- Excellent written and oral communication skills.
- Ability to work in a team environment.
- Ability to learn in a fast-paced environment.
- General computer literacy including proficiency in Microsoft Word® and Excel®.

Please apply directly to James Sorbon, Director of Personnel.

Exercise 14–6 [Tax]

The job listing for a tax analyst for National Chemical Corp., shown in Figure 14–6, is typical of many job listings for this type of job. Assume you have all the qualifications for this position. Write your résumé and a letter of application to respond to this listing. Address your application

---

FIGURE 14–6   Typical Entry-Level Job Listing for a Tax Analyst in Industry

National Chemical Corp.
756 Petro Lane
Tulsa, OK 74103

Opening for Tax Analyst

National Chemical Corp. (NCC) produces a broad range of specialty chemicals and fibers that are marketed globally in over 80 countries. In 2016, NCC had revenues of approximately $4.2 billion. The company is based in Tulsa, OK, and employs more than 10,000 people worldwide.

Job Responsibilities

- Assist with preparation and filing of Sales and Use tax returns in numerous jurisdictions.
- Assist with external Sales and Use tax audits.
- Assist with various special projects.
- Assist with management or issuance of customer and vendor exemption certificates.
- Assist with preparation of property tax returns, and monitor tax assessment notices and bills.
- Assist in preparation of monthly journal entries, reconciliation of applicable general ledger accounts, monthly and quarterly tax payments, returns, and submissions to various jurisdictions.

Requirements

- Degree in accounting or related field.
- Demonstrated analytical and problem-solving skills.
- Ability to communicate effectively, both orally and in writing.
- Ability to work in a team setting.
- Detail oriented and strong research and analytical skills.
- Ability to use tax research software.
- Proficiency in computer skills using MS Office.
- Willingness to learn new computer software.
- Knowledge of accounting principles and corporate tax law.
- Ability to multitask and work under tight deadlines.
- Strong interpersonal skills.

Apply directly to Susan Charon, Director of Human Resources.

to Susan Charon, Director of Human Resources. Invent any facts you may need to complete this assignment.

Exercise 14–7 [Managerial]

The job listing for a corporate accountant, shown in Figure 14–7, is typical of many job listings for this type of job. Assume you have all the qualifications for this position. Write your résumé and a letter of application to respond to this listing. Address your application to Thomas Lombardo, Director of Human Resources. Invent any facts you may need to complete this assignment.

FIGURE 14–7   Typical Entry-Level Job Listing for Corporate Accountant

Allegheny Industries
8005 Allegheny Drive
Pittsburgh, PA 15250

Opening for Corporate Accountant

Allegheny Industries is an international, publicly traded company manufacturing heavy equipment for the construction and shipping industries. The equipment it manufactures is marketed globally. In 2017, NCC had revenues of approximately $2.3 billion. The company is based in Pittsburgh and employs more than 6,000 people.

Duties

- Prepare financial statements and various financial reports for internal and external use.
- Perform accounting activities relating to the maintenance of general ledger accounts and the month-end closing process, including journal entries and reconciliations.
- Assist with various treasury duties including cash reconciliations, deposits, refunds, vendor and debt payments, and loan compliance.
- Assist with preparation of budgets and forecasts.
- Assist with federal, state, and local tax compliance.
- Assist with other functions as needed.

Job Requirements

- Bachelors degree in accounting.
- Good knowledge of U.S. GAAP and able to research new issues.
- Ability to work with people from all departments.
- Strong written and verbal communication skills.
- Strong problem-solving skills.
- Proficiency in Microsoft Excel® and Word®.

Apply directly to Thomas Lombardo, Director of Human Resources.

CHAPTER 15

Writing for Publication

Learning Objectives

After studying this chapter, you should be able to

15.1 Plan an article you will submit for publication.

15.2 Research, draft, and revise an article for publication.

15.3 Submit an article for publication in a professional, effective manner.

As a practicing accountant or business services professional, you may decide at some point in your career to write an article for publication. This might be a short article for a newsletter, perhaps published by the organization for which you work, or it might be a longer article for a professional journal, such as the *Journal of Accountancy* or the *Management Accounting Quarterly*. You might also write a blog related to your work or respond to an article you find online. Most of the techniques discussed in this book apply to writing for publication, but in this chapter, we consider some additional pointers.

PLANNING YOUR ARTICLE

LO15.1   Plan an article you will submit for publication.

To plan your article, start by considering the publication that you want to write for and the topic you want to write about. Most likely, you'll be writing about your experience in practice, such as a better way to approach an accounting procedure or solve an accounting problem. You may also write a document to express your opinion on some controversial accounting or business issue currently under discussion in the profession. This document might take the form of a letter, essay, or discussion paper. Earlier chapters of this book discuss these formats.

Whatever the topic you've chosen, target your writing to the editorial practices and readers of the publication to which you're submitting the article. One of the best ways to have an article published is to write on a subject that is interesting and relevant to a wide range of the publication's readers.

Consider the type of writing typically published by the targeted publication. You will probably want to write for a journal that prefers practical articles about the practice of accounting. The *Journal of Accountancy*, *The CPA Journal*, and the *Management Accounting Quarterly* publish articles on practical concerns shared by accountants. Journals and newsletters published on the state or local levels might publish articles of general interest to accounting professionals, but they also include articles of local interest. Other publications such as the *Accounting Review* prefer academic articles on scholarly research. Figures 15–1 and 15–2 show some accounting journals of interest to

---

FIGURE 15–1   Some Accounting Publications Available Online and in Print

CPA Magazine
This is the leading accounting publication for Chartered Professional Accountants of Canada. www.cpacanada.ca/en/connecting-and-news/cpa-magazine

The CPA Journal
This journal is a publication of the New York State Society of CPAs. It publishes articles on accounting and auditing, taxation, finance, management, responsibilities and leadership, and technology. www.cpajournal.com/.

The International Journal of Accounting (IJA)
The IJA is published by the University of Illinois and publishes articles explaining international accounting practices including theoretical justifications and criticisms. www.sciencedirect.com/science/journal/00207063.

Journal of Accountancy (JOA)
The JOA is published by the American Institute of Certified Public Accountants (AICPA). It contains articles on auditing, career development, consulting services, ethics and independence, financial management, financial reporting, forensic and valuation services, fraud, internal controls, personal financial planning, practice management, risk management, tax, and technology. Available to members of the AICPA, or you can just subscribe to the journal. www.journalofaccountancy.com/.

Journal of Accounting Research (JAR)
The JAR is an academic journal focused on academic research. It is published by The Accounting Research Center at the University of Chicago Booth School of Business. http://onlinelibrary.wiley.com/journal/10.1111/(ISSN)1475-679X.

FIGURE 15–1   *(Contd.)*

Accounting Review (AR)
The AR is published by the American Accounting Association and contains articles "reporting the results of accounting research and explaining and illustrating related research methodology."
http://aaajournals.org/loi/accr.

The New York Times (NYT)
The NYT's articles on accounting and accountants are available at www.nytimes.com/topic/subject/accounting-and-accountants?8qa.

FIGURE 15–2   Some Accounting Publications Available Online Only

CCH Daily inc accountancy LIVE
This journal is published in the UK. It publishes articles on international accounting in addition to those more focused on the UK. www.cchdaily.co.uk/.

Accounting Today
This is a good source for all news and opinion aimed at the CPA. Two blogs—*Accounting Tomorrow*, which deals with the future of the accounting profession, and *Debits&Credits*, which deals with the latest developments in accounting, tax, and client advisory services—are also published by this journal. www.accountingtoday.com/.

AccountingWEB
This is a very good source for news on topics that include tax, accounting and auditing, technology, practice, and education. The Web site also has links to several useful blogs including the IMA Young Accounting Pros Blog, on which members of the IMA's Young Professionals Committee discuss advice and experience highly useful to entry-level accountants. www.accountingweb.com/.

Big 4
This is a useful blog covering career opportunities and significant developments in larger accounting firms and other companies. Its contributors are current employees or alumni of those companies, but it is not affiliated with any company or group of companies. www.big4.com/blog.

CPA Trendlines
Published by Bay Street Group LLC, this publication contains useful articles on tax, accounting, and finance. cpatrendlines.com/.

Management Accounting Quarterly (MAQ)
The MAQ is published by the IMA (Formerly the Institute of Management Accounting) and contains articles "by and for academics

FIGURE 15–2 (*Contd.*)

and practitioners of accounting and financial management." Topics include (among others)"cost/management accounting techniques, ABC/ABM, RCA, GPK, statistical process controls, target costing, theory of constraints, methods of calculating stock options, techniques to improve account-ing and finance education, new theories in finance and accounting, and much more." www.imanet.org/career-resources/get-published-with-ima/management-accounting-quarterly?ssopc=1.

SmartBrief
This is a source for several useful newsletters: *CPA Letter Daily* (for CPA news), *BusIndNews* (for accounting and finance news), *Financial Planning Digest (for CPA personal financial planners)*, *IIA Glaobal SmartBrief* (for global internal auditing news), *IIA SmartBrief* (for news for internal audit professionals), and *Institute of Internal Auditors Global SmartBrief* (for world-wide internal auditing news), www.smartbrief.com/.

practicing accounting professionals. Figure 15–1 lists publications that are available both in print and online; Figure 15–2 shows accounting publications that are available only online.

Blogs on topics of interest to accountants have become com-mon, and their use will likely become even more prevalent in coming years. Chapter 12 discusses writing for blogs more fully, but most of the suggestions you find in this chapter will also help you write effectively when you publish online.

Here are other questions to consider about the publication in which you hope to publish your writing:

- Who are the readers of the publication? What are their interests and concerns? How much technical expertise on your topic are they likely to have?
- What format, organization, and length do the publication's editors prefer? You can learn this either from an editorial policy state-ment or by studying articles already published.
- What style of documentation does the publication use? If the publication doesn't specify a documentation style, follow the guidelines for documentation given in Chapter 8 of this book.
- What writing style do the editors prefer? Articles in professional accounting publications may be written either in a serious, schol-arly style or in a light, conversational one. A blog will usually be informal, though it should be written clearly and correctly. All publications prefer prose that is clear, readable, and concise, with little, if any, unnecessary accounting jargon.

PREPARING YOUR ARTICLE

LO15.2   Research, draft, and revise an article for publication.

After you've chosen a topic and publication to target, find out what else has been written on the topic lately, especially if you are hoping to publish the article in a national or regional journal. You can search the Internet or visit a good library to find this information. This research will help in several ways:

- You'll find out what has been published recently on the topic so your article will not repeat what has already been done.
- You'll find out what issues or approaches are of current interest in the profession.
- You may find references that you can use in your article to support your position. Alternatively, you may find positions taken by other people that you want to refute.

In addition to this background research to find out what has already been published on the topic, you may need to do original research to back up your writing with sound observations and reasoning, and perhaps with authoritative accounting pronouncements as well. You may find it helpful to review Chapter 8 of this text, which discusses accounting research in more detail.

After you have planned the article and done any necessary research, you're ready to begin writing. Draft and revise your article according to the guidelines discussed throughout this book. Chapter 3, which discusses document organization, may be especially helpful. When you feel reasonably satisfied with the article, ask colleagues to critique it. People who have successfully published may be particularly helpful.

For the final manuscript you will submit for publication, pay particular attention to a professional presentation, including accurate and complete documentation of any sources you have used, prepared according to the guidelines of the publication to which you're sending the article. Professional appearance of the document pages is also important, and grammar and mechanics should be flawless.

SUBMITTING THE ARTICLE

LO15.3   Submit an article for publication in a professional, effective manner.

When you're ready to submit your article to the targeted publication, send it along with a cover letter addressed to the editor by name. If you submit the article electronically, you will send it with an email that functions as a cover letter. This cover letter or email should be concise and courteous, and it should mention the title of your article. Explain briefly why you think the article would interest the publication's readers.

Be sure you have complied with the publication's submission requirements. For example, the publication may require that you write the article in Microsoft Word® and submit it electronically. A publication may also require that you submit multiple hard copies of the article. Whatever the submission requirements are, follow them precisely.

After all this preparation, your article should have a good chance of acceptance for publication. However, be prepared for the possibility that your article will be rejected by the first publication you send it to. If your article is rejected, turn it around and send it somewhere else. Revise it to suit the readers and editorial policies of the new journal: type of articles published, interests and needs of the readers, length and style of writing, and style of documentation.

Writing for publication can be a rewarding component of your professional accounting career, but like all the writing discussed in this book, it requires planning and attention to detail, including a concern for the readers.

EXERCISES

Exercise 15–1 [General]

Obtain a recent issue of several professional business publications. For each of these publications, answer the following questions:

1. What type of writing do these publications publish? Possibilities include academic research, practical accounting applications for public or managerial accountants, articles of organizational or local interest, or articles addressed to some special-interest group.
2. Who writes the articles for these publications? They may be written by members of a sponsoring organization, professional writers, professors, or other accounting professionals.
3. Analyze the specific articles published. Are they all the same length, format, and style? Some publications may publish a variety of articles, such as short notes and longer essays and articles.
4. What are the standard editorial practices, such as article length and style of documentation?

Exercise 15–2 [General]

Choose an article from a recent edition of an accounting journal such as the *Journal of Accountancy* or *The CPA Journal*. Analyze the effectiveness of the writing using the "Tips for the Effective Writer" shown in Figure 1–1 in Chapter 1. Then summarize your evaluation in a short memo to your instructor. Alternatively, your instructor may ask you to prepare an oral presentation of your analysis. Whether you present your analysis in written or oral form, back up your findings with specific examples from the article you analyzed.

Exercise 15–3 [Tax]

Identify a tax article that has appeared in the *Journal of Taxation*. Summarize the article in a style that would be appropriate for the readers of *The Wall Street Journal*. Remember to document your sources properly and prepare your article according to the submission requirements for *The Wall Street Journal*.

Exercise 15–4 [Financial]

Identify a recent FASB Accounting Standards Update (ASU). Summarize the ASU in a style that would be appropriate for the readers of *The CPA Journal*. Remember to document your sources properly and prepare your article according to the submission requirements for *The CPA Journal*.

Exercise 15–5 [Auditing]

Prepare an article for *Accounting Today* on the role of auditing in helping to protect investors. In your article, explain how an audit is undertaken, the reliance on internal controls put in place by management, and the responsibility of management for the financial statements.

Remember to document your sources properly and prepare your article according to the submission requirements for *Accounting Today*.

CHAPTER 16

Oral Communication: Listening and Speaking

Learning Objectives

After studying this chapter, you should be able to

16.1 Explain the importance of good listening skills and apply those skills in conversations with others, as well as in larger groups.

16.2 Prepare an effective oral presentation: planning, researching, and composing.

16.3 Prepare effective visual aids.

16.4 Practice your presentation.

16.5 Complete your preparation: room and equipment; appearance and dress.

16.6 Make an oral presentation with poise and confidence.

16.7 Manage stage fright.

16.8 Explain the special considerations involved in presenting financial information.

Communication is a multifaceted process. It includes verbal skills such as reading, writing, listening, and speaking, as well as various forms of nonverbal communication—gestures, facial expressions, and other forms of body language. Moreover, all of these components of communication are interactive, making communication a complex process indeed.

So far in this text we've focused primarily on the writing skills you'll need as a professional accountant. This final chapter examines two important oral communication skills, listening and oral presentations, both of which will play an important part in your professional success.

LISTENING SKILLS

LO16.1   Explain the importance of good listening skills and apply those skills in conversations with others, as well as in larger groups.

In Chapter 1 we pointed out that listening skills are an important part of effective communication. What you hear from other people often provides much of the information you need to perform your job well. When you listen carefully, you'll find out what other people may know about the situation you're involved in, what their expectations are, what their attitudes are, and ideas they have about the work in progress.

In addition, the willingness and ability to listen carefully to what others say contributes to good relationships between you and your colleagues. In fact, listening attentively to what other people are saying might even be considered an ethical issue, because it involves respect for others. Here are some guidelines to keep in mind as you learn to be a good listener. Some of these skills apply to one-on-one or small group communication, and some apply to listening in a larger group setting, such as a meeting. Many of the guidelines apply to all situations in which good listening is important.

Conversations with Another Person or in a Small Group

When you are part of a small group conversation or your conversation is with only one person, the people you interact with will form an opinion about you that they will long remember. Thus, the care with which you listen to others is not just a matter of politeness, but will also contribute to your professional reputation. Keep these pointers in mind:

- Focus your attention on what the speaker is saying and don't let your mind wander to other topics. Don't rehearse your own response to what is being said while the speaker is still talking.
- Don't interrupt the speaker. If you must interrupt for clarification, wait for a pause and then apologize: "I'm sorry to interrupt, but I want to be sure I understand this point before we move on. Did you mean . . . ?"
- Look at the speaker, maintaining good eye contact. Your face should express sincere interest and, where appropriate, empathy with what the speaker is saying.
- Leave your cell phone or other electronic equipment turned off and put away.
- Avoid distracting gestures or movements, such as playing with a pen.

- When the situation requires that you understand and remember precise, accurate information, summarize what the speaker has said and ask whether you've understood correctly.
- For some more formal situations, such as an interview, prepare topics for discussion or questions in advance. Anticipate what questions you'll be asked, and have answers in mind. Think also about the questions you'll want to ask. Take your notes with you to consult as the discussion progresses. Leave space in your notes to record important information.

Large Group Discussions, Lectures, and Meetings

In large group discussions, lectures, and meetings, the guidelines for discussions in small groups are still important. And remember these additional tips:

- Take notes so you won't forget important information. This advice applies especially to an interview, meeting, or lecture.
- Listen attentively. Maintain steady eye contact with the speaker. Sit quietly and avoid distracting others. Leave electronic equipment turned off and out of sight.
- Don't become involved in side conversations during a meeting, for example with the person sitting next to you, even if the side conversation relates to the topic of the meeting. These side conversations are distracting to others, including to the speaker.

When you master listening skills such as these, you'll have much better information to use as the basis of further work. You'll also have contributed to a respectful, professional environment and better relationship with your colleagues.

ORAL PRESENTATIONS

LO16.2 **Prepare an effective oral presentation: planning, researching, and composing.**

Speaking before a group, like writing, is often an important part of an accountant's professional responsibilities, yet public speaking creates anxiety for many people. If you learn a few strategies for public speaking, however, and practice as often as possible, your fear of these situations will diminish. With guidance and practice comes mastery, and with mastery comes confidence. In the remainder of this chapter, you'll see that effective oral presentations, like writing, result from a process: preparation, practice, and delivery.

The time you spend preparing and practicing for your oral presentation will help ensure your success. Preparation involves several steps, as the following sections will discuss. You will analyze your purpose and audience; conduct any necessary research; compose your speech; prepare your notes and visual aids; and—perhaps most important—practice your presentation.

Planning the Presentation: Analyzing Purpose and Audience

The first step in planning your presentation is to analyze its purpose. Perhaps you need to inform the listeners about the progress you've made on a project, or propose that the decision makers in the group approve a new project. You may want to convince senior management to invest in a new computer system or explain to coworkers how to implement the system already adopted. Remember that no matter what the primary purpose of your presentation, it has an important secondary purpose as well: your desire to impress your listeners as a competent professional.

As you analyze the presentation's purpose, think also about the audience. How many people will you be speaking to? Will they be a fairly homogeneous group, or will you be speaking to people with different degrees of knowledge about your topic and different interests? An important consideration is which decision makers will be present. In planning your presentation, the needs and interests of these decision makers should be a primary concern.

Higher order thinking skills, including analysis and evaluation, apply just as much to an oral presentation as they do to a written document. Think in advance about the questions the audience will have about the topic, whether or not there will be a formal question-and-answer session as part of the presentation. By anticipating listeners' questions, you can explain your ideas in a convincing way. Anticipating listeners' questions and having the information ready to answer them also shows the audience that you are thoroughly prepared, credible, and professional.

Throughout the planning and preparation of the speech, always think about the audience: what they know about your topic, what they need to know, what their concerns and interests are, and what their attitudes may be toward your point of view and the information you'll present.

Other Things to Consider

In addition to analyzing your purpose and audience, determine how much time you'll have for the presentation. Find out also how you will be speaking to your audience: formally from a podium, or perhaps informally from your seat in a conference setting.

Yet another consideration is whether to illustrate your speech with visual aids, such as charts or other graphic material. If you decide to use visual aids, consider the room where the presentation will be made. Will the space and facilities allow you to use the visual aids you prefer? A later section of this chapter discusses how to prepare effective visual aids. For now, the important point to remember is that you need to start planning visual aids early.

Finally, budget your time so you can complete the work needed to gather information, compose the speech, make notes, prepare visual aids, and practice the presentation. All these steps take time, particularly if your topic requires much underlying research.

The key to handling all these tasks is to make a schedule with dates for completing each step. It's important to plan your work and budget your time.

Gathering Information

The next step in preparing the presentation is to gather the necessary information. Be thorough in your research so that you can answer any questions the audience may raise. When you are thoroughly prepared, you'll seem competent and professional, and your presentation will have an excellent chance of success. Before you begin, you may want to review Chapter 2, which discusses how to generate ideas, and Chapter 8, which covers accounting research.

Composing the Speech

After you've gathered the information you need, organize the material into an outline. Keeping in mind the purpose of the speech and the interests of your audience, identify the main points you want to make. *Your speech should contain no more than three to five main points.* These main points, with an introduction and conclusion, are the outline of your presentation. Let's look now at how to fill in that outline.

Introduction

The introduction should do two things: get the listeners' attention and preview the main points you will cover.

When you plan the opening sentences of the presentation, consider the listeners' point of view. Why should they listen to what you have to say? Will your speech be meaningful to them, perhaps helping them solve a problem or accomplish a goal? What makes your topic particularly timely and relevant to your listeners? Why are you qualified to speak on this topic? Questions such as these can help you compose the opening sentences of your presentation to get your audience's attention. Here are a few additional suggestions:

- Begin with an interesting story or example to introduce your topic.
- Cite a startling statistic.

- Ask a rhetorical question—one that you don't expect your audience to answer, but that will start them thinking about the topic.

After your opening sentences, provide a brief preview of what the speech will cover. If you tell the audience what the main points will be, you'll help them remember what's important as you progress through your presentation.

Body of the Presentation

In the body of the presentation, you present again your main points and develop them in detail. Be specific and concrete: Use facts, examples, and, where appropriate, statistics.

As you move from one main point to the next, you can help your listeners remember main ideas with two techniques: internal summaries of what you've already said and clear transitions that lead into the next main topic. For example, you might say something like this:

> So one advantage of this new software is that it would reduce the time needed to process customer accounts. [This is an internal summary. We know it's a summary because of the word *so*.] The second advantage is that the software would provide us with better records for our sales managers. [This sentence provides a transition into the next major section of the speech and identifies the second main point for the listeners.]

By providing internal summaries and obvious transitions, you can help your listeners remember main ideas as you give your presentation.

Conclusion

The last part of the formal presentation is the conclusion. Once again, summarize the main ideas you want your audience to remember. Your presentation will be most effective if you end with a forceful closing. Here are some suggestions:

- Ask your audience to do something. This call to action may be low key—a request that they consider your recommendation, for example. However, you may want to be more forceful, and sometimes even dramatic, if you think the topic warrants this approach and if this tone is suitable for your audience.
- Refer again to the opening sentences of your presentation. If you used a story, example, or statistic, suggest how the ideas expressed in your speech relate to these concepts.
- Remind your audience of the benefits they will receive if they follow your recommendations.

For additional help in composing your speech, review Chapter 3, which covers the principles of coherent organization.

Making Notes

After you have gathered your material and completed the outline, you are ready to put your notes in final form—the form from which you will actually speak. Notice that this section is not called "Writing Your Speech," and for a very good reason. Most experienced speakers find it unnecessary to write down every word they want to say. In fact, having a word-for-word manuscript of your speech could lead you to make two mistakes in your presentation: reading the speech or trying to memorize it (more about these pitfalls later).

The most helpful way to prepare notes is in outline form. You should already have this outline because you prepared it as you gathered information and organized your materials. Whether your outline appears in a computer file or is hand written, write in a large font that you can read easily from a distance and highlight key words and phrases.

If you plan to speak from a computer, keep in mind the possibility of a technological glitch: unlikely, but possible. As a backup, print your outline on hard copy, again using a font that will be large enough for you to see easily.

Here are a few pointers:

- Include main points in your outline, as well as supporting details and examples.
- Write out the opening sentences and the conclusion. (This is the exception to the advice not to write out the speech word-for-word.)
- Indicate in your notes where you will use your visual aids.
- As you review your notes, highlight key phrases in a contrasting color or font. When you make the presentation, these highlighted phrases will remind you of the points you want to make.
- Number the pages of your backup hard copy outline and clip them together.

When we discuss practicing and delivering your presentation, you'll see how notes prepared in this way will help you make a smooth presentation.

VISUAL AIDS

LO16.3 Prepare effective visual aids.

To appreciate how visual aids can contribute to an effective presentation, consider your audience's point of view. When people read, they have a number of visual cues to help them identify and remember main ideas. They have titles and headings, paragraph breaks to signal a shift in topic, and often graphic illustrations. If they need to review something that has already been covered, they have only to turn back the page to see that material again.

Listeners to an oral presentation have none of these visual cues to help them follow the flow of thought, unless the speaker provides them with visual aids. A major advantage of visual aids is that they help listeners identify and remember main ideas. They offer another advantage as well, because well-constructed, attractive visual aids make the presentation more interesting.

To some extent, which visual aids you use will depend on where you'll be speaking. If you are making a classroom presentation, for example, you can prepare handouts; write on the chalkboard, whiteboard, or easel pad; prepare posters and charts; or use electronic slides created by Microsoft PowerPoint®, Apple Keynote®, or similar programs.

You may decide to use more than one kind of visual aid. For example, handouts give your listeners something to take with them to reinforce what you've said, especially when you want to give them lengthy or detailed information. However, you don't want them reading the handout instead of listening, so illustrate your presentation with posters, charts, or electronic slides, and distribute the handouts after the presentation.

Let's look more closely at guidelines for preparing visual aids that you can use during your presentation:

- Be selective in planning your aids, and limit the amount of information you present visually to key ideas. If your audience is constantly occupied reading material presented visually, they may not listen to what you're saying.
- Keep your aids simple. Use key-words and phrases rather than sentences, and limit each aid to about five or six lines.
- Be sure the writing is legible and large enough to be read from the back of the room. If possible, use bright colors to make your aids more attractive. (Avoid yellow, which is often hard to see from a distance.)
- Make your aids neat and professional looking. A computer with a graphics package will help you achieve a professional appearance.

You can include any information on your visual aid that will help your listeners understand and remember your message, but visual aids are particularly helpful in identifying your main points, summarizing your recommendations or conclusions, or providing a vivid illustration. You can also summarize statistical information in a table or graph. (Chapter 6 provides additional information on the preparation and use of charts and graphs.) Yet another technique is to reproduce cartoons to amuse your listeners as you illustrate a point.

Be aware of potential risks in using computer-generated aids. If you use too many visual aids, you may lose eye contact with the audience, and the audience may not pay careful attention to what you're saying.

After you have prepared your visual aids and notes, you are ready for the next important step in the preparation of the oral presentation: practice.

PRACTICE, PRACTICE, PRACTICE

LO16.4 Practice your presentation.

Practicing the presentation is essential for several reasons. For one thing, the more often you review the speech, the more familiar you become with it, so that when you speak before an audience, you will appear knowledgeable and convincing. You'll also feel more confident that you have mastered the ideas you want to present. When you practice, especially before other people, you also identify in advance any potential problems that could occur, such as a presentation that is too long or too short for the allotted time.

Here are some strategies that will make your practice time most useful:

- Practice the speech out loud. Pay attention to your voice, posture, and gestures.
- Time the presentation to make sure it is the appropriate length.
- Practice using the visual aids, including any equipment you will be using, such as equipment for an electronic slide presentation.
- If possible, practice in the actual room you'll be using for the presentation.
- Practice before a live audience, such as friends, family, or coworkers. Ask them to be critical of the content and delivery of the speech.
- If you have access to video recording equipment, ask someone to record the presentation so that you can identify and correct any problems.

Finally, avoid this common pitfall: Never read or try to memorize your speech! The only exception to this guideline is that you may find it helpful to memorize your opening and closing sentences.

FINAL CONSIDERATIONS: ARRANGEMENTS AND DRESS

LO16.5 Complete your preparation: room and equipment; appearance and dress.

Checking the Arrangements

For some oral presentations, preparations include arranging for a room and equipment. Even if someone else is responsible for these duties, it may be a good idea to check them yourself. Be sure that the room will be unlocked in time for the early arrivals at the presentation and that the equipment will be delivered and set up in working order.

Check again on these arrangements a short time before the presentation begins. If there is some unforeseen problem, such as malfunctioning equipment, you'll have time to correct it.

Appearance and Dress

A final consideration in the preparation for your presentation is appearance and dress. As in any professional situation, your grooming should be impeccable. The clothing you wear will depend to some extent on the situation, but professional styles and colors are almost always preferable. If you are in doubt, it's better to err on the side of conservatism.

MAKING THE PRESENTATION: POISE AND CONFIDENCE

LO16.6   Make an oral presentation with poise and confidence.

We discussed the steps of preparing an oral presentation before you actually give it: planning, composing, and practice. Now we'll look at the qualities of effective delivery and strategies to help you become an accomplished public speaker. The effect you should create on your audience is one of poise and confidence.

Eye Contact

A secret of public speaking is to maintain eye contact with the audience. When you look your listeners in the eye, you involve them in the topic and help ensure that they listen carefully. Establish eye contact when you first stand before the audience: stand straight, smile with confidence, and look around the room. Look briefly but directly at various people at different locations. This initial eye contact should last for a few seconds.

As you begin the presentation and progress through it, continue to maintain this eye contact. Hold the eye contact with each person for several seconds, perhaps the length of a complete phrase. Shift the contact from one side of the room to the other, front to back, and at various points in the middle. If your audience is small, you may be able to make eye contact with everyone in the room several times.

Regardless of the size of your audience, it's essential to establish eye contact with one important group of listeners: the decision makers. They will be judging the ideas you present and your effectiveness as a speaker. Good eye contact will help you keep their attention. You'll also seem confident and in control of the situation.

You may also find it helpful to look frequently at the listeners who seem most interested and supportive of what you are saying. You can recognize this group by their expressions of interest and attention, or perhaps even nods and smiles. Their enthusiasm can give you extra energy and confidence.

Here's a final word about eye contact and the use of visual aids, including electronic slides. When you refer to your aids, don't turn your back on the audience except briefly if you need to locate and point to something specific. Maintain eye contact as you refer to the aid so that your audience will listen to your explanation.

When you think about the importance of maintaining good eye contact with the audience, it's obvious why you shouldn't read your speech and why you should be so familiar with your notes that you only glance at them from time to time.

Body Movement and Gestures

Poised, natural use of your body and gestures also contributes to an effective presentation. Stand still, with good posture, and look directly at the listeners. Don't move about, except to use your visual aids (for example, to point to something on a chart or to change a slide).

Natural, expressive use of your hands is an effective way to emphasize ideas and feelings. For this reason, it's better to place your notes or computer on a table or lectern so that your hands are free for gestures.

Voice

Three elements of your voice contribute to a presentation's effectiveness: pitch, volume, and speed. Pitch is the high or low tone used for speaking. Most people's natural pitch is fine and requires no modification for public speaking. A few people need to pitch their voices a little lower than normal, especially if they are nervous when they speak.

Volume and speed may require more attention. The key to speaking at the correct volume is to speak loudly enough so that people in the back of the room can hear you. Be consistent; don't let your voice drop at the ends of sentences, for example, so that your audience misses the last words or must strain to hear you.

When you practice the presentation, pay particular attention to the speed at which you are speaking. You should speak slowly enough to enunciate each word clearly. Some speakers have a tendency to speak more rapidly when they are nervous. If you fall into this category, make a conscious effort to slow down.

STAGE FRIGHT

LO16.7   Manage stage fright.

Now that we've introduced the topic of nervousness, let's think for a minute about how to manage what for many speakers is the worst part of public speaking: stage fright. Notice that the objective for this section is "*Manage* Stage Fright," not "*Eliminate* Stage Fright." Even the most experienced, effective speakers may have some stage fright; in fact, they use this emotional energy to help them make a more effective presentation. The emotion, if kept in control, can give you the extra charge to make an energetic, enthusiastic, and convincing presentation.

Of course, too much stage fright is counterproductive. Let's look at some strategies you can use to manage stage fright before and during your presentation.

Prepare Well in Advance

One advantage of thorough preparation and practice is that they help prevent stage fright. When you know you thoroughly understand the topic, and when you have thought in advance about the questions and interests of the listeners, you will *feel* prepared, and thus competent. A feeling of competence, in turn, gives you confidence in your ability to do a good job. Actual practice, especially before a live audience, will also increase your confidence.

Just Before You Speak

Two tricks may be helpful in the last few minutes before you are scheduled to speak. The first is to use this time to go over your notes one last time to be sure your main points, as well as your opening and closing sentences, are fresh in your mind. The second trick is this: Don't think about how you're feeling!

If you think about being nervous, you'll only increase the feeling. Instead, think about something pleasant that is completely unrelated to your presentation. Perhaps you can think about some pleasant activity you have planned for later in the day.

During the Presentation

Most speakers find that their stage fright goes away after the first few minutes of their presentation. When you are speaking, look directly at your listeners with poise and confidence: They'll probably reflect these positive feelings back to you. Notice which of your listeners are most interested and receptive to what you're saying, and make frequent eye contact with these people. Their enthusiasm will add to your feelings of confidence and help to ensure that your presentation is effective.

PRESENTING FINANCIAL INFORMATION

LO16.8 Explain the special considerations involved in presenting financial information.

The standard techniques for presentations given in this chapter apply to accounting presentations, of course, but you should bear in mind a number of special considerations when you are presenting financial information. Most of the time, presentations of financial information contain numbers, tabular data, and charts that may be shown on electronic slides. The following points apply in this type of presentation:

- Make sure your numbers are consistent. For example, if "Sales are expected to reach $7.25 million in 2018" appears on one slide, make sure your other slides don't contain some other number. It's easier to make this kind of error than you might think. When you develop a presentation, you will revise it several times before you produce your final version. When numbers are changed during the revisions, it's sometimes difficult to find all the places in the presentation where they appear. As a result, conflicting numbers end up in the final presentation.
- Make sure your numbers "add up." For example, if your presentation includes a statement such as "Sales are expected to grow 20 percent from their 2017 level of $7 million, reaching $8.4 million in 2018," make sure that $7,000,000 × 1.20 does in fact equal $8,400,000 (which it does).
- Make sure the audience can read the charts or slides in your presentation. This applies to the size of the charts or slides as well as their design. Many audience members would have difficulty making out the slide in Figure 16–1. Although the slide illustrates

FIGURE 16–1 Example of a Poor Slide

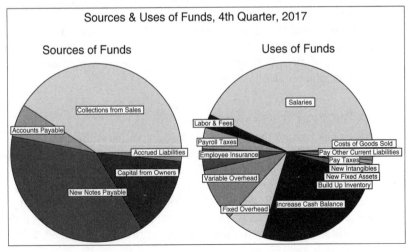

where the company's funds came from and where they went, the labels on the pie slices are too small to read, particularly from the back of the room. Also, there is too much information on the slide to take in at once. In this case, the presenter should separate the charts into two slides and increase the font size in the labels.

- Use computer-assisted presentations wherever possible. Presentations developed in graphics programs look very professional, and they may well make the difference between your recommendations being accepted or rejected.

A FINAL WORD

Public speaking may always fill you with some apprehension. With practice and the mastery of technique, however, you will become much more sure of yourself and your ability to be an effective oral communicator. For that reason, it's a good idea to take advantage of every opportunity to practice your public speaking. The payoff will be greater professional success.

EXERCISES

Exercise 16–1 [General]

Select one of your classmates as a partner for this exercise. Imagine that you have been asked to introduce your classmate before a professional meeting of your peers. Interview your classmate, taking notes as you ask questions. Review your notes for accuracy and organize them into an outline that you can use for a two- or three-minute introduction. (Hint: Analyze the interests of your audience as the basis for the questions you ask in your interview.)

After you have completed one interview, you and your partner can switch roles so that you are interviewed for an introduction your partner will make.

Exercise 16–2 [General]

Select one of the following topics and prepare a 5-minute presentation to give to your class:

- Career opportunities in accounting
- ISACA (Formerly: Information Systems Audit and Control Association)
- The Impact of social media in public accounting firms
- The *FASB Accounting Standards Codification*®
- Content and format of the CPA, CGMA, or CMA exam

Exercise 16–3 [General]

Assume you have been asked to give an oral presentation to a group of local business leaders on the role of ethics in accounting. Your audience will be knowledgeable about business and current events, but they are not themselves accountants. Your presentation, which will be the program of a business luncheon, will be 15 minutes long.

Research the issue of ethics in accounting and prepare an outline for your presentation. Then deliver the presentation to your class or to a group of friends.

Exercise 16–4 [Tax]

Prepare an oral presentation on itemized deductions that may be taken by an individual for tax purposes. Assume the audience for the oral presentation is a group of young people just beginning their careers. Prepare any visual aids needed for an effective oral presentation. Your presentation should be about 15 minutes long.

Exercise 16–5 [Systems]

Prepare an oral presentation on the extensible business reporting language, XBRL. In your presentation, discuss what XBRL is, how it is used, and its advantages. Assume the audience for the oral presentation is a group of young people just beginning their financial data management studies in school. Prepare any visual aids needed for an effective oral presentation. Your presentation should be about 20 minutes long.

Exercise 16–6 [Tax]

Prepare an oral presentation for class from a recent article in the *Journal of Taxation*. Remember to adapt your information and presentation to the needs and interests of your classmates. Your presentation should last about 10 minutes.

Exercise 16–7 [Financial]

Prepare an oral presentation for class from a recent article in the *Journal of Accountancy*. Remember to adapt your information and presentation to the needs and interests of your classmates. Your presentation should last about 10 minutes.

Exercise 16–8 [Auditing]

Prepare an oral presentation for class on the Public Company Accounting Oversight Board (PCAOB), and why it was formed. Remember to adapt your information and presentation to the needs and interests of your classmates. Prepare any visual aids you think may be helpful to your audience.

Exercise 16–9 [Tax]

Your school's honorary society has asked you to give a presentation at its monthly meeting on "Objectives of the Federal Tax Law." Your audience will be primarily other accounting students, but will also include professional accountants who are in attendance to recruit new hires for their firms. (You hope to be one of these new hires.) Prepare notes to use for your presentation. Your instructor may ask you to make your presentation to the class.

Index